BLUE STOCKING IN PATAGONIA

BLOODSTOCK
IN PATAGONIA

ANNE WHITEHEAD

BLUE STOCKING
IN PATAGONIA

To dearest Tony —
who makes an appearance
somewhere in this book —
and often in my thoughts!
Love
Anne

P

PROFILE BOOKS

For Luis

First published in Great Britain in 2003 by
Profile Books Ltd
58A Hatton Garden
London ECIN 8LX
www.profilebooks.co.uk

10 9 8 7 6 5 4 3 2 1

Typeset in Minion by MacGuru Ltd
info@macguru.org.uk

Printed and bound in Great Britain by
Clays, Bungay, Suffolk

A CIP catalogue record for this book is available from the British Library.

ISBN 1 86197 504 x

Overleaf: Mary and Will Gilmore (at left) and expedition party at
Estancia Killik Aike, Patagonia, in 1901

CONTENTS

There is a curious Argentine film, *Miss Mary*, starring Julie Christie, about an upright English governess on an estancia or ranch on the pampas. She struggles with isolation, social dislocation, authoritarian employers and her own sexual frustration, against a background of war in Europe and impending dictatorship in Argentina. Directed and co-written by the late Maria Luisa Bemberg in 1986, the story is, I understand, fictional. Certainly it is not about my 'Miss Mary', whose actual experiences in South America included being a governess on an estancia. But as André Gide said: 'Fiction is history which *might* have taken place, and history fiction which *has* taken place.'

I

WATERWAYS

Squealing cockatoos shredded pine cones above me, four people were practising tai chi, suspended in the graceful gestures of 'passing clouds', an elderly couple shared their sandwich with the pigeons, and sounds of young kids playing soccer came from the grassy field nearby. In the late afternoon I was sitting on a bench under century-old trees – jacaranda, fig, camphor laurel and Norfolk pine – in the grounds of Stanmore public school, unusually extensive for Sydney's inner west and now made available after hours as a common for residents of this newly gentrified area. Ahead of me was the handsome main school building of russet brick and sandstone, erected in 1883, boasting three sets of stone stairs to a colonnaded verandah. It is a monument to the New South Wales colony's pride in its programme of 'free, compulsory and secular' education, which in the 1880s had rapidly expanded literacy among the working class.

Mary Jean Cameron, an inspirational young teacher posted to the school in May 1891, welcomed her appointment there. But because of events that had their origin in Queensland in the very month of her arrival, she stayed just four years before resigning, leaving her pupils in tears as she departed. One of them recalled that she 'said goodbye to us and went away to a distant land but she was the kind of personality whose memory never fades'.[1]

I had come to the school in September 2002, as a ritual starting point for my own expedition, trying to imagine it when Mary was there, when the great trees were mere seedlings, for I was about to set off for that 'distant land' on Mary's trail.

Some time before her departure, Mary had set down her dilemma in deceptively confident handwriting in her journal:

> This day my feet are set on the junction of three paths. It is imperative that I should choose one (or that I should drift along one). I know that if I choose I shall very likely take the wrong one, that I shall be some distance on my way before I find that out and that it will be then impossible to return ...[2]

It was 1895 when she embarked on her intrepid journey from Sydney to the heartland of South America to join an experimental socialist utopia in Paraguay.

After the armed suppression of a five months' long strike of over 10,000 shearers in Queensland in 1891, hopes of a social revolution, a republic, or just a better way of life in Australia had faded for many bushworkers. Then they listened to William Lane, a British journalist whose vision owed more to mateship than to Marx, a fiery supporter of their cause during the strike, who in his editorials in the *Queensland Worker* proposed a better way of life.

He called on the disenchanted to uproot themselves and sail to a faraway place where they could build a secular heaven on earth: a communal society in the backwoods where all would be equal, regardless of class, education and gender. From there they could one day emerge, a disciplined army of thousands, to lead the workers of the world to socialism. This was not 'a wild dream, an impossible hope', he insisted, all it took was the daring to act on it – somewhere far from the contaminating influence of class. Somewhere in South America. They could be an inspiration for workers in all lands, for the industrial poor of England, France and Germany, even perhaps for the peasants of Russia. They could write the future history of humanity on the rocks of the Andes!

In 1893 over 500 Australians, mostly male bushworkers and trade unionists, followed Lane to Paraguay to found their New Australia. But, by the time of Mary's passage two years later, the utopian dream had fragmented: it had become a nightmare of harsh words, occasional punch-ups, litigious threats and two implacably opposed rival colonies.

Despite this alarming development, Mary made her way to the breakaway settlement, Colonia Cosme, deep in the interior of Paraguay – by mailboat to Montevideo, by paddlesteamer 1,600 kilometres up the great rivers, Río de la Plata, Paraná and Paraguay, then by steam train and at last by horseback, 'hearing the oranges go squish, squash under our horses' feet', to reach a ragged collection of thatched huts in a jungle clearing. It was an extraordinary journey in the mid-1890s for a lone female with no language other than English, but Mary Cameron was an extraordinary young woman.

She was twenty-seven years old in 1892 when she met William Lane – who was to change the course of her life – at one of the radical discussion evenings held above McNamara's bookshop in Sydney. She still had something of the country girl about her – tall and lissom, with wide, brown eyes and auburn hair hacked unfashionably short by her own hand. One of her Stanmore pupils later recalled that 'Miss Cameron's short crop of hair was a never-ending source of interest', and her jaunty appearance was accentuated by 'a sailor hat, a small hard straight-brimmed straw hat'.[3] Often too she wore a red sash at her waist, which she said was a declaration of her socialist beliefs.

Lane, the notorious newspaper editor, four years her senior, had been described by a cabinet minister as 'the most dangerous man in Australia',[4] but he was physically unprepossessing. Prematurely balding, short-sighted behind gold-rimmed spectacles, he walked with a limp caused by a crippled left foot. But when he spoke he was compelling: he could focus on one person and inspire with his passion and sincerity or electrify hundreds with his eloquence.

Mary was ready to listen. Her very first teaching posting, in 1887, had been in Silverton, a silver-lead mining town near Broken Hill on the parched red plains of outback New South

Wales. There her political beliefs had been shaped by observing the brutal working conditions of the miner fathers of her pupils, and the way concessions were only forced from the employer, the monolithic Broken Hill Proprietary Company, by the men's newly formed trade union. Her first political poem, 'Unrest', was published in July 1888 in the local newspaper, the *Silver Age*.

By the time she was appointed to a school in Sydney in 1890, more of Mary's verse had reached print in the *Town and Country Journal*. She gravitated to the literary and radical milieu that converged on McNamara's bookshop and its upstairs room where the Australian Socialist League had its meetings. Here, she attracted the attention of the writer Henry Lawson, two years younger than herself, shy, deaf and formidably talented, with an insight into the lives of ordinary bush people which she envied and a way with alcohol, she soon discovered, that she feared.

It was a strange meeting, that between the young Lawson and me. I had come down permanently to the city from Silverton; he had come from Mudgee and the mountains … Tremulously we met, for we were both exceedingly thin and over-strung; he nervous because he thought me a scholar, I humble because I knew him a genius. Afterwards he said he fell in love with me at first sight.

'But I am not pretty!' I said.

'It was your eyes …' he answered.

There seemed no passion in Mary's response – to her

there was 'a curious immaturity about Lawson at that time
... he was in the sappy twig stage of development' – but she
rejoiced in his company. They walked the streets of the city
together, discussing poetry and social injustice, landlordism,
class distinction, 'title worship' and all the other 'dust-
covered customs', Henry said, that England had lumped on
them. She had been disturbed by the hard lives of the
outback miners; he showed her the social misery behind the
glittering harbour and the fine new city buildings: 'He used
to take me out to see the wrong things, the things repressive
of the rights of Australia; the things like a blot upon her and
which prevented her being herself – the low wage workers,
the Chinamen working at treadle-saws in underground
cellars lit only by a grating in the street, the huddled houses
... the pale seamstresses ... the neglected children of the
Quay and elsewhere.'[5]

Henry's formidable mother, Louisa Lawson, was the
editor of Australia's first feminist journal, the *Dawn*. Mary
attended one of her lectures and agreed that 'an advocate of
women's rights' was not to be dismissed by 'the repulsive title
"blue stocking"', nor categorised as hanging 'half way over
the bar which separates the sexes, shaking her skinny fist at
men and all their works'.

Not long afterwards, no doubt at Henry's urging, Mary
moved into the Lawson household as a paying boarder, but it
was soon clear the two women did not rub along well
together. It seems Henry proposed marriage, but was
encouraged by Louisa (surely a ruse to get him away) to first
set himself up financially by trying his luck on the West

Australian goldfields with his younger brother. According to Mary's account, Henry then begged her to elope with him, but 'some sense of unfitness, some realisation that I was not ready for marriage made me say no ... Affection I had and always would have for him – the affection of a friend who thought him wonderful and for whom he had opened a newer and a wider world.' (However, much later she claimed the two of them might have ended up together after all, if Louisa had not intercepted and destroyed the letters meant for her, sent by Henry from the west.)[6]

At the time Henry was clearly devastated by Mary's refusal, for his poem 'The Rejection', not published until 1893 in the *Bulletin,* is believed to be about her. The first of the nine verses is enough to convey his despair:

> She says she's 'very sorry' as she sees you to the gate,
> You calmly say 'Goodbye' to her while standing off a yard,
> Then you lift your hat and leave her, walking mighty stiff
> and straight –
> But you're hit, old man – hit hard.[7]

The relationship between Mary and Lawson had developed at a time of bitter industrial turbulence along the eastern seaboard of the country – the so-called Great Maritime Strike – involving seamen, wharf labourers, miners and shearers. In the end the dispute was decisively quelled by government forces. The following year, 1891, the five-month-long shearers' strike in Queensland was viewed on both sides as an explicit war between labour and capital. Mary wrote feisty verse in support of the shearers, who were holding out in primitive bush camps, surrounded by troopers armed with Gatling guns and Nordenfeld field pieces. Newspapers from the southern states sent 'war correspondents'. Henry Lawson warned, in his famous poem 'Freedom on the Wallaby':

> We'll make the tyrants feel the sting
> O' those that they would throttle;
> They needn't say the fault was ours
> If blood should stain the wattle.[8]

William Lane was effectively one of the generals in this war and his editorials in the Queensland *Worker* made him a household name. It was after the strike was ignominiously defeated – though with remarkably little blood spilt on either side – that he produced his master plan for a communal society of 'mates' in South America, an example to the world of socialism in action. He began seriously to recruit for it, not only among the disillusioned shearers of Queensland, but as far south as Tasmania.

Mary was tremendously flattered when Lane paid her a visit in October 1892. Soon she was working for the cause, after school hours writing for and sub-editing their recruiting journal *New Australia*. 'I know', she wrote, 'that the men and women who are carrying this thing on are actuated by true and honorable motives' and, because of that, 'I do give my faith to the movement and my heart to its working'.[9]

But more than ideology attracted her to the New Australia movement. She was overwhelmingly smitten – for the first time in her life – by one of the organisers and Lane's favoured lieutenant, David Russell Stevenson. A cousin to the writer Robert Louis Stevenson, he was a tall, muscular Queensland shearer with a swashbuckling ginger moustache. The man was the embodiment of *machismo,* even though he had not yet learned the Spanish expression for assertive masculine pride. Lane even made him the model for his hero in his rambling recruiting novel *The Workingman's Paradise*:

> He was strong and straight and manly … so broad and strong that he hardly looked over medium height. He had blue eyes and a heavy moustache just tinged with red. His hair was close cut and dark; his forehead, nose and chin were large and strong … a breath of the great plains came from his sunburnt face and belted waist …[10]

Stevenson was often to be seen in Mary's company at social evenings of the New Australia Co-operative Settlement Association. Sometimes, so the talk went, he would linger so long chatting to her that he would miss the last ferry, and would have to strip off his clothes and swim across the harbour, risking the sharks. The gossips wondered if she was still with him when he stripped. It is certain that Mary – as well as William Lane and most of the other communards – had expectations that she would marry him.

A barque, the *Royal Tar,* 598 tons, built of bloodwood and blue gum, was purchased and refitted for the grand exodus – for thousands were eventually expected to make the journey.

The first emigrants arrived in Sydney from all over the country. Mary was disappointed, but accepted the logic when Lane decreed that only bachelors and families should be among the pioneers. Single women would be more than welcome once the colony was established. Still, she envied an attractive young nurse called Clara Jones who was travelling without family because government regulations insisted that a certificated sister be aboard.

On a grey, rainy day, 16 July 1893, well-wishers, cynics and the curious lined Sydney's rocky foreshores to bid farewell to the 220 brave or foolhardy souls crowding the decks of the *Royal Tar*. Mary had a privileged position, with other key supporters, on a chartered launch which followed the little three-masted barque across the harbour. She waved, she recalled, until her arm was numb, and no doubt it was Stevenson she was still trying to make out among the rain-blurred figures on the deck as the little ship unfurled its sails and passed through the Heads, bound for South America.

Before a year was out, despite the departure of another 200 hopeful colonists, there were compelling reasons for Mary to abandon any idea of finding a communal or personal utopia in Paraguay.

The original colony, Nueva Australia, had broken up in acrimonious circumstances after just a few months. It had begun with chairman Lane expelling three men for breaking the colony's teetotal pledge – they had returned merry from the nearby village but claimed to have merely taken a little wine with the local priest. Then they conceded that they had observed a Paraguayan woman roll a cigar on her naked thigh, and were accused of breaking another pledge, fraternising with the locals and crossing the 'Colour Line'. Eighty other individuals walked out in protest at such a harsh enforcement of the rules after only one infringement. British Consular officials in Asunción were appalled to discover penniless Australians on their doorstep, begging Her Majesty's Government to fund their passages back to Australia. A suave British diplomatic envoy was sent from Buenos Aires to plead tolerance but found Lane implacable. The commune committee, wishing their wandering brethren to return and having had enough of William Lane, pushed through a vote of no confidence in the chairman instead. The Australian press enjoyed a field day. The Sydney *Bulletin* crowed:

> It has proved itself just like every other expedition and the result is only what might reasonably have been expected. Man will drink and gamble and prowl round to the backdoors of the dusky daughters of the land till the end of time, and every scheme that fails to take these facts into consideration is certain to come to grief …[11]

Lane and sixty-three of his most loyal followers walked out and – with another grant from the remarkably tolerant Paraguayan government – re-established themselves on remote, more inaccessible land, between two rivers liable to flood, some 130 kilometres south-east of their rivals.

Declaring they would even refuse to get up a cricket team against their former comrades, they threw up a few grass and mud huts and called the fledgling commune Colonia Cosme. Their new constitution still endorsed socialist principles but, unbeknown to Mary, the male majority had peremptorily scrapped the ideal of gender equality.

Mary by then was running the old New Australia office in Sydney almost single-handed after school hours, as a very partisan Cosme recruiting office. If she had more personal reasons in persisting with the idea of making the journey to Paraguay herself, it is a wonder she was not deterred by the fact that she had not received a single communication from Dave Stevenson. Perhaps she invented excuses to herself – such as the unreliable mails from Paraguay – although she regularly received bitter diatribes from Lane, denouncing the backsliders at New Australia. Then his own wife, Anne, returned and stayed with Mary at her modest lodgings in Sydney's Marrickville, sent by her husband to recruit single women for the bachelors at Cosme. As it turned out, the single women of Australia stayed away in their proverbial droves. But it is remarkable that Mary had apparently heard nothing of a romance between Stevenson and the nurse Clara Jones on the outward voyage of the *Tar,* a flirtation so flagrant that William Lane had insisted on putting a stop to it. He had told the nurse in no uncertain terms that Stevenson was already engaged. Soon after their arrival at the settlement in Paraguay, he had been more than happy, as village magistrate, to marry her off to another man. If Anne Lane told Mary nothing of this it was probably because she, like her husband, favoured the match with Stevenson; if any rumours came through by mail, she may have diffused them by assuring Mary that Clara was now happily married to a Queensland bushman, Billy Laurence. Perhaps Mary excused Stevenson's silence with the rationalisation that he was a bushman, after all, vigorous and assertive when action was called for, but not a *writing* man.

But one particular writing man *was* paying her attention once again. Henry Lawson had come back from Western Australia, bereft of gold nuggets; he had visited the outback towns of Bourke and Hungerford and hated the experience, then spent a miserable eight months in New Zealand. On his return he hit the bottle more than ever, and was often staggering when he arrived at Mary's door. Anne Lane wondered aloud why Mary bothered with him.

To Mary, a man like Stevenson, still a Lane loyalist, a bachelor and a teetotaller, a bushman who could turn his hand to most rugged tasks but who enjoyed reading the classics – Shakespeare, John Donne, Robbie Burns and even the works of his famous cousin – must have seemed better husband material, even if he had been neglectful as a correspondent.

After Anne Lane returned to Paraguay in March 1895, William beseeched Mary to follow. He emphasised how badly they needed a schoolteacher: the woman who performed the role had stayed with the rebels at New Australia. His brother John had been filling in but, as a qualified botanist with a diploma from Kew Gardens, he was needed for their agricultural projects.

The impetus for Mary's decision was very likely her thirtieth birthday, which she celebrated, or rued, in Sydney on 16 August 1895. Thirty was an age when the term 'spinster' was often replaced by 'old maid', a condition her notebooks indicate she devoutly feared. It may have been then that she described her perilous position at the junction of three paths and gloomily predicted:

> … One leads to the desolate regions of old maidism; the second to the devil; the third to marriage and probable misery.[12]

Three months after her birthday, Mary was ready for her momentous expedition. She even packed a length of white hailstone muslin in her saratoga trunk, suitable for a wedding dress.

In her memoirs she described Henry Lawson's despair at the prospect of her going:

> The night before I sailed he broke right down. He knelt to me and begged me not to go. 'If you go I am ruined,' he said, 'my life will never be worth anything again.'

The next day, 15 November 1895, Henry was at the wharf to see her off. He appeared in a frantic state, even talking of stowing away among the cargo. 'Henry's sad face was the last face I saw,' Mary wrote, 'his voice the last I heard. He looked like one lost and hopeless.'[13]

In committing to the voyage – to Auckland and then on in

a little mailboat, the SS *Ruapehu*, for a rough three-week passage around Cape Horn to Montevideo – Mary had determined on her chosen path. The next entry in her notebook reads: 'I am tired of the gilded chaff of single life and my being craves for the more substantial food of married life – even though it be rye bread.'[14]

According to William Lane, Mary's craving would soon be fulfilled. He had tried desperately to attract single Australian women to his scheme and, in recruiting speeches in country town halls, he had promised them that in the Paraguay settlement they would be overwhelmed with offers of marriage. But apart from the two certificated nurses required by governmental order to accompany the pioneers to South America, he was disappointed that single women unaccountably stayed well away. Mary was the only one who responded to the call.

After an unsteady embarkation, Mary enjoyed her two-week trip upriver in a paddlesteamer to Asunción, Paraguay's capital, locked in the fastness of the continent:

> When I went aboard the *Olimpo* I was obliged to take a boat to go out to her. It was a rough day and I had to get a four-oared boat. She danced so that everything loose had to be stowed and I had to watch that I did not lose my balance and take an unexpected dip.

She was well aware of the sensation she caused among the native crew as 'an English lady' travelling alone, how eccentric she seemed as she stood for hours by the steamer's railing,

Mary Cameron, aged 30 in 1895, the year she sailed for South America

mesmerised by the great Argentine pampas, green and billiard-table flat to the horizon, and by the phosphorescent glow of swarming fireflies at night. Once they entered the tropical waters of the Paraguay river, she would sip iced lemonade and fan herself, the perspiration running off her in streams as she peered into the tangled wall of rainforest as they chugged past, hoping for a glimpse of a jaguar, the brilliant flash of a macaw. She wrote about herons dreaming on a sandbank, and flamingoes, startled by the ship's engines, taking off in a fluttering cloud of pink and white.

The English chief engineer, Thomas Dysart, was kind to Mary, possibly because he felt attracted to her, although she no doubt indicated she was pledged to a man she would join at the small colony of Australian socialists. But she dined with Dysart and the captain every evening, and later recalled how the engineer allowed her the use of his private bath each morning: 'The whole ship's crew, cooks, stewards and all not on actual duty, used to gape with astonishment.'[15]

Buenos Aires had been left far behind. I stood on the top deck of a big white ship, mesmerised by the intricate network of islands and channels, luminescent in the moonlight. The islands were flat, just above the level of the water, overgrown by shadowy vegetation. Brigands and pirates used to live on them, gauchos who had traded their horses for canoes. Any actual mainland, I was told, was impossible to see. On the starboard side it was fifty kilometres away.

This was a research trip to Paraguay that I made almost a decade ago, timed to coincide with the centenary celebration of the Australians' arrival in that country. I was cruising the same waterways towards Asunción that Mary had in 1895, two years after the pioneers. Her steamer was a cargo boat with only a few passengers. That sort of river transport does not exist anymore, so I was making do with a gleaming white tourist cruiser, the *Cuidad de Paraná*.

On the second day I woke to brilliant sunshine and what seemed to be the ocean outside my cabin window. We had entered the great Paraná river. Over 3,000 kilometres further upstream, it roars through the jungled ravines of Brazil, advances in a body of water said to exceed the combined volume of all the rivers of Europe, through rainforest and rich farming land, past the cities of Posadas and Encarnación and the ruins of the old Jesuit missions, to join the Paraguay river, then takes a vast horseshoe turn, the converging waters sweeping silt from the Mato Grosso and melted ice from the Andes, before becoming this majestic waterway flowing through the Argentine pampas to the Atlantic. The Guaraní people call the Paraná the Womb of the Mother of the Sea.

As night fell, the throb of guitar and *bandoneón* came from the nightclub below, moonlight rippled the water and stars appeared in the enormity of vaulting dark. I located the Southern Cross and felt comforted to have come so far and still to have the company of an old friend. With a sudden judder our ship lost its forward momentum; the engines heaved, laboured and then abruptly shut down. The tango music stopped. Passengers discussed the development excitedly. We had simply stranded, explained an officer, but there was no cause for alarm. The tide would refloat us in an hour or two.

A man leaned against the railing and started singing in a calm pure voice, in a language that was not Spanish. People gathered to listen; someone whispered that he was singing in

Guaraní. As the notes of his song rippled out over the water, no one moved until he was finished. We were all entranced.

I discovered he was Paraguayan and a doctor. He said he had been singing about the river, it was in his blood. His father had been in Paraguay's Prefectura Naval, the Maritime Police, and often used to talk about the old days. When I told him I was researching an Australian woman poet who came this way on the paddlesteamer *Olimpo* over a hundred years ago, he remembered his father had often spoken of that boat: it was one of the last paddlesteamers still working from the early days. Owned by a Paraguayan shipping company called Camihort, it did the run from Buenos Aires to Asunción right up until 1930. 'Your poet would have had a good trip,' he grinned. 'Her boat probably didn't get stuck like this. The river was deeper in those days.'

Mary Cameron disembarked at the wharf in Asunción on 31 December 1895. The city was full of New Year's Eve revellers and the train schedules more lax than usual. She booked into the Hotel de Paris near the railway station, where Cosme people enjoyed reduced rates, and sent a telegram to the colony, 224 kilometres south-east, giving her expected time of arrival the following day. As she walked the streets of the capital, new and exotic wonders confronted her, filtered through a haze of golden dust. The public buildings with Palladian façades, domes and cupolas were grander than most of Sydney's, the little hovels in the back lanes heart-breakingly worse. Orange trees fringed the pavements where all kinds of people jostled and paraded: barefooted soldiers carrying swords and muskets, street vendors with baskets of bananas, papayas and trussed live chickens; a raptor-faced Indian with a monkey on his shoulder; a group of *guapos,* posturing local toughs, in highheeled lacquered boots out to find trouble; and señoritas, half-veiled by lace mantillas, shepherded by their mothers on their way to evening mass. The cacophony of noise would have been exhilarating: bells tolling from a dozen churches, the clatter of horse-drawn trams and hansom cabs, the rumble of bullock wagons along rutted, potholed roads, the cries of vendors and urchins, the neighing of horses, braying of donkeys, barking of dogs, the strumming of a harp from a café doorway and a choir in full-throat from within the great twin-towered cathedral. Mary slipped inside it and was struck by the sight of choristers and incense bearers 'in vestment trimmed with almost priceless lace, yet with bare feet'.[16] Even long after she had retired for the night in her tiny hotel room, the life of the city still intruded:

Once in Asunción,
Long, long ago in Paraguay,
I woke to hear the sentries' call,
The hours of night go by.[17]

Next morning a porter from the hotel accompanied her through the gothic-arched cloisters of the grand railway station and stowed her bags and large saratoga trunk on a belching steam train. All day the train travelled at a sloth's pace, allowing Mary ample opportunity to take in the landscape of the country she had adopted as her new home. She saw low rolling hills covered with dense primeval forest and wide flat grasslands, studded with palm trees and watered by streams. Near every railway siding were clusters of mud and thatch cottages, surrounded by vegetable gardens, patches of maize and groves of the ubiquitous orange trees that the Spanish Jesuits had first brought to Paraguay. At many of the countless stops, women in loose white chemises leaped into the carriages with baskets of oranges and mandioca bread, shouting '*Naranjas! Chipá!*'

It was nearly dusk when the train paused for just a few moments at Sosa, a lonely siding twenty kilometres west of the Australian colony. Mary struggled down with her luggage, friendly passengers assisting with the trunk. She had expected, and hoped, that Dave Stevenson would be there to meet her. But no one was. Her sense of disappointment and isolation must have been devastating as she approached the startled villagers at a cantina near the siding. She spoke no Spanish and the local people at Sosa, like many *campesinos,* may only have spoken the Indian language, Guaraní. I imagine myself as a firefly watching from the encroaching shadows as the tall, important but very flustered woman mimed that she wanted to find the *australianos* – producing blank stares from the little group of locals.

The *colonia socialismo* …?

Looks of sheer bewilderment.

The *inglés?* You know the *ingles* …?

Ah *claro*! Why didn't the señora say so the first time!

21

The villagers would never have heard of Australians or socialists and certainly nothing as bizarre as the two in combination, but they had certainly heard about the *inglés* and it seems they made an intelligent though mistaken supposition. It would have been with the generosity typical of country Paraguayans that they transported the problematic stranger woman by cart to the next settlement of González. This was a government-funded agricultural colony for a very mixed bag of immigrants. Mary was not at all impressed:

> The colonists were Paraguayan with an odd German, English and Frenchman. Here one learned what a 'poor white' is. He is the most miserable and squalid of beings, living on his wife if he has one, or his mistress if he has not, and when he has neither, living anyhow.[18]

One of the 'mistresses' ran what passed for a boarding house – it was most likely an amateur brothel as well – and Mary had decided there was no other option but to stay the night when a European man came riding into the village, leading two horses. Once again she was crushingly disappointed, for he was not Stevenson but John Lane, brother of William, the Australian colony's chairman.

According to a later account by his daughter, John was none too happy about his mission: Stevenson had bluntly refused to do the honours, as he was 'a bit of a Casanova … and didn't consider himself engaged to Mary'; instead, 'poor Papa had to ride twenty miles through the pampas'.[19] And when John Lane arrived at Sosa he discovered that the train had come in earlier than expected and the strange señora had gone on to González. He and his wife had known Mary in Sydney and as an honourable man he was no doubt sympathetic to her embarrassing situation – possibly making it more so by awkwardly deflecting her enquiries. They accepted the rough accommodation offered, and Mary's emotions must have been in tumult on that first night of the new year and her new life.

Next morning they set off on the arduous ride to the colony, wild oranges squish-squashing under their horses' hooves as John Lane led the packhorse bearing Mary's trunk – which contained the length of muslin for a wedding dress.

It was late afternoon when they clattered over the substantial wooden bridge the colonists had built over the Pirapó river and came into Colonia Cosme – a timber barn and a collection of mud huts with thatched roofs in a grass clearing surrounded by rainforest. Mary had expected the settlement to be primitive – after all, she had been editing their association journal in Sydney and had often emphasised the roughness of living in order to encourage only the sturdiest kind of recruit. She had also heard about the indigestible diet, although she still found it a shock: 'At the time of my arrival in the settlement things had not long passed the stage of utter and continued hardship, the time when food consisted solely of beans relieved by an occasional monkey.'[20] She also realised that she was only the third single woman in a colony overwhelmingly populated by bachelor bushworkers who knew little of social or intellectual niceties. But Stevenson knew something of both; what she was not prepared for was the way in which she was spurned by him and the devastating rudeness of his rejection, which soon had the little colony buzzing.

A 'welcome dance' was put on for Mary that evening in the social hall, an open pavilion structure with a thatched roof. It may have looked romantic, with the moon riding high and oil lamps suspended from the joists, but a colony descendant recounted the tittle-tattle that 'the men drew straws – the unlucky ones with the long straws had to dance with her'.[21] Mary's biographer William H. Wilde suggests (with assumptions that would displease most feminists) that she would have frightened most of the men as 'a somewhat daunting person – a radical bluestocking, competent, assured and forthright'. [22]

There is no record of Stevenson dancing with Mary that first evening. The presumed reason for his behaviour need not detain us for long, for he is very soon to disappear from our story. In Australia he had been known as a ladies' man and this is indicated by his jotting in a notebook:

> The girls are the boys for me,
> Bright faces all spanking with glee,
> Roguish and sly, some are modest and shy,
> But all are attractive to me.[23]

Perhaps Mary Cameron, remembered by a male colleague on the journal in Sydney as 'a tall straight, lissome, alert-eyed and jolly-voiced maiden in a white blouse and a scarlet belt',[24] had presented a challenge to Stevenson – until she ceased to be jolly and became too serious about him. However, most of the colonists knew that on the pioneering voyage of the *Royal Tar* Stevenson had fallen genuinely in love with the nurse, Clara Jones. She had returned his affections, until told by the interfering and manipulative William Lane that Stevenson was already betrothed to Mary. Clara reacted by making an unhappy marriage with another man instead. It was all a fiasco, blighting the lives of Stevenson, Clara and Billy Laurence, the simple farmer from Queensland whom she had married without love.

Stevenson blamed Mary and believed she had overstated the attentions he had paid her in Sydney. Now, despite the desperate shortage of women at Cosme, he rejected her in a public and humiliating way.

That Mary eventually forgave him for the pain he caused is suggested by a poem she wrote many years later:

I had a lover,
He loveth me not,
His way he went
And me forgot;
Yet may his sleep
Be soother and sound
As though he had never
Dealt me a wound.[25]

She gamely settled into community life, writing to a friend in Sydney:

Cosme colonists in 1896. Mary Cameron in dark dress, straw boater and white apron. Clara (Jones) Laurence to her left in white dress and hat

> I am satisfied of the justice and the possibility of communism. I am satisfied with my own lot, I am contented and I feel I have learned more since I came here than I had ever hoped to learn in Australia.[26]

Perhaps Mary was protesting too much, for a few months later she penned a rather desperate note to her old suitor, Henry Lawson, encouraging him to come to Paraguay after all:

> Communism as we have it is alright, Harry, and we are getting on – slowly of course, but in a year or two what now is, will have gone, drowned by prosperity. And the country! – It is a constant wonder to me, so beautiful, so rich in bird, insect and plant. And the history! – and the stories of the

war! If you were only here, Henry. Don't let someone else snap your chances. Come while the field is new ... You know I wouldn't ask you if I didn't think it worth it – even from your standpoint.

M. J. Cameron.

PS I didn't get married.[27]

When Lawson failed to respond – she did not know that he had recently married – Mary astonished the gossips at Cosme by showing interest in William Gilmore. He was a quiet and diffident bushman, though undeniably a handsome one, described by an envious male colonist as having 'the sort of head that young girls rave about, clean cut features, nose somewhat aquiline and forehead crowned by a big bunch of bushy black curls'.[28]

Gilmore was incapacitated for a time by a lacerated back and a sprained ankle, the result of an accident which revealed his generous nature: he had seen a post collapsing on the children's swings and took the weight himself, so saving the children from mishap. The shy, reticent man became the hero of the hour. While he was laid up in the small colony hospital, Mary took to visiting him every day to read to him. 'She had a wonderful speaking voice and they loved to hear her read,' a colonist remembered, 'but she *would* sing!'[29]

When Gilmore recovered, he accompanied Mary on her regular evening strolls in the rainforest – the *monte* – which she thought magical with its profusion of palms, ferns, cedars and entwining creepers, 'like some vast Botanical Garden let loose'.[30]

It was probably on one of these twilight walks that the couple agreed to marry. If it was Gilmore who proposed, he showed an uncharacteristic assertiveness. Mary was more likely the one who put the question, perhaps not so much out of any sudden infatuation but as a desperate measure to salvage her dignity. She still planned to stay in this small and resolutely isolationist community in the Paraguayan rainforest for the remainder of her life and Gilmore – a skilful hunter, axeman, carpenter and also a sensual lover (as her poems soon suggested) – was a suitable husband for the frontier.

It could be that their physical attraction startled them both. And the rest of the community, who soon heard about it. For one of the men wrote rather spitefully to friends in Australia that the engagement was not the surprise it might have been:

> An accidental *rencontre* with an agouti shooter in the *monte* a few nights previous had prepared us for the announcement. Neither of the two look any the better for it. He is quieter than ever and the lady looks as if she has had a fit.[31]

The couple were married on 29 May 1897 in a forest clearing with orange blossom falling over them. She wore a dress made of the hailstone muslin she had brought in anticipation of another groom at her side, mosquito netting covering her auburn hair. Gilmore had trouble pushing the chunky ring on to her finger, a crude one he had fashioned by cutting the centre from a shilling piece. They were an oddly matched pair.

Although he was a capable shearer from the Australian colony of Victoria, Gilmore had received no formal schooling after the age of ten. His grammar and spelling were atrocious. Unfortunately Mary, his bride, did tend to notice such things. She was not only an experienced teacher, a newspaper columnist and an occasional editor for their journal, but she had begun to make a small name for herself as a poet.

A spate of ingenuous, simple, happy poems in the colony journal, *Cosme Monthly*, left no doubt that she had fallen deeply in love – or lust – with her new husband:

> It's us two when it's morning,
> And us two when it's night;
> And us two when it's troubled,
> And us two when it's bright;
> And us two don't want nothing
> To make life good and true,
> And lovin'-sweet, and happy,
> While us two's got us two.[32]

By August 1898 Mary was nine months' pregnant. She was thirty-three years old, then considered a perilously advanced age to be giving birth to a first child. However, to avail herself of the assistance of a midwife, she needed to travel into the large country town of Villarrica, eighty kilometres away. Because the colony could only afford one train fare, she was obliged to make the journey alone among a crowd of country people, both Indians and *mestizos* (people of mixed Indian and European blood). This was discomfiting to her,

Mary Gilmore's pupils with artwork at Cosme c. *1898*

accepting as she did the prevailing British notion, questioned by only a few brave individuals, that as Anglo-Saxons they were superior in all things and must set an example:

> I got into the train wet, cold and alone, for we did not feel justified in spending money on a ticket (1s 8d) for my husband. And there I travelled in a filthy third class carriage full of natives, of whose language I was quite ignorant – all smoking, men and women alike, with baskets of meat here and there on the floor – game-cocks perched on the backs of the seats, and young pigs in bags among our feet …[33]

Mary rented a small cottage in the town for her confinement and later claimed the midwife was drunk during her labour. However, on 21 August, she gave birth to a boy and promptly named him William Dysart Cameron Gilmore. But it was two weeks before she could manage the journey back to Cosme.

Will Gilmore was enraptured with his son and set about making a cot for him out of the beautiful, heavy *lapacho* wood from the forest.

Billy would remain a joy and a loving bond between the couple in a community where everything else seemed to be disintegrating. The little settlement was riven by factionalism and feuding over William Lane's autocratic chairmanship, his enforcement of teetotalism, strict communal sharing and the 'Colour Line'. Fraternising with the local Paraguayans, particularly the attractive women, was strictly forbidden. This was testing the faith rather too sternly in a colony made up principally of single men, and in a country populated overwhelmingly by women without men, a result of the devastating War of the Triple Alliance which had ended just over twenty years earlier. Paraguay, resoundingly defeated by its neighbours Argentina, Brazil and Uruguay, had lost literally 90 per cent of its manhood. A culture developed where the male was prized. The temptations for the colony bachelors were irresistible. There were further expulsions. More colonists walked out in solidarity.

One thing needs to be said, and clearly: this was a colony predicated on racism. Lane had envisaged an 'Anglo-Saxon enclave' which would emerge as some kind of world socialist – but very white – vanguard. His followers, mostly bush-workers, accepted this because it endorsed the unformed fears and prejudices of the labour movement back home. Mary accepted this at the time, too, although her own father had brought her up to think very differently. The Australian colony's decline is a long story in itself, and one that I have told elsewhere.[34] It continued on a fading note for another ten years. But William Lane abandoned the last shreds of his socialist and isolationist dream by walking out with his family just one year later, in August 1899.

Mary and her husband had always supported Lane and two weeks afterwards they also resigned. However, lacking money, they had to find a way to earn their passages home to Australia.

Some of the former bushworkers who had already left the colony had found shearing work on the great sheep estancias of southern Patagonia which were mostly in British hands. Gilmore went down for the summer shearing season while Mary stayed on at Cosme with baby Billy for another nine months, a disillusioned and peevish woman, expressing her anxieties almost daily in letters to her husband, even though she could not afford to post them until they became a batch: 'I often dread your feeling sorry you left the Colony. Don't for my sake, darling. We can't be much poorer than we were here, you surely won't have to work harder ... Surely it will never be as bad as that again'; 'I must not grumble – only I sometimes grow so sick of it all. The gossip and the spite and the jealousies, and sometimes I overstep the mark and say things my better self despises me for and then I feel worse than ever.'[35]

The mail arrived from Australia with a copy of the Sydney

Bulletin. It contained a small advertisement which should have made her elated – but Mary mentioned it to Will in only a desultory way:

> They advertise 'In preparation: A *volume* of verse by Mrs Gilmore (M.J.C.)' They think more of my stuff than I do. I hope it will sell.[36]

She seemed more concerned to apologise to her husband for not being 'a very handsome or a very robust mother', but believed they should still have 'real clean healthy children' because 'you have form and physique – enough to make up for my lack of both'. She fretted when she had not heard from Will for two months and ached at the thought of losing him:

> I don't suppose, if anything happened to you I would die or go mad – though I could easily enough go mad if I chose to allow myself. I would probably make an idol of the boy but life would be a living death and the spring would never bloom again for me.[37]

On 15 December 1899 Mary wrote a letter which I find painful to read. She expressed her great love for Gilmore, though she knew, because of her failed relationship with Stevenson and the literary ambition evident in her poems, that the colony people doubted it. Perhaps she suspected that her husband, always modest and self-deprecating, might have insecurities himself. So she made what was for her an ultimate sacrifice, an offer to give up her vocation as a writer:

People here say I mean to be a writer, and that is why we resigned. They know nothing about it. I wouldn't be a writer
in case I should let the love of it grow into my life and perhaps owe to it what I only want to owe to you – or that it
might set up another aim or tie in which you would not be
the centre.[38]

In her next letter she despaired that the original aims of the
community had almost completely eroded: 'The idea of
Communism is practically dead and the well doing financially of the Colony is the one thing. "What will pay best?" is
the idea.' The place no longer offered anything 'to balance its
snakes, its fever, its jaundice, and its generally infernal climate' and she longed to leave.

Mary spent a wretched Christmas Day with only her son
for company and a storm raging outside:

The house is full of leaks, and the driving wind has sent the
rain in at the back bedroom window ... I feel half afraid of
the lightning, and I am quite nervous ... I have been thinking of you all day, and I ate my dinner with tears, wondering
all about you. Will, dear, you must never leave me again. I
can't spare you.[39]

Colonia Cosme was providing me with the same infernal example of its climate. As darkness fell, lightning flared above
the *monte*, thunder rolled and the rain sheeted down. I took
shelter with my Paraguayan friends, descendants of Aus-

tralians, in a farmhouse at the old settlement, 224 kilometres from Asunción.

The previous night in the city we had all attended the centenary celebration hosted by the Australian ambassador from Buenos Aires. Almost 200 descendants of Australian pioneers had gathered together in a grand old ballroom to commemorate their forebears' arrival in Paraguay. They were a handsome group of people, most of mixed Paraguayan blood and coppery complexions, who unlike their teetotal ancestors, were not averse to the good Argentine wine. Only a handful of them spoke English. They were cattle ranchers, businessmen, peasant farmers, a doctor, an architect, a political candidate for the right-wing Colorado Party and a veterinary surgeon who was the only one to profess himself a socialist. I moved among them, recording what they felt about the occasion, about Australia and, indeed, about their socialist antecedents. 'I think that company of people,' said one of them, Carlos Jacks, 'like most socialists, had more good intentions, poetry and dreams than they had clear plans or understanding of human reality.'

That evening, out of wine and nostalgia a plan emerged for a few descendants to make a visit to the old settlement the following day and I was invited to join them. Apparently times had changed since my previous visit: the road had become impassable except by four-wheel drive, and even then it was very treacherous, with at least five of the bridges that had to be traversed now just narrow planks. It might be my only chance to see the old colony again.

The following morning we set out cheerfully with Randolf

Wood, a Paraguayan architect and great-grandson of an Australian shearer, as our expedition leader. Most of the other passengers were related to him in one way or another, including the glamorous Mercedes, a Paraguayan colonel's daughter, who was married to his cousin. We had reached deep Paraguay when we saw the little mud-and-thatch ranchos, oxen *carretas* and horsemen in wide flapping trousers called *bombachas*.

We crossed the bridge over the Pirapó river, notorious for its sudden floods, and we had arrived. But there was an elegiac quality to our day in the beautiful and remote village of Cosme. The tall blue gums, planted by the colonists, were thriving near the old brick pit pond, but there was no longer anyone there who spoke English and only one resident with any interest in the settlement's obscure connection with Australia. The last of the original homesteads was a ruin, its timbers sagging under the weight of the rusting iron roof, vines forcing their way through holes in the walls.

Dark clouds rolled across the sky as we walked in a straggling group to the cemetery. The grassy streets were wide – a legacy of the masterplan for a great communist city – only at their centres scarred red by the furrows of *carreta* wheels. Cows ambled along, a gaggle of geese flapped across our path. Paraguayan villagers stood and watched at the doorways of little houses with thatched or tiled roofs. A dozen children trailed us, their fascination undisguised, giggling as Mercedes' strappy gold sandals sank in the mud.

The cemetery was unrecognisable from my previous visit. Newly constructed bungalows surrounded it and beaten-earth pathways now separated the brick and concrete vaults of Paraguayan Catholicism. The weed-covered mounds of the colony graves, many lacking headstones, were barely discernible.

In the late afternoon the black clouds burst with an astonishing ferocity. As the cyclonic storm gathered in power, we took shelter under the drumming roof of a modern brick farmhouse. We were an oddly assorted group as we sat in a huddle, dolefully drinking *yerba maté*. I recalled that someone once wrote that there is nothing quite so depressing as a defeated, written-off utopia. The hours ticked by and the rain roared down relentlessly, flickering the oil lamps. There was still no electricity at the old colony and the tiny telephone booth had closed at dusk.

At midnight, Randolf determined that we should make a start regardless, otherwise the Pirapó could rise and maroon us for days. Our vehicle sloughed through the mud, the windscreen wipers having little effect. The village might not have existed in the watery blackness, but for the blur of a few lamplit windows.

'I won't be in a hurry to come here again,' Randolf muttered darkly.

'There's nothing to come here for anyway,' snapped Mercedes, who had been reluctant to make the trip at all. '*Nada!* Absolutely *nothing!*'

∞

Mary stayed on at Cosme until mid-May 1900, aware that she was a financial burden, isolated and critical of almost everyone around her. When a pregnant 18-year-old girl became engaged to a man twenty-five years her senior, Mary vented her righteous outrage in a letter to Will: 'I have only a contemptuous pity for the girl … For the man I feel the utmost scorn.'[40]

She made an abrupt decision to leave the colony and rent the cottage where she had given birth to her son in Villarrica. The tall red-haired woman with the baby in her arms became a distinctive figure in the town's muddy streets, picking her way around puddles and cowpats in her long blue skirt. She employed sign language to shop at the market, her Spanish limited to a few words, and anyway the country people mostly spoke Guaraní.

Mary came to depend on her confidences to her husband in almost daily letters, saved up until she could post a bunch together. In just the fortnight since she arrived in town, she wrote to Will, 'I have 120 pages of daily letter stuff for you, mostly taken up with the boy.' She reminded him that Tuesday 29 May would be their wedding anniversary:

> Three years married. It seems little and yet it seems a life –
> it is a life indeed, for what would either be, the other being
> lost? Every day brings me nearer you and my heart will be
> glad indeed when the last day of this separation is over, and
> I too hope we may never be parted again.[41]

Her landlord, Señor Ortiz, was kind, and fussed ineffectually about her security:

I used to sit in the verandah at sundown and even till nearly dusk. After a week of this my landlord and his six daughters came one evening to see me and remonstrate. It wasn't safe, they gave me to understand; there were bandidos about … Some weeks afterwards, finding the door rattle in a high wind, I examined the hinges. There were no screws in them, only nails, old rusty nails, about two to each hinge. I smiled. The thing was so like Paraguay.[42]

She was touched by another act of generosity. In a note she sent to Thomas Dysart, the riverboat engineer, she had mentioned that if she ever ran short of funds she would apply to him. 'The next post brought me $50. Wasn't it kind of him? For however kind anyone may be, to ask is always a little unpleasant. I am very glad to have it as I can spend some of it for clothing for Billy and have him warm going down the river.'[43]

At the end of July 1900, Will Gilmore returned for Mary and she packed up their few possessions to go back with him to Argentina, where he had been offered more work for the summer shearing season.

The family made their departure from the country in which they had invested so much optimism on the paddle-steamer *Olimpo*. Mary stood at the railing as the boat edged out into the wide bay of Asunción in the pearly morning light, sounded its hooter, its paddles churning the muddy waters and headed down the great complex of rivers – the Paraguay and Paraná and on to the noble estuary of the Rió de la Plata.

II

TANGOS

The Gilmores would have seemed a shabby couple as they came down the gangway from their paddlesteamer, the muscular bearded man struggling with luggage and the tall woman, her dark skirt and jacket neatly patched, holding a young child. But to be threadbare and travel-worn in Buenos Aires in August 1900 was commonplace, and in the raffish port of La Boca, almost mandatory. The big ocean liners bringing the immigrants across the Atlantic from Europe docked in the new port dredged at vast expense to the east of the Plaza de Mayo, but the riverboats still came here, to moor, jammed bow to stern in the turgid, noisome waters of the Riachuelo, next to the brightly painted craft of the Genoese fishermen who had made this area their home.

But the woman, Mary, would still have been an object of interest, not only for her pale skin and dark red hair, but also because she was most likely taller than any other woman in the milling, noisy crowd on the wharf. However those men adopting the *machismo* of their new country would not have approved had they known that she called herself a socialist, believed in votes for women and tended to be more assertive than her husband.

The family was guided through the tangle of people, horse-drawn carts and wagons on the wharf by the *Olimpo*'s engineer, Thomas Dysart. He had known Mary since she came to South America four years earlier and after her marriage had taken an instant liking to her husband as well. Dysart proved a good friend to the couple – between voyages delivering special parcels rather than entrusting them to the mails – and had recently sent Mary a welcome $50. He had been charmed when their son had been named in his honour, William Dysart Cameron Gilmore.

Mary was avid to take in the scene as their carriage lurched through potholes and around tramcars towards the city:

> In the old Port of Buenos Aires one finds narrow winding streets as in Sydney, in some places so narrow there is barely room for the carriage traffic to pass the trams, and one could easily throw oranges from house to house or talk from window to window across the street.[1]

Mary's is a noticeably more romantic view than that offered by old photographs from the Archivo General de la Nación in Buenos Aires of the the badlands to the city's south at that time. These show the *cinta negra,* or black belt, as a clutter of factories, workshops, the municipal slaughter-house and meat-packing plants, all disgorging wastes into noxious lagoons where women washed clothes, while ragged children played in the sludge among a tangle of scrap iron.

The riverfront in Buenos Aires, c. 1900

As I am driven in to Buenos Aires from Ezeiza International Airport in October 2002 – nine years since I travelled on that riverboat to Paraguay – my heart is in my mouth. While planning this trip I had known about the rapidly revolving doors of the president's office, the US$140 billion external debt, the collapse of the peso, the restriction on cash withdrawals; I had known about angry *porteños* (the name for the citizens of Buenos Aires) beating the bank doors with pots and pans, had heard about the barter markets and the demonstrations in the streets. But still I had not been too alarmed.

I studied Spanish irregular verbs and determined to get past the present tense: 'I walk post office, tomorrow I walk post office, last year I walk post office' might have done last time, but now I could do better. I took tango lessons two nights a week: 'Slide your feet across the floor, slide, mesh your footwork with your partner's, torso upright, now twirl and dip, flick your leg back …' I had put aside for the journey my strappy dancing shoes and a sleek little black silk skirt.

But shortly before I departed, a Buenos Aires friend had e-mailed urging me to leave my laptop and jewellery at home and to wear shabby clothes. 'Don't look like a tourist,' he warned. 'If you must bring a camera, make it a small one you can carry in your handbag.' I consulted the Australian Department of Foreign Affairs' 'Advice to Travellers' on its website:

> The situation in Argentina is volatile with significant social and political tension resulting in regular mass rallies that occasionally become violent. Australians in Argentina should exercise caution, closely monitor developments that may affect their safety and avoid street gatherings which may occur as a result of the country's continuing economic problems. Crime, including hold-ups, muggings and armed robberies, continues to be a problem.

Not encouraging. The dancing pumps went, to be replaced by some old scuffed shoes and an anorak like a plastic mattress. The next bit of advice was a real worry:

> 'Express kidnappings' are becoming a problem in Buenos Aires. Victims are selected at random and held hostage for several hours until a ransom is paid, at which time the victim is usually released.

I didn't care for that 'usually' either. The *Guardian* reported how some ordinary Argentinians were held until a ransom was paid and then killed anyway, a teenage student whose corpse was found floating in a canal after a ransom approximating £3,000 had been delivered. Witnesses described men in police uniform as his abductors. 'Before it was just the rich who were targets of criminal activity,' said a Buenos Aires university professor, 'now you don't have to be wealthy to become a victim of robbery or kidnapping.'[2] And your captor could be your peer. With half the middle class now deemed to be below the poverty line, some of them, their lifestyles and expectations destroyed, had turned their resourcefulness to crime in an attempt to claw their way back. The online *La Nación* had a feature on techniques to guard against kidnapping attempts, which were happening at the rate of one a day: 'Remember to walk on the sidewalk against the oncoming traffic …' Police, overworked and underpaid, had been implicated in some crimes, while those still enforcing the law put themselves in great danger; over sixty officers had been killed in the previous six months in the capital and its surrounding province.[3]

As we drove along an arching freeway, high above squatters' houses thrown together from plywood, cardboard and tin, I felt both compassion and a deep sense of personal, selfish fear. This trip was going to be different. Why had I left my comfortable home to follow some fool story about a woman, however worthy, who came here over a hundred years ago? It was not as if I spent my life – though even to me it sometimes seemed like it – researching Mary Gilmore and the Australian colonists of Paraguay. In the past nine years I had been doing other things – screenplays, a thesis, and had been researching a story which had taken me to India twice – but somehow I had not finished with Mary, and in the New South Wales Mitchell Library I had found a cache of her writings, most never published, about her time in Argentina. So, for better or worse – and I hoped not for a great deal worse – I was back.

We arrived in the city proper with its grandiloquent architecture, but the streets were much scruffier than I remembered. I had wanted to stay in bohemian San Telmo, but my friend advised that it was not too safe there at night. I was booked instead into a small hotel in the centre of the city. On the broken pavement outside, a pleasant-looking family – mother, father and two very young children – were scrounging through bags of rubbish.

It was almost certainly Thomas Dysart who arranged for the Gilmores to stay at the Salvation Army hostel in San Telmo, a place suitable for *los ingleses* like themselves – those who were genteel but not well-heeled, especially if they spoke very little Spanish.

San Telmo was by then a *barrio* of poor immigrant workers. The rich had abandoned the district after the ferocious yellow fever epidemic of 1871, when more than 13,000 people had died within three months. Convinced the river fogs had brought on the disease, those who could afford to had relocated themselves on the higher ground in the city's north,

Crowded patio of a typical Buenos Aires conventillo, *c. 1900*

now the exclusive Barrio Norte. The tall mansions of San Telmo, with ironwork balconies overlooking narrow streets, formerly serviced by black slaves, had been converted into boarding houses, known as *conventillos,* for the city's labourers and the never-ending stream of new arrivals coming steerage class across the Atlantic.

The less fortunate lived on the street. But some found shelter with the Salvation Army at its hostel on Calle Humberto Primero. The main building had once been a gentleman's mansion; its nobly proportioned rooms with huge double doors opened to a tessellated-tiled verandah along the front of the building which was bright with potted flowers. A former grand salon was used as a dining room for the first-class boarders, which select community the Gilmores now joined.

Although Mary later admitted she had arrived with 'a fine Presbyterian prejudice' against the missionaries, she was soon won over to the Jayets, the couple running the institution. He was a Swede and she was Swiss-French, a tall, capable woman who already spoke ten languages and was about to embark on Norwegian. Mary remarked on her shrewdness: 'she never forgot a face and she read every man's character in his face'.[4]

Will Gilmore was not able to linger at the hostel. The family were still scratching for every peso they could put towards their return fares to Australia. He was due back at a ranch in Patagonia, Estancia Killik Aike, for the summer shearing season, but this time he would be taking Mary and young Billy with him. Meanwhile, here in the milder north, shearing took place in spring and he was hopeful of finding work with a reference from Agar, Cross & Co., the big estancia agents in Buenos Aires: 'The bearer, William Gilmore, is an Australian shearer we beg to recommend to you for shearing with Wolseley machines and who is desirous of finding employment.'[5]

But in the end it was a former Cosme friend, Jack Black, a New Zealander, who organised a job for Will at Santa Rosa, an estancia on the pampas almost 400 kilometres south of Buenos Aires. Black's laconic directions formed the entirety of his communication: 'The trains leave Plaza Constitution on Mon, Wed, Sat, change trains at Las Flores, take train for Tandil. Station master at Santa Rosa speaks English, will show you my house.'[6]

For three months Mary and Billy stayed on at the hostel, with Gilmore unable to visit them.

The First Rule of Travel, according to the writer Pete Mc-
Carthy, is to buy the local paper and go for a drink. 'The
court cases, property prices and obituaries will tell you more
than any guidebook, and the drink will help you feel you understand things that in reality are beyond your comprehen-
sion.'[7] Quite so, I agreed as I ordered a *vino tinto*, costing just
4 pesos, or US$1. A glass of good wine was even cheaper else-
where, but I was in the gloriously rococo Café Tortoni, with
its marble tables, leadlight ceiling, paintings and mirrors on
the walls. It was crowded with smart *porteños* taking aperi-
tivos; if 50 per cent of the population was below the poverty
line, then this must be the other half. I opened the daily English-language *Buenos Aires Herald* and flicked through its
pages: 'Pickets block bridge in homage to killed comrades…
IMF deal around the corner – Duhalde government exul-
tant… In the north-eastern province of Misiones some 500
teachers and state workers staged a march yesterday… Benefit performance of *Hamlet*… Kidnapped car dealer released
after 10 days when 2500 pesos ransom finally paid. Police
were not involved in the negotiations… RBL Women's Meeting Oct. 8, Mrs Mary Cherry Walmsley will give a talk on
"Opera Houses around the World". For bookings call Gertie
or Molly… Menem may be arrested if he again fails to testify
as a suspect in an investigation as to why he kept a secret
bank account in Switzerland… Escort Barbie. Argentine top
model. Only for you. Age 24. Discretion assured.'[8]

Plaza de Mayo, Buenos Aires, early 1900s

Mary made forays into the city, laid out on a grid pattern beside the broad brown estuary, with the green ocean of the pampas encroaching on its other sides. The grasslands were the source of the fabulous new wealth from beef transported to Europe in fast refrigerated ships, and from wheat, linseed and maize.

Just fifty families at the time were recorded as owning 4,600,000 hectares in the fertile Buenos Aires province.[9] Most of them had acquired their land and their influence during the colonial period and those with an old respected Spanish name such as Paz and Anchorena still enjoyed the greatest social prestige. But after the boom of the 1880s they had developed links, through obligation, marriage and mutual self-interest, with major industrialists and business people of the capital and leading figures in government, law and the military. The financial and political power of this group *el oligarquía* – perhaps 200 families in all – seemed impregnable against the demands of the working and middle classes for a greater voice. Presidential contenders and congressmen only emerged through the oligarchy's ranks, and political office, with its opportunities for corruption, ensured an even greater accumulation of wealth.

The landed gentry built mansions on their country estates and bought fine horses for playing polo, a game introduced by the British but passionately embraced by Argentines, or sometimes *pato,* an authentically local and violent horse sport, originally played by the gauchos with an unfortunate duck in a basket. When these favoured members of the upper class travelled abroad, they inspired a new saying, 'rich as an Argentine'. They returned from their sojourns in Europe with antiques, *objets d'art* and a love of French style. They demolished the old Spanish colonial city of Buenos Aires and with imported architects and teams of immigrant artisans – stonemasons, carpenters, tilers and plasterers – they remodelled it as a Francophile fantasy. Grand public buildings – all domes, cupolas, columns and caryatids – rose on the widened avenues. Sumptuous private *palacios* sometimes occupied a whole city block. And in the narrow cross streets the workers huddled in the cramped accommodation of the *conventillos.* Fifty thousand of them were *golondrinas,* 'swallows' visiting from Europe for the pickings of the season.

While Mary writes vividly about the people she met in Buenos Aires, her descriptions of the metropolis are blunt and prosaic. She was overawed by its size and sophistication; comparisons with Paris were meaningless to her for this was the largest city she had seen. She was, after all, only really acquainted with two:

> Buenos Aires is a very large city, having a population as great as that of Sydney and Melbourne put together. It is built on the edge of the Argentine pampa so that in situation it is quite flat. In all the newer parts the streets are wide, set at right angles to one another as in Melbourne, and planted with trees. Under these trees the coffee houses place seats and little tables where, in the evenings, thousands of people sit in the cool and drink coffee, eat ices, and take chilled milk through straws.[10]

She would have had no access nor presumably any desire to observe the upper classes in their exclusive haunts: playing polo and cricket at the Hurlingham Club or gathering at parties at the sumptuous Jockey Club with its colonnaded foyer on Calle Florida, its walls hung with paintings by Goya, Corot and a priceless Gobelin tapestry. The favourite watering place for British men – women were excluded – was the English Club, which occupied a rambling house in the centre of the city, where papers and publications from 'home' were subscribed to and English gin was always in stock. The wives met at the genteel, wood-panelled Richmond Café or the tearooms of the British-owned department store, Gath and Chaves, until that was superseded as the place to be seen by the opening of Harrods' a decade later.

The old Harrods' department store occupied a city block but was lacking customers and staff, many of its windows, its past elegance and any apparent future. Directly across from it, also closed and boarded up, was the gracious *belle époque* Phoenix Hotel. The Prince of Wales had been a guest here in 1926 and, on my previous visit to Buenos Aires, even I had enjoyed the faded charm of its marble floors, palm-filled atrium and gilded elevator cage.

I passed banks clad in corrugated iron sheeting as I made the short walk from my present modest hotel to Calle Florida, the famous pedestrian boulevard, alive and crowded as always. On the racks of the news kiosks three faces from bygone years were endlessly repeated on the displayed magazines – Evita Perón, Ché Guevara and the tango singer Carlos Gardel – in their personal variations of the brave smile, the revolutionary scowl and the languourous leer. Just how much *more* was there to say about them? Perhaps a people who feel diminished have a need for former heroes, especially those who seemed to represent the underdog. Ché was the undisputed winner at the T-shirt stalls, often with a message beneath his image, just in case anyone dared to forget his birthplace, *El Ché es nuestro!* – 'Ché is Ours!'

During the month that I made my many evening strolls along the Florida promenade (despite the official advice), there were always two or three people with the white sticks of the blind, a man with a card saying he was diabetic and no longer able to afford insulin, '*Soy diabetico. No trabajado*'; but they stood silently, passively, holding out their little cups. The only aggressive beggars I encountered, who physically detained me every time, were young women in floral skirts, usually holding babies to their breasts. I had laughed at the knee-jerk chauvinism when Argentine friends insisted they were Romanian gypsies, working in teams for a boss. One day I photographed a tiny sleepy boy, unhappily playing a squeezebox. 'Where do you come from?' I asked him as I dropped a peso into his tin. 'Romania,' he replied listlessly.

But every day and evening on the promenade there were young people scratching some kind of living with ingenuity and imagination. Musicians, buskers, artisans with the usual New Age handiwork spread out on the pavement, and the money-change touts, who offered only a fraction more than the bank rate but seemed officially tolerated. And every night a young couple – he in black shirt, white braces and two-toned 'correspondent' shoes, she beautiful but achingly thin in a brief slit skirt – danced the tango with perfect precision and gymnastic bravura. There were the living statues, staying still to stay alive: Carlos Gardel, naturally, immobilised under his fedora; inscrutably Charlie Chaplin; and the black-masked *El Zorro*, the Fox, of film poster fame.

The Fox – that was the nickname of one of the country's most famous past presidents, Julio Argentino Roca. The Gilmores' arrival in August 1900 came two years into Roca's second term. He was the hard man who had led an extermination drive against the country's Indians just twenty years earlier, opening up the pampas to settlement and becoming a national hero himself. The former professional soldier was

Living statue of Carlos Gardel

a wily politician who had well earned his vulpine sobriquet. During his corrupt authoritarian regime he advanced his own fortune, but also the nation's economy. A network of British-built railroads extended over the great flat land, new ports were dredged for ships taking Argentina's wheat and refrigerated beef to Europe and, with the orgy of public building and beautification, a dusty colonial town was turned into the endlessly extolled 'Paris of South America'.

Mary understood little about the politics of Argentina and no doubt her husband knew even less. The systematic and brutal way Roca had settled the 'Indian problem' may not even have been known to her, still less overly concerned her, given her views on the superiority of the Anglo-Saxon race. (It was to be another fifty years before Mary became active in Australia for Aboriginal rights.) The few scraps of information she did have about President Roca – his blue eyes and fair complexion much remarked on in the press – she absurdly romanticised: 'The handsomest man I ever saw. He had, in addition to physical perfections, the beauty of strong, just intent and mind.'[11]

In fact, in 1900 there were 40,000 unemployed in Buenos Aires and regular demonstrations in the Plaza de Mayo, with socialists and anarchists voicing their protests in front of the pink presidential palace, the Casa Rosada.[12] The previous year, when the secretary to the chief of police had the temerity to issue a public statement suggesting that the unemployed were not working because they did not wish to, he received a nasty shock: 'The next day several thousand fliers appeared on the streets; they offered employment and gave the secretary's home address as the place to which to report. The following morning unemployed workers packed that street and the adjoining blocks. Police reinforcements finally had to be called in to disperse the crowds.'[13]

A wave of political assassinations by Italian anarchists – of President Carnot of France, Empress Elizabeth of Austria and King Umberto of Italy – had recently shocked Europe. The *Buenos Aires Herald* warned *porteños* that the criminal anarchist existed among them, waiting to strike from the dark, 'from a fanatical, abnormal idea of his duty'.[14]

Anarchists and socialists had forged an uneasy alliance in Buenos Aires. But Mary, refugee from a socialist colony, made no comment on these developments, isolated by her lack of Spanish, and crucially by her almost total disillusionment with left-wing politics. 'I have come to the conclusion', she had written to her husband, 'that Communism is a failure – is not attainable, real Communism, that is, and enforced Communism is worse than none.'[15]

Her main concern in the sprawling city was the safety of herself and her son.

It was 3.30 on a Thursday afternoon and I had come to see the Madres of the Plaza de Mayo marching in the square in front of the Casa Rosada, as I knew they would be. Wearing their distinctive white headscarves, these 'Mothers of the Disappeared' were keeping their grim and regular appointment as they have been doing for a quarter of a century. I was startled to see heavy iron barricades, at least two metres high, right across the square between the Mothers and the palace, and behind the barrier a line of maybe sixty riot police in flak jackets with shields and full combat gear. This seemed astonishing overkill. There were only perhaps a dozen of the women, most of grandmotherly age, walking silently in a straggling group, accompanied by a man on crutches, a few other male sympathisers and some children.

I went over to three elderly white-scarfed women, presiding at a table of pamphlets and books, and asked about the show of force. A kindly woman explained that a big demonstration of rural workers and the unemployed was expected to join them in solidarity in the square that afternoon. Many of them had been organised to come by bus from other parts of the country. But she had heard they had been delayed at the edge of the city by a police roadblock, and all were being searched.

In April 1977, early in Argentina's seven-year state reign of terror by the military junta, a group of fourteen mothers gathered in the plaza, at great personal risk, protesting the disappearance of their sons and daughters, husbands and brothers.

Up to 30,000 mainly young people were abducted, tortured and killed by death squads in the regime's brutal 'Dirty War' against leftist guerrillas, outspoken students and anyone even vaguely suspected of sympathising with them. The mothers had no bodies to bury and grieve over, no death dates to mourn, no explanations for what had happened. The numbers of women silently protesting in the square grew.

A few months before my departure I had attended a talk in Sydney by their internationally famous spokeswoman, the feisty and combative Hebe de Bonafini, a tall, imposing 72-year-old with a large, squarish face. She could be mistaken for a provincial mayor, a magistrate or an accountant. After her passionate speech I was introduced to her and felt her assessing me shrewdly behind rimless glasses. The force of her moral authority was palpable. She gave me her card and agreed to meet with me later in Buenos Aires, but only if she had the time, 'as things are desperate there, as you must know'. Just a few days before she travelled, two demonstrators had been shot dead by police. In protest at the killings, 14,000 people had marched on the presidential palace demanding the resignation of the Duhalde government. It was forced into unprecedented action resulting in two police officers being arrested.

Now I was in the plaza at Buenos Aires and about to witness a demonstration. I could hear chanting and shouts in the distance. I asked the Mother at the literature table if Hebe de Bonafini would be coming to the square today. She looked at me drily. 'I'm not sure. She may come with the unemployed. But I don't think she'll be giving interviews …'

During the Dirty War, in 1977, Hebe's two sons Jorge and Raoul, university students in their twenties, were kidnapped and 'disappeared'. Afterwards she and forty of the newly formed Mothers of the Plaza were for a time imprisoned in a cell they shared with the corpse of a young man who had been tortured beyond recognition. 'On seeing him,' she was quoted as saying, 'we didn't know if he was one of our sons. The authorities do these kinds of things to put pressure on us, to show us how regrettably powerful they are.'[16]

In her Sydney talk Hebe explained why the Mothers wear white headscarves instead of carrying individual portraits of their missing loved ones. It was because they had resolved to 'socialise' motherhood, share their grief and anger:

> We travel the world and are in solidarity with all mothers of the world who suffer. Their lost children belong to us all. Our fight is to gain justice for *all* of them.[17]

She said when the 'so-called' democratic governments came to power in Argentina, people thought the Mothers would stop, their purpose over. 'But we did not believe in the promises of politicians. We continued to march every Thursday.' The uncompromising stance split the Mothers' movement. Some of the women wanted the satisfaction of a trial, an exhumation, a grave to visit, a memorial, some form of reconciliation; others accepted financial compensation. But the radical group of mothers, standing firm with de Bonafini, rejected any attempt at closure.

> We denounced and rejected all the palliatives that were offered to us. We denounced the exhumation of corpses. We mothers began to reject death and everything that symbolised death – the offers of museums, monuments, flowers thrown in the river, solemn ceremonies – we rejected them all. We rejected the very idea of our children's deaths – for we shall not allow them to die.[18]

A handful of top-ranking officers, including the former

dictator Jorge Videla, were tried and sentenced in 1985. But the Mothers believed their distrust of politicians well founded when President Carlos Menem signed a pardon for the guilty men of the junta in 1989. Videla was allowed home under comfortable house arrest.

The Mothers became involved in many projects as Argentina's economic crisis worsened: barter-exchange markets and an attempt, with the voluntary labour of over a hundred young people, to bring an abandoned flour mill back into production. They allied with another group, *Hijos* – the children of the *desaparecidos*. Most ambitious of all, in 1999 they set up a co-operative university with voluntary teachers and 580 students. Though a critic described it as an 'unrecognised pseudo-educational entity',[19] today de Bonafini claims the university has thousands of students. 'It is so beautiful to go there,' she told us in Sydney, 'to this place full of young people who have so much energy and optimism.'

In 1999 the Mothers were awarded the UNESCO Education for Peace prize. They were even tipped as possible candidates for a Nobel Peace prize – that is, until 11 September 2001. While doing some research before my departure for Argentina, I was startled to read that, on a Buenos Aires television programme, Hebe de Bonafini had apparently rejoiced at the attacks on New York and Washington as 'a blow to the belly of the beast!'[20]

It is not surprising that hard remark cost this brave, indomitable woman many supporters in the West. If I had met her again in Buenos Aires, I would have wanted to question her about her lack of empathy for those other suffering mothers whose children too were victims of hatred.

The chanting and shouts had become louder and suddenly a great throng of people surged from the Avenida de Mayo and into the square, waving flags and banners, placards and shovels. Thousands filled the vast space, as I had seen it happen so often on archive film. But this was no adoring populace waiting for Evita to wave from the balcony; instead, it was a swarming, angry mass of people: peasants from the northern provinces; workers laid off when factories closed down; municipal public servants who had not been paid for months. The poor, the desperate and the shirtless. There were women in the throng and perhaps Hebe was there somewhere with a flag, like Delacroix's Liberty, pressing forward to the barricades – metaphorically, that is, for I witnessed no violence from the protesters. But the riot police held up their shields and spread themselves out in a taut, tense line, facing the protesters through the iron mesh. Now I saw other police at the rear of the plaza. A helicopter clattered above, using state-of-the-art technology, I was told, to photograph people in the square. The friend who was with me, a mild-mannered accountant, had been reluctant to be there at all. Now Luis was in real panic, rasping that we had to get out. 'The police might use tear gas!' We fled away down a side street. I watched the event, described as 'a near-riot', on television that night in my safe hotel room and next day read about it in the newspaper.[21]

I never did get my interview with Hebe de Bonafini, whose contacts would inevitably have been recorded by state security. She was probably right in what I sensed was her steely assessment of me. I was a coward.

Mary Gilmore had repudiated politics for the time being, but she still had an insatiable curiosity and a compulsive need to write, 'observing people, their circumstances and their ways'.[22] She began to make notes about the people among whom she lived, starting with the formidable Madame Jayet.

Buenos Aires' unsavoury reputation at the end of the nineteenth century had brought various moral and social reformers to Argentina. The Jewish Association for the Protection of Girls and Women and the British Immigration Society were pledged to save young female immigrants from prostitution. Madame Jayet's father had been a watchmaker, she had lost her mother when she was still a young girl and soon after had joined the Salvation Army. Mary described how the Jayets arrived among 'the first handful of Salvationists in Buenos Aires and perhaps in South America'. She thought their story was one 'of courage, of hardship, of peril' in the face of the country's overwhelming Roman Catholicism. They had taken a single room in one of the poorer parts of the city, and gradually they made their mission known.

> Sometimes they went out in the streets unmolested, sometimes they had to fly for their lives. A while all would be quiet; then would come persecution; sympathisers lost their situations, friends dared not sit with open doors or win-

dows for fear of stones, and the houses of members were known by their battered doors and smashed windows.

But the small band of Salvationist believers gained a following; they expanded to two rooms and then to four, with furnishings and patronage provided by 'certain people of standing'.

Little by little persecution ceased. As numbers grew, money came in; with money, visions of what could be done for the needs of a teeming city in which no minimum wage, no eight hours, no restriction of contract immigrants, operates to keep down the number of desolate and destitute. Buenos Aires is neither India, China nor Japan, but the taint that comes from inmixture of racial standard of a low grade and the seething poverty that makes it impossible for the unskilled and even skilled labour to rent more per family than one quarter of a room, fill the streets with homeless wanderers, almost whose only hope of food is crime and whose only chance is charity.

Madame Jayet took Mary on a tour of the public dormitory for the second-class residents, to the converted carriage house for the third-class boarders, and finally to the night refuge for homeless men – an iron shelter on the adjoining block containing trestle tables for meals and 'eighty wooden bedsteads each with mattress, pillow and a pair of strong blue police blankets. Going in to have a look at it I found it spotlessly clean and smelling as strongly of carbolic as a hospital.'

Mary felt ashamed of her initial prejudice and concluded, 'I had no feeling save of admiration and respect and a wish that all Christian bodies would take up the waif of the street and feed and shelter him in the same impersonal kindly way. All classes came to them, all religions. They met all alike, they fed all alike.'[23]

The *Buenos Aires Herald* estimated that in the month of August 1900 alone, the Salvation Army had sheltered 3,929 people in its night refuge and supplied 8,036 meals. The following month the night refuge 'for the Relief of needy and homeless persons' was moved to a new location further up the street and the army opened a Free Labour Bureau to supply 'Peones, Cooks, Clerks and Domestic Servants at shortest notice. Estancieros and Employers of Labour are invited to write to the Bureau when requiring servants.'[24]

I made enquiries of the Salvation Army, still carrying out its mission in Buenos Aires but housed in new premises. The old hostel had closed many years before, they told me, and no one could remember the street number, but I would be able to recognise the big empty building down at the end of Calle Humberto Primero.

San Telmo had long been a haven for artists; now, even in the current economic crisis, the *barrio* was fashionably bohemian, with bistros and tango clubs, art galleries and antique shops. As I walked along the narrow street I learned from my guide-book that it could boast quite a history. Number 555 was the location of the famous publishing house, Sudamericana, founded by an exile from Franco's Spain who published the unknown Colombian Gabriel García Marquez's *Cien años de soledad* (*One Hundred Years of Solitude*) in 1967.

One building had a grim façade. A plaque indicated that it had been built in 1735 and was now a penitentiary museum. A volunteer guide, a man of military background, explained that it had been the Buen Pastor prison for women, run by nuns. I learned later that the wealthy and influential writer and publisher Victoria Ocampo was imprisoned there for twenty-six days in 1953 because of her vocal opposition to the Perón regime. Later she published the Spanish translations of Graham Greene's political novels, banned in Franco's Spain; in gratitude Greene dedicated *The Honorary Consul* to her.

Just down the road, at 250 Calle Humberto Primero, I found a derelict mansion I was sure must be the old Salvation Army hostel. Near the entrance gates men were cooking over a brazier. French windows blocked off with corrugated iron once opened on to a verandah which I imagined as it might have been, bright with potted yellow flowers. The blotched, crumbling walls looked unstable, there were gaping holes in the roof, but the building was still accommodating the homeless. Damp shirts and trousers flapped on strings along the verandah. A woman was washing clothes in a bucket while her baby played in the dirt where once there had been a garden. Upper windows were broken, in darkness. Others glared where the squatters had rigged makeshift lights. A young couple, the girl with various face piercings,

The derelict former Salvation Army hostel in San Telmo

came from a front room through a tie-dyed curtain. The aroma of marijuana, not Madame Jayet's carbolic, floated on the evening air.

But former homeless people such as these, now occupying substantial vacant buildings, were the lucky ones compared to those sleeping rough in the parks or on the streets. Well after midnight I emerged from an elegant restaurant, having dined sumptuously with friends. As we hailed a taxi I saw that a family of rubbish fossickers, parents and three small children, were bedded down on the pavement against the restaurant wall, asleep under some rags and sheets of cardboard.

'It's terrible!' I expostulated, as we crossed the street for a taxi. 'Yes, it's terrible,' said Luis, my Argentine friend, 'it's terrible and it's wrong. But with the elections coming there are populist politicians who tell these people that all humans are born equal, that they have a right to their share.'

'That's right! I agree with that!' I shouted at him, so easy on a full stomach to assert my position on the side of the angels.

'But if they rise up to demand their fair share,' he answered quietly, 'it will bring the military back. That's the fear a lot of us have.'

For Argentina it has been a shocking descent since 1900, when the country was the world's largest meat producer and the second largest supplier of wheat. It was commonly seen in competition with Australia, but it was also judged a potential economic rival to the United States. Carlos Pellegrini, a former Argentine president, predicted in 1906 that his nation would win the race for economic superiority by the end of the century.[25] The expression 'God is Argentine' became a popular saying.

But Marcelo T. de Alvear, president from 1922 to 1928, warned his people of the danger of too much hubris:

Argentines refuse to accept any truth which makes them inferior to anyone else. Theirs is the greatest city in the world, their frontier mountains the highest and their pampas the widest; theirs the most beautiful lakes, the best cattle, the richest vineyards, and the loveliest women. They accept no qualifications nor the fact that there might be some other country which surpasses them in anything … perhaps it is this overwhelming pride of the Argentines that leads them to believe they can live aloof from any interdependence of nations; that they are self-sufficient without possessing even elementary industries; and that they need have no fear of whatever changes may come.[26]

The changes have come with a vengeance. While Argentines act out their fear and desperation with almost daily demonstrations in the capital, they have become dangerously subdued in their expression of *argentinidad,* their sense of national esteem. Over 100,000 mostly professional people have left in the last two years. A recent BBC documentary compared the formerly rich country to the shell of a five-star hotel: 'People are still demanding comforts and room service that are no longer available and no one is listening.'[27]

But some developers show defiant optimism. As this book was going to press I had news from Buenos Aires that the squatters have been evicted from the old Salvation Army hostel building and the bulldozers have moved in to make way for a shopping centre. Public outcry and a court order have apparently stayed further demolition for the present.

Some of the other guests in the first-class dining room at the hostel attracted Mary's attention. One claimed to be a lineal descendant of Oliver Cromwell, another was said to be related to the Duke of Somerset, although a third she dismissed as 'a cowboy'.[28]

One dining companion, in particular, captured her imagination: a Chilean businessman called James McGregor Finland, son of a Scottish father, 'educated at the grey old University of Edinburgh, inheritor of his father's estates, master of half a dozen languages, and son of a *criolla*-Chilean mother. He had the look of it in his flattened Indian face. He had the way of it in his great brute strength, his magnificent physique, and, above all, English taught as he was, in his typical South American fiery patriotism.'

They sat at the same table at meals and Mary was grateful to converse in English. She never forgot the Indian in him, she wrote, 'and, truth to tell, he never let anyone else forget it. Yet somehow I liked the man in spite of myself and my foreign upbringing.' She liked him because he was her type – a manly man.

> There was about him an air of strength, of virility, that attracted one, especially a woman, a capacity for immediate action, action absolutely devoid of the element of the uncertain, that drew admiration and attention in spite of a constant undercurrent of repulsion. One looked at his strong white teeth and felt health and strength. One heard him speak of his country, and dreamed patriots. 'My country, Chile!' he would say, and as he said it the smoky eye would deepen and flash under the depressed eyebone, the head thrown up with all the pride of a Highlander among Lowlanders.[29]

The wealthy McGregor Finland was in Buenos Aires for business, but could achieve little because of the simmering argument between Argentina and Chile over the demarcation of their border in southern Patagonia. There was talk of war. 'The country from end to end, from Argentine Atlantic to Chilean Pacific', Mary observed, 'was in a state of tumult over the Chilean–Argentine boundary question.'[30]

The southern areas of Patagonia and the island of Tierra del Fuego had long been claimed but neglected by the Argentine government, while large numbers of land-hungry Chilean peasants had been moving across the *cordillera* since the 1830s and assuming ownership of the territory. In 1881 a settlement was reached between the two countries which provided for a division of Tierra del Fuego between them and set a vague international boundary along the line of the 'highest peaks of the Andes'.

But in the intervening years the Chileans had reoccupied the southern region and the Argentinians, under the forceful dictatorship of President Julio Roca, were ready to take them on. As the *Buenos Aires Herald* reported in October 1900: 'Chilli will never be quite satisfied until she has been "sat upon".'[31]

Chileans were distinctly unpopular in the city. McGregor Finland admitted that he felt unsafe in the streets. Potshots from the high buildings were common. 'He was too big a man to be mistaken for an Argentine,' Mary wrote, 'who is a small "neat" man, leaning more to the Spanish type than does the Chilean.'

It is likely that McGregor Finland walked with Mary through San Telmo's narrow streets, perhaps pointed out his vulnerability against the defensive architecture: window bars 'half an inch thick, suggesting nothing so much as gaols or private lunatic asylums', and the parapets looming above: 'We learned the use of these things later... you can shoot from behind a parapet into the street in almost perfect safety.' He may have told Mary the story – little known in England, but frequently recounted in Argentina – of how those narrow streets had played a key part in defeating an invasion by the British.

In June 1806 Commodore Sir Home Popham was returning from South Africa in command of a British naval squadron, accompanied by General William Carr Beresford and a Highland regiment. Acting on their own bungling initiative, they led a combined force of 1,600 men in an insouciant invasion of Buenos Aires, declared the Spanish-ruled city a British possession and occupied it for two months. The astonished Spanish viceroy fled to the interior, pausing only to make off with the bullion from the treasury.

The Foreign Office in London reacted in consternation, unsure whether to be embarrassed or gratified. Meanwhile, a resistance army of 12,000 patriots, led by a Frenchman, Santiago de Liniers, joined with the residents of Buenos Aires to repel the insolent invaders. After a skirmish, the British surrendered. The captured officers were placed under house arrest on an estancia on the pampas and spent their days delightfully, fishing, hunting and playing cricket.

His Majesty's Government hastily dispatched reinforcements to Argentina, with Lieutenant-General John Whitelocke in command. But the *porteños*, the people of Buenos Aires, had now gained a new sense of confidence and were determined to repel the next British onslaught. They enlisted and trained their own militia. When Whitelocke's force of 7,000 red-coated soldiers entered the narrow streets of San Telmo on 5 July 1807, the citizens crowded the flat rooftops of the houses and tipped barrels of boiling oil from the parapets; they bombarded the troops below with 'musketry, hand grenades, stink pots, brick bats, and all sorts of combustibles'.[32] In that one day 'half of the British assault force were casualties: 401 dead, 649 wounded, 1924 prisoners'.[33] General Whitelocke abandoned the battle and evacuated his troops. Further disappointments awaited him in London where, for his troubles, he was court-martialled and cashiered.

But for the Argentines the victory instilled a tremendous sense of nationalist pride, and with it a growing determination to govern themselves. In 1810, taking advantage of Spain's occupation by Napoleon's forces, an autonomous government was set up in Buenos Aires, ostensibly pledging loyalty to the deposed King of Spain, Ferdinand VII.

However, a war of resistance ensured that Spanish rule was never reimposed. General José de San Martín extended the nationalist struggle, in 1817 leading his 5,000 soldiers in an epic crossing of the Andes to join with Simón Bolívar's forces in Peru. Today in Argentina, as *El Libertador,* Martín is to be found in stone or bronze sitting triumphantly astride his horse in almost every town and city square. He had a belief, later more honoured in the breach than the observance within the country he liberated, that 'The army is a lion that must be kept in a cage and not let out until the day of battle'.

Evidence of the British invasion was there for Mary and

McGregor Finland to find in their own street, Calle Humberto Primero, near their hostel. In the church of Nuestra Señora de Belén they could have found a marble table in the sacristy with a plaque indicating that it was used as an operating table for the wounded during the hostilities. Across the way, another small plaque called attention to the site of a bar run by a local woman, Martina Cespedes. When British soldiers captured and occupied the church, the woman and her many daughters enticed them, one by one, into the bar and tied them up. Martina handed over eleven of her twelve British captives to the Argentine militia – the twelfth stayed on to marry one of her daughters. The story goes that the mother was rewarded for her brave deeds with the title of Captain of the Argentine Army.[34]

Mary's writings indicate that she frequently walked the streets of the *barrio* with only her 2-year-old son for company. I can picture her in her long dark schoolmarmish dress, striking if not beautiful, with her deep russet hair and fine dark eyes, deflecting the hungry stares of lonely immigrant men. When a *guapo*, a city dandy with slicked-back hair, moves towards her, bowing, mouthing felicitudes she does not understand, she holds her son tightly against her body.

'*Permiso, Señor, no comprendo. Me inglesa.*'

She usually found it more prudent to pass as *inglesa*; to say she was *australiana* would have invited an enquiry, further conversation. Grasping the small boy's hand she would hurry on.

Mary apparently did not know that Buenos Aires at this

time had a lurid reputation as the port of missing women, its bordellos said to harbour countless young European women kidnapped and sold into the South American sex trade. 'If anybody wants to find out how the girls are treated,' proclaimed the National Vigilance Association in London in 1899, 'they may simply take a walk along the Calle San Juan and the Calle Lavalle, those two streets that have been nicknamed by the people Calles Sangre y Lagrima (the streets of blood and tears).'[35]

Calle San Juan runs through San Telmo, with Mary's hostel on Calle Humberto Primero just around the corner. Mary had an innocently benign view of it: 'Calle San Juan is one of the finest streets leading from the city, long, broad and beautifully planted; where trams fly all day long and notices order you "*Guardar la Izquierda*" (keep left) every few yards.'[36]

There were in fact many brothels in the neighbourhood but, despite the claim that 'the English girl commands the highest price and it is to the Argentine that she is generally exported',[37] the British had little actual cause for alarm. Very few of their women ended up in the bawdy houses of Buenos Aires. Between 1889 and 1901 almost 5,000 foreign prostitutes were registered with the municipal authorities, as was required of them (unlike the local women, who generally preferred to work freelance from the streets and tango halls). Some were from Italy and France, a negligible number from Britain, but an overwhelming 65 per cent were Polish, Russian or Austro-Hungarian. Most of these women were voluntarily escaping poverty, social upheaval or persecution at home and saw a chance for survival in the overabundance of

Street mural, La Boca

lonely men in Argentina. A large number of them were Jewish. As one rabbi conceded in 1899: 'One must have seen the misery of the Polish Jewish cities ... to understand that a trip to Buenos Aires is not frightening.'[38]

In the clubs, cafes and bordellos of La Boca and San Telmo, immigrant men were escaping the crowded tenements to try out the steps of a new dance – with a prostitute if they could afford her fee, otherwise with each other. To the strains of piano, violin or mandolin the dancers' sliding, swaying movements melded the sinuousness of Spain's flamenco, the throb of gaucho tunes, the wistfulness of the countryside *milonga*, the rhythm the black slaves brought from Africa. But the tango's final distinctive sound arrived with the *bandoneón*, a small accordion brought from Germany by sailors.

The dance has been defined as 'a sad thought that is danced', or 'a game of chess', played between 'a fatal man and a femme fatale', their mutual attraction and repulsion 'prolonged into an unbearable, endless tension'.[39] Not every Argentine loves the tango: Ezequiel Martínez Estrada has called it 'a dance without a soul for automatons', parodying 'the seriousness of copulation because it seems to engender without pleasure'.[40] By 1900 the tango had become an obsession in the working-class barrios, although it lacked respectability and social acceptance.

In San Telmo Mary could not have avoided seeing a huddle of lonely men on a café corner or at the doorway of a bar or tenement patio, as one of them, partnering a prostitute or another man, gave an impromptu demonstration of the sultry, gliding motions, pelvis to pelvis, the strutting, suddenly precise steps, the twirl and languorous, scandalous embrace. She would not and could not have approved. She would have gathered her long dark skirts about her and hurried on.

The tango eased the loneliness and hardships of the poor. It alarmed the Argentine élite who feared both its blatant sensuality and the social danger that it represented – that the masses were finding expression. Soon the dance was exported to Europe, titillating and scandalising; it became a sensation in Paris, while the British royal family, recognising disgusting foreign habits when they heard of them, officially made it known that they would decline attendance at parties where it was performed.

❧

In a smoky nightclub in San Telmo, the crypt of a deconse-
crated convent, a couple glide under the spotlight, limbs
meshing in moody coquetry. At a change in the music, *ban-
doneóns* growling, they step, turn, twirl, rock. He forces her
backwards and low, the threat of violence lingers between
them. White throat exposed to the light, she hangs there,
then stretches, springs, advances, all feline aggression and
challenge. Her beauty is dangerous, cropped black hair stark
against her pallor, black dress split to the thigh, a sleek black
panther stalking her prey. With sudden mastery, her partner
turns, pushes her back, and predator is prey once more.

Likenesses of the great tango singer Carlos Gardel brood
down from every wall. It has been said that if the bordello
phase, with the emphasis on the dance itself, was the first era
of the tango, then Gardel's, from roughly 1919 to 1935, was the
época de oro, the golden age. He is still revered as the greatest
exponent of the *canción*, the tango song. Most of his mourn-
ful lyrics have a dark hint of misogyny, and warn against
women who are too independent:

> It's best not to talk about women;
> none of them, friend, give you any reward,
> and today I assert this from experience.
> Take my advice: don't fall in love,
> but if it should happen you have to surrender,
> have strength! Suffer it, and don't cry,
> for a truly macho man should never cry.[41]

The writer Jorge Luis Borges wrote that the mission of the tango was 'to give Argentinians the inner certainty of having been brave, of having performed in accordance with the requirements of daring and honour'.[42] But to feminist historians the tango expressed a deeply conservative *macho* vision of Argentine society.[43]

Gardel's image is still everywhere in Buenos Aires: on the covers of magazines and books in Calle Florida; in bas relief in a technicolored tourist alley in La Boca; painted on building façades in San Telmo; as a statue in working-class Abasto where he grew up and the Subte (subway) station was re-named in his honour. A radio station – FM Tango – still plays his recordings for one hour each day. He belongs to the Argentine people, who do not care to be reminded that he was born in France.

Gardel's image is darkly narcissistic, enigmatic and languorous in the shadow of his fedora, forever youthful, forever loved. He died romantically and tragically while still young and beautiful in a plane crash at Medellín, Colombia, in 1935; at least three people committed suicide on hearing the news. On impact a money belt of gold sovereigns was said to have fused into his heart, piercing it with golden slivers. He became a myth. People lined the streets for seven kilometres to watch his funeral cortege pass by on its way to the Chacarita cemetery.

Una sombra ya pronto serás,
Una sombra, lo mismo que yo …
A shadow you soon will be,
A shadow just like me …[44]

Luis drove me to the Chacarita, on the western fringe of the city, on his way to an appointment beyond it. We wandered the aisles of the vast necropolis, among the imposing vaults, mausoleums, marble obelisks and fanciful statuary of the affluent Argentine dead, those who could not quite make it to the infinitely more exclusive Recoleta cemetery near the centre of town. But Juan Domingo Perón lies here in his family tomb – a less successful eternal address than his heavily embalmed spouse, Evita, who is in Recoleta, surrounded by the upper-class families who detested her.

But the star of the Chacarita is the grandiloquent tomb of Carlos Gardel with its huge, dinner-jacketed bronze statue. The plaques on its base, from admirers all over the world – a convent in Paris, factory workers in Mexico, miners in Bolivia – are partly obscured by all the floral wreaths. On every anniversary of his death the cemetery is said to be a crush of the devoted and traffic comes to a standstill outside.

I decided Gardel had received quite enough attention. I had another purpose in coming to the Chacarita – to search in the British Section, the Cementerio Brítanico, for the grave of an obscure Australian bushworker and Mary's friend, Billy Laurence.

Billy had been the husband of Mary's former rival, the nurse Clara Jones, who had wanted to marry Dave Stevenson instead but was talked out of it by William Lane. But Billy had been much loved by the Cosme community for his open cheerful nature and his 'golden tenor' voice, which made him a favourite of the colony's glee-club evenings.

With the outbreak of the First World War Billy Laurence,

Stevenson and a dozen other Australian colony men from Paraguay had declared themselves ready to die for King and Empire, for the red patches on the map they had learned about at school. They travelled to Buenos Aires and signed up at the British Army depot. They provided yet another bizarre variation in the motley crowd the *Buenos Aires Herald* described:

> Ties of blood and kindred and devotion to the Motherland brushed all other considerations to one side. There one rubbed shoulders with reservists, old soldiers, old volunteers, many of whom had seen active service in the South African war, and others anxious to give the most practical evidence of their patriotism.[45]

Billy, who was forty-nine years old, was rejected as unfit, but he refused to leave it at that. He insisted on an operation at the British Hospital to cure his condition, a stone in the kidney, so he could do his bit for the Empire. He died on the operating table. His mate Dave Stevenson arranged for him to be buried in the Chacarita. Stevenson, meanwhile, went on to the war and was wounded on the Western Front, a bullet lodged near his heart. He was discharged in 1916 and returned to Paraguay to marry Clara, the woman he had always loved.

It seemed to me Billy's life had always been something of a disappointment and that the Chacarita was a lonely place for such a simple bushman to finish up – and he had been an atheist to boot. The neighbours would hardly be sympathetic and I doubted that he had received a single visitor in the last ninety years. I planned that, as soon as we located his grave, I would buy a sheaf of yellow broom at the kiosk, the nearest thing they had to Queensland wattle. I thought Billy would enjoy it.

After over an hour in the British Cemetery we had found not a single grave as early as 1914, so concluded that segregation must have occurred later. We returned to the main Chacarita. Luis consulted a cemetery worker passing by with a wheelbarrow.

'He says unless you've paid for a vault at the Chacarita, if you only have a grave in the ground, it's dug up after six years and the bones are cremated. This has always been the system here. You never get longer than six years in the ground.'

'What happens to the ashes?'

'If someone claims them, they can be placed in an urn in the cemetery wall. Otherwise, well, they're just thrown away.'

Sorry, Billy …

On the way out we passed by the tomb of that *other* tenor. I noticed that one of the faithful had contrived the visual joke which is a regular attraction at the Chacarita. They had left a half-smoked cigarette between the statue's metal fingers. '*Cada día canta mejor,*' the *porteños* say. 'Gardel sings better every day'.

I made the longish return trip to the city alone by Subte, the underground metro. I knew that tourists were advised against the Subte, but thought if I kept my mouth shut I would merge with the other bottle blondes.

A young man came into the carriage with an electric guitar and portable amplifier and launched into some *canciónes,* tango songs, his tenor voice magnificent. Far from averting their eyes – as Australian people do with intrusive buskers – these *porteño* commuters, from some of the poorer barrios of the city, sat up and welcomed him, made requests, discussed possibilities across the aisle, disputed whether he should do this one or that, and spiritedly clapped each of his three songs. When he passed around the hat – and this in a country where half the people are now below the poverty line – almost everyone found a coin for him, even a toothless old woman with rustling plastic bags of scavenged paper. After a gracious speech – oratory was a bonus – and more applause, the young man moved on to the next carriage. We were all left smiling a little foolishly at each other. It was a sweet moment.

III

GRASSLANDS

In Buenos Aires one has a sense of a city lapped by two swirling tides – the wide brown Plata, which in the morning can assume the silver of its name, and the illimitable green of the pampa, flowing to the foothills of the Andes. The great flat grasslands, with deep black soil free of stones, broken by rare atolls of the native *ombú* trees, as if put there to offer shade for sheep and cattle, produced the country's stupendous wealth of its glory days. The American writer Archibald Macleish wrote a paean to the pampa:

> It is a country in which the distances from house to house are too great for the barking of dogs even on the stillest night, a country in which the cocks crow only twice because there is no answer. It is a country so level that even time has no hold upon it and one century is like another; a country so empty that the watchers at night put their eyes along the ground to see the circle of the horizon; a country in which the sky is so huge that men plant islands of eucalyptus over their houses to be covered from the blue; a country in which space is so great that all the

visions end in eternity. It is a country of grass, a country without stone ...[1]

It must have been frustrating for Mary not to travel across the great grasslands to visit Will at his estancia near Tandil, almost 400 kilometres south, in a remote area of parched hills and rocky streams, but there is no evidence that she did. She could not have afforded the train fare or had anywhere suitable to stay when she arrived.

However, she certainly fantasised about the life her husband was living, and she seems to have been taken in by what Bruce Chatwin has called 'all the cant about the gaucho'. While the 'real' gauchos of the early days were by then receding into frontier myth, a few colourful characters may have been employed at Estancia Santa Rosa. Mary had certainly heard about their accoutrements, such as the 'Argentine saddle, high at the back with a horn in front for the *riala* or lariat, huge stirrups, *cojonilla* (sheepskin), *fierza* (saddle mat or cloth), broad cinch and a bridle with bells on reins'.[2] She was an omnivorous reader and might also have come across Charles Darwin's journal writings from his 1832–33 voyage on the *Beagle*. He was fascinated by the gauchos' proud, dissolute appearance, their long black hair curling down their backs, and with 'great spurs clanking about their heels, and knives stuck as daggers (and so often used) at their waists, they look a very different race of men'.[3] Whether Mary ever actually encountered any of these wild horsemen or simply appropriated a description of them from other writers, she seems to have considered them a mandatory exotic subject for her potential Australian readers:

> The gay *gaucho* having pride in his appearance wore a yard-wide panama with a tall top and cord tassells or tiny silver bells around the edge, wide topped bombachos, thrust into *potro* boots with tiny bells set round the tops, a tucked and feather-stitched shirt, short jacket and broad sash ... As he walked he sounded like fairy bells ... Men were very proud of their spurs. They were always oiled and well polished. Also they loved that they should clank. Men walked in such a way that they would. Not to clank marked the greenhorn ...[4]

At the end of September 1900, the shearing and therefore Will Gilmore's employment at Santa Rosa, came to an end. His contract may have been shortened by a climatic and economic catastrophe. In 1900 there were extensive floods in southern Buenos Aires province resulting in 'the loss of fourteen million head of sheep'. The ultimate effect was to reduce the importance of sheep raising on the pampas, with much of the area turned over to crops and cattle.[5] Meanwhile, Gilmore needed to find more work in the north if he could.

On either side of the road, I observed, there were sudden lakes on the low-lying paddocks, fence posts and trees sprouting up from them. This was the end of a season, in October 2002, of sustained rain. My companion fretted that almost half the property to which we were heading was under water. And when the flood recedes, she said, it leaves the grass 'sour', bad for the sheep.

I was travelling across the pampas in a burgundy Fiat with Señora Elisa Magrane de Boote, the aristocratic Hispanic flow of her name brought up rather short by that 'Boote', the surname of her husband who is the fourth generation of a British family in Argentina. 'Call me Minnie,' she told me, everyone who knew her did, a pet childhood name which had stuck. She and her husband John usually stayed in their Recoleta apartment during the week and went to the property, Estancia Los Yngleses, 320 kilometres south-east of Buenos Aires, at weekends. This was the first time in six months that her husband had allowed her to drive this road by herself, 'and you're the reason for my sudden independence,' she grinned.

A handsome sixtyish woman, understated elegance in cashmere, she had clearly been a great beauty – and my view was confirmed when I saw pictures of the young blonde debutante back from 'finishing' in Europe in old clippings of Argentine society at play. I could tell she had been less than impressed by my little hotel when she picked me up in the city, so, two hours later, I was glad we were easier in our conversation and I enjoyed her natural vivacity.

We passed billboards, a house or two, some industrial development, the outskirts of a town. 'This is Chascomús,' Minnie said, 'the halfway point on the road to the estancia … Of course for Gilmore and the other men, it would have taken all day to travel to here … They would probably have put up for the night … Oh no …! I was afraid this might happen! Quick, sit on your handbag.'

She slowed right down. Ahead of us a dozen men stood right across the road, blocking it to traffic. There were other men at the sides. They had red flags and rough signs with various desperate messages in Spanish: *'Por los niños es necesito comida'* – 'Our children need food' – 'Please you must help us' – 'No jobs. No food. We are starving.' – and *'Trabajadores via extinción'* – 'The working class is on its way to extinction'. But there was a threat in their stout sticks and a couple of the men had knives in their belts.

'Who are they?' I asked.

'Highway robbers! *Piqueteros*! I'll handle this. Don't you say anything.'

The men surrounded us and peered into the car. Minnie lowered her window and handed the leader a negligible amount, about five pesos, less than US$2. They stood aside to let us through, almost deferential, vaguely apologetic. I felt I was experiencing what Australian Cobb and Co. coach passengers reported in the goldrush days – that when they were held up by bushrangers, they found some of them almost gentlemanly.

'They say they have no jobs because that milk factory over there closed down,' said Minnie, accelerating, 'but they'd rather stand about all day stealing money from people than go and look for other work!'

Later my informative friend Luis explained that a milk-processing plant called Gandara had closed down at Chascomús, throwing about a hundred people out of work. 'They have no hope of any other jobs now,' he said, 'so they block the roads to draw attention to their plight, to demand their jobs back, to get money to survive, and they share this between themselves and their families. They're like another road toll.' He told me they were called *piqueteros* after the English word 'picketers', and that there were groups of them all over the country. 'Sometimes they surround the entrance to a supermarket and demand bags of meat and groceries. Two months ago, at a gasworks in Comodoro Rivadavia, they threatened to blow up the tanks unless laid-off workers had their jobs restored. They are an organised force. When they want to cut a road or bridge, they delegate. When they want to stage national roadblocks – and that happened last holiday weekend – they can.' But it was usually only the leaders, he said, who had a political ideology; most of the men taking part in the protests just wanted their jobs back, roofs over their families' heads, meals on the table, even to *have* a table again, for many of them were sleeping rough.

For the moment, said Luis, especially after the police shooting of two of them nearly brought the government down, the authorities were leaving the men alone, letting them blockade the highways. At least until after the April 2003 presidential elections. 'The danger will be when they don't. These people have lost nearly everything. They don't have much more to lose.'

Minnie had no patience at all to discuss the *piqueteros,* although she was happy to tell me about the Gibson family and the history of the estancia. The fact that I was with her at all was the result of extraordinary luck, of reading the right book at the right time – or just in the nick of time – and so tracking down the property where Will Gilmore landed a job…

The next shearing contract Gilmore had formally arranged was in Patagonia, but that was two months away, in December 1900. In severe climates such as the high country of South Island New Zealand, the Falklands and Patagonia, shearing is not risked until high summer. He desperately needed more work if he could find it. One of Mary's letters home suggested that Will was fortunate enough to obtain a short stint of shearing on an estancia close to the mouth of the Rió de la Plata. The details she gives are vague, mentioning only that his employers were Scots.[6] Certainly that would have pleased her, for she had always taken pride in both her own Scottish ancestry and that of her husband. On the previous New Year's Eve she had written to Will from Cosme: 'We have been seeing the old year out, Scotch fashion.' She had sung 'Annie Laurie' and danced the Highland Schottische.[7]

I had wondered about these Scottish employers and whether James McGregor Finland, the Chilean-Scottish businessman, had provided the introduction for Will. Being a frequent visitor to Buenos Aires, he would very likely have made contact with those of his ilk – or that half of his ilk – at the annual Caledonian balls and Hogmanay celebrations.

Then a friend, knowing of my fascination with the country, gave me a handsome coffee table book called *Argentina: The Great Estancias*.[8] It was a visual delight to leaf through the colour plates: images of the pleasure domains of the Argentine oligarchy when they were one of the richest groups of people in the world, acting out their fabulous fantasies: a mock seventeenth-century French château; an ivy-clad English castle; a dazzling white Moorish palace set among palms and cypresses; a *faux* Norman manor; a German hunting lodge with massive chimneys; a long low-roofed Spanish hacienda with russet adobe walls.

The verdant pampas and the shorthorn, Hereford and polled Angus cattle which produce the wealth are artfully viewed through filigree entrance gates or at the end of long avenues of Lombardy poplars. Gardens are landscaped with cedars, palms and pools, wrought-iron follies and marble cherubs on plinths, tiled courtyards, urns of geraniums, fountains playing and inviting crocheted hammocks. The interiors suggest a feverish trawling of Europe for heavy Spanish furniture, iron candelabra, crystal chandeliers, carved wooden doors, silver candlesticks, leather-bound volumes, four-poster beds, portraits of haughty *hidalgo* ancestors in gilded frames and sensuous doe-eyed gauchos by the French painter Monvoisin.

And there are photographs of those who assumed the lifestyle as their birthright: two women with fashionably bobbed hair and jodhpurs, seemingly straight out of the pages of English *Country Life*, but they are María Teresa Bosch Alvear de Dodero and Stella de Morra de Cárcano in 1931 at Estancia San Miguel, entertaining the similarly jodhpured Edward, Prince of Wales. The prince grins sidelong, a pipe clenched in his teeth, as if gratified to have discovered such a delightful and neglected British colony. And a woman on horseback, caught in mid-canter across the steppe, hair tousled, smiling to camera through dark glasses, plaited belt at her waist and kerchief at her neck, is Jacqueline Bouvier Kennedy in 1966.

It was only a month before my planned trip to Argentina, when I was going through the book again, that I made the discovery. It *had* to be the place where Gilmore worked for Scottish sheep ranchers. In my earlier superficial browsing I had passed over it, misled by the property's name: Los Yngleses (The English People). With growing excitement I read:

> Inland from Cape San Antonio, where the estuary of the Río de la Plata meets the Atlantic Ocean, lies a historic estancia bought in 1825 by the Scottish Gibson family and still owned by their descendants. The estancia's name was Rincón del Tuyú, but after the Gibsons acquired it, the natives preferred to call it Los Yngleses (The English) in spite of the family's true nationality. Sheep ranching in Argentina began at Los Yngleses, and the estancia played a pioneering role in refining sheep breeds and in developing techniques to make productive use of wool.[9]

I keyed in the relevant names on an Internet search engine and came up with 'Gibsons – in Argentina from 1819' – the home page of a real estate company specialising in estancia land. There was a photograph of Prince Charles, wineglass in hand, with one of the directors. I wrote to the e-mail address and Herbert Gibson promptly replied. Another branch of the family now owned the property and he had sent my enquiry on to them. A letter duly arrived from Minnie Boote. 'Have no doubt,' she wrote, 'that Los Yngleses is the estancia where Gilmore worked. I wonder if this Will is related to Matthew Gilmour, who was brought out by the Gibsons from Scotland as a shepherd?' She extended an invitation for me to visit.

Minnie's connection to the estancia was by marriage, but, although she had an illustrious Argentine, Spanish and British background herself, she was very proud of the Gibsons and their almost two centuries in Argentina. The first of the family to arrive was John Gibson, the son of a Glasgow textile exporter, in 1819. A few years later he was joined by three brothers from Scotland – George, Robert and Thomas.

In 1825 they bought the 30,000-hectare estancia, then called Rincón del Tuyú. Three years later, after the premature death of John, the remaining brothers were running 600 head of pampa sheep, which they eventually crossbred with merinos to improve wool production; they experimented with Lincoln, but today the Romney Marsh is the property's exclusive breed, farmed for both meat and wool. By 1844 the brothers were packing wool at the estancia using the first mechanical baler in Argentina and shipping it from their own wharf to Liverpool and the weaving mills of Manchester. They had become seriously successful, running 100,000 head of sheep, and had acquiesced to the local name for the property, Estancia Los Yngleses. But there were Indian raids, and newspaper research informed me later that 'the list of stores sent down by sea included gunpowder, two cannons, eight muskets, 20 sabres and lead and stone cannon-balls'.[10]

The brothers had brought a few crofters with them from Scotland, including a man called Matthew Gilmour, as shepherds and labourers for the property.

Soon one Gibson brother, Thomas, emerged as the main *estanciero*. Although he bought other farm properties – at Azul in Buenos Aires province, Mendoza, and even in Paraguay – Los Yngleses was always the one that engaged his interest most. In 1862, he and his wife returned to Scotland leaving the running of the estancia in the hands of two of his sons, Ernest and Herbert. However, Thomas retained effective control for another thirty years, sending thunderous letters from his home at 1 Eglington Crescent, Edinburgh, even though they took eight weeks to arrive. He was still exerting power when Will Gilmore was employed there.

Minnie stopped at the village of General Lavalle, population today 1,000 inhabitants. Once it had been part of the estancia, but in 1866 the Argentine government summarily expropriated 8,000 hectares for a town settlement and with it took its port. A few boats were moored beside the wharf on the Ría Ajo, a navigable stream which flows into the last bay of the mighty Río de la Plata before it merges with the Atlantic Ocean. The village is nondescript, built on a grid pattern, like most settlements on the pampa; it is distinguished only by its beautiful 1892 Roman Catholic church largely funded by the Presbyterian Gibson family. There are many Scottish graves in its cemetery, the cause of death baldly announced on one headstone: 'Drink'.

We drove into Estancia Los Yngleses through an avenue of tall eucalyptus trees. I was enchanted to see flocks of rheas, the South American ostrich, among the sheep and Aberdeen Angus cattle. 'They're a pest!' cried Minnie.

The Big House, a rambling white-washed building with red-tiled roofs over its various sections, was set among spreading oak and chestnut trees and expansive lawns. The household staff having taken my luggage, I was introduced to Minnie's husband John Boote, a tall, rangy affable man, his conventional country clothing made distinctive by a 'gaucho' belt of silver chains and, appropriately enough, knee-high leather boots. Over lunch he expressed disappointment at the results of a cattle sale. Although the remaining 5,600 hectares of Los Yngleses is still primarily a sheep property, he also runs Aberdeen Angus and a herd of long-horned *criolla*, the native cattle.

Afterwards I walked with Minnie and admired the vast mown parkland – as if Capability Brown had been busy in Argentina, the trees in blossom, the wisteria arbour and beds of bright annuals. But she was furious about the damage some wild deer had done the previous night. Then we saw him, a distance away through the trees, a magnificent stag with huge antlers, his does behind him. 'That's the brute!' she exclaimed.

The *Great Estancias* book had noted that the Gibsons were fortunate in the property's unique terrain. Marshes, gullies, lagoons and woods of native *talas* and *coronillo* trees

Homestead, Estancia Los Yngleses

discouraged attacks by Indians, 'who bypassed the area in their raids, fearing that their horses would not be able to cross the marshes and crab beds'. The Gibson men and their workers repelled a determined Indian raid in 1831, fighting at close quarters in the woods, and against another attack in 1855 they used heavy artillery. I considered the damage that heavy artillery would do to Indians riding bareback ...

Minnie told me that what turned out to be worse for the Gibsons was the occupation of the estancia in the early 1830s by General Rosas and his 4,800-strong private army. The dictator had stopped off here while pursuing *unitario* 'revolutionaries' and *all* the cattle had been killed to feed his men.

A portrait of Thomas Gibson presides above the fireplace in the drawing room, his flowing white beard making him resemble an Old Testament prophet. On another wall are his

Thomas Gibson 1838 watercolour of gauchos branding at Los Yngleses

paintings of the property. He had been a dab hand at water-colours and some of them, from the 1830s and 1840s, I recognised from my book: the first modest, thatch-roofed ranchos built at Los Yngleses, nestled among Lombardy poplars; gauchos branding cattle; the Gibson men, in overcoats and scarves, standing beside their covered wagons to mark a boundary post in the frosty grass while servants in ponchos look on and birds wheel in the wintry sky behind them.

Between 1864 and 1873, after Thomas Gibson had returned to Edinburgh, he arranged for some forty workmen to be sent out from Glasgow as estancia labourers or *peones*. Minnie showed me the original list – many of the men had already taken Spanish first names in deference to their adopted home: Alfredo Taylor, Diego Boe, Tomás Nicholson, José McKenzie and Roberto Clark.

Thomas Gibson had worried at the time about how these men, mostly Borderers, would fit in. He wrote to his brother-in-law: 'As to what the men will be like, time will tell. Perhaps many are too well bred and intelligent. We will see whether this is good or not. Perhaps shepherds from the highlands would be more docile.'

As a strict Presbyterian ruling the estancia by mail from Scotland, Thomas Gibson forbade any work on Sundays. He expected his sons to read the Bible to the *peones*, even if he had to bribe them to do it. But he despaired of his elder son Ernest in regard to this matter, as he wrote to the younger Herbert:

> I would like very much for you to read prayers on Sunday morning at 10 am. I will pay you to do it. Ernest has no will to do it. You can take 15–20 minutes to do it. I will pay you six shillings and eight pence for each person present. You will receive benedictions yourself and the estancia will also.[11]

Squelchy earth sank beneath my feet as I picked my way through natural groves of *tala* trees, jumping from one firmer tussock to the next, to emerge at a wide lagoon. Ibis pecked at the water's edge, and wild ducks took off in a flurry at my appearance. I was encroaching on one of Ernesto's favourite haunts.

Apparently he had inherited his mother's dreamier nature, and during his schooldays in Scotland had developed a passionate interest in bird-watching. On returning to Argentina, he was sometimes accompanied on expeditions at

Los Yngleses by his friend, the naturalist and writer William Henry Hudson, who was making observations for his books *Argentine Ornithology* and *The Naturalist in La Plata*.

Together they enjoyed scenes Hudson later described:

> [T]he western sky flushed with sunset hues, the calls from the reedy marshes of ibis and spoonbills, storks, swans and spurwing lapwings, the cry of the upland plover, mellowed and made beautiful by distance and the profound silence of the moonlit world.[12]

Hudson was born in 1841 at Quilmes in the La Plata region, to American parents who had migrated to Argentina. When he was six years old, he and an elder brother visited a property on the Plata marshes which could well have been Los Yngleses, for a biographer describes the owners as 'Scotch'.[13]

On that property young William Hudson had a powerful experience:

> It was all like an English meadow in June ... An astonishing number of birds were visible – chiefly wild duck, a few swans, and many waders – ibises, herons, spoonbills, and others, but the most wonderful of all were three immensely tall white-and-rose-coloured birds, wading solemnly in a row a yard or so apart from one another some twenty yards out from the bank. I was amazed and enchanted at the sight, and my delight was intensified when the leading bird stood still and, raising his head and long neck aloft, opened and

shook his wings. For the wings when open were of a glorious crimson colour, and the bird was to me the most angel-like creature on earth.[14]

The boy learned it was a flamingo, and this vision, a true moment of epiphany, set him upon a course. Watching birds and writing about them was to become his life's work.

In 1874, after a last journey to Patagonia, Hudson left South America for ever. He moved to England, to him at first a country 'of glorified poultry-farms'.[15] His life there was mostly self-imposed loneliness. Joseph Conrad, who admired him, once remarked: 'If I were a beastly bird Hudson would take more interest in me than he does.'[16] And he remained obsessed with the land of his youth.

∾

By the early 1890s, Ernesto and Herbert were running Los Yngleses together and were Will Gilmore's employers when he took up work there in late September 1900. But behind them both loomed the stern father, firing off authoritarian letters from Edinburgh.

Minnie showed me an example, a letter Thomas sent to his sons in 1903, just one month before his death. He was incensed that fewer lambs had been born that season than expected – surely the result of pulling the rams away too early? The emphases are his:

…[I] hasten to write being shocked to learn … about failure of lambing. *This must be done* [leaving rams with the flock] and Herbert should consider himself to have *failed as a sheepbreeder* in this part-increase. Try to get my 46,000 lambs in the Yngleses alone. Try to get the blessing of your father back, and put lots of rams in all paddock flocks particularly, as Mr Corbett showed was necessary, because they are not brought up to the rodeo every evening. *Now I must be obeyed.*

Your administrator, Th. G.[17]

There is no record of Will Gilmore's experiences on the property three years earlier. Probably he never came to the attention of He Who Must Be Obeyed in Scotland. Will was not a good correspondent at the best of times, and few of his letters from any place of employment have survived. Mary was always the one to depend on for an account, and she never went to Los Yngleses. But Will's accommodation in the long galleried single men's quarters would have been more comfortable than on most estancias, and the men had their own *matédero*, a large room where they met – as they do still – to barbecue meats at the huge fireplace and share *yerba mate*, the Paraguayan herbal tea popular throughout the southern part of the continent

I walked back to the rambling, white-washed homestead along the avenue of arching century-old eucalyptus trees which must have been planted about the time Gilmore was there. I imagine they would have given him a pang of homesickness. But I wondered exactly how he had landed the job.

⌘

Above the dining-room mantelpiece, with its china Stafford-shire dogs, was a competent portrait in oils of four bearded 'Scottish ranch hands at the estancia'.

Minnie introduced me to Roberto Boe, the last of the farmhands directly descended from the Scots brought out to Argentina in the 1860s. He allowed me to photograph him, his boots, blowsy pants and chunky belt thoroughly criolla-Argentine, although there was still something Scottish about his rakish black beret.

However, a few shepherds had come from Glasgow before that main immigrant group, soon after the Gibsons took up the land. One of them, Matthew Gilmour, arrived about 1844, and was described as 'a good and reliable worker'. He eventually bettered his position and bought a small property of his own called Montes Blancos, not far away, near the coast.

He was living there with his family in 1900, by then a very old man, but he was still on good terms with the Gibsons. Minnie had a theory that he might have had a family connection with Will Gilmore, and so may have recommended this Australian relative for a short contract. I liked the idea, but wanted more support for it. Certainly in many documents I had come across, the surname for Mary and Will was spelled 'Gilmour'. With illiteracy widespread at the time, spellings of surnames were often in flux. But Mary would surely have mentioned such a good story as this fortunate family connection?

However, Minnie had an even better story to tell me, a very famous one in Argentina, written up in the newspapers of the time, and she directed me to other versions of it, written by W. H. Hudson and – this was *serious* recognition – by Jorge Luis Borges. It was the story of 'the Gilmour child'.

∾

Borges was succinct in his short story 'The Captive':

> A boy disappeared after an Indian attack. People said the Indians had kidnapped him. His parents searched for him in vain. Then, long years later, a soldier who came from the interior told them about an Indian with blue eyes who might well be their son.[18]

From local knowledge, Minnie informed me that the young boy was named Matthew – or Mateo – after his father, and was indeed a very beautiful little boy with pale skin, blue eyes and fair hair. His mother adored him.

In Hudson, and his is the more detailed account, Matthew Gilmour advertised the loss of his child, offered a large reward and sent agents out to look for him. 'Mr Gilmour spent a large part of his fortune, and eventually it had to be dropped.' Only Mrs Gilmour continued to believe that her lost son was still living.

Then one day a traveller, an educated man, came to their gate at noon and asked for hospitality, 'as the custom was in my time on those great vacant plains where houses were far apart'. He entertained his hosts over dinner 'with an account of some of the strange out-of-the-world places he had visited'. But when one of the sons of the house, 'a tall slim good-looking young man of about thirty' came in, he could not stop staring at him.

The stranger continue to fix his gaze on the young man until eventually Mrs Gilmour demanded the reason. The guest explained that two years earlier, at 'a military outpost, on the extreme north-eastern border of the republic' (and this puts it at Corrientes, across the river from Paraguay, as confirmed in a newspaper account), he had seen 'someone so like the young man before him that it had almost produced the illusion of his being the same person'. The memory had stayed with him because the garrison was such an unlikely place to see such an apparently refined individual:

> It was composed of the class of men one usually saw in these border forts, men of the lowest type, *mestizos* and *mulattos* most of them, criminals from the gaols condemned to serve in the frontier army for their crimes. And in the midst of the low-browed, swarthy-faced, ruffianly crew appeared the tall, distinguished-looking young man with a white skin, blue eyes and light hair – an amazing contrast!

This was the first clue the parents had received of their son's whereabouts in thirty years. In Hudson's story the young man of the house, Robert, then made the first of three epic journeys to find his lost brother.

At the end of his third expedition, three years from when he began, 'he succeeded in finding the object of his search, still serving as a common soldier in the army. That they were brothers there was no doubt in either of their minds, and together they travelled home.' The old father and mother embraced their lost son and told him how they had always loved him and prayed to have him back.

The story should have had a happy ending, but the blue-eyed soldier 'had no recollection of his child life at home – no faintest memory of mother or father or of the day when the violent change came and he was forcibly taken away'. He remembered only a man who had 'owned him', who became so 'exacting and tyrannical, and treated him so badly that he eventually ran away', and was dragooned into the army.

But, according to Borges, he did in fact respond to one other memory:

> The man, buffeted by the wilderness and the barbaric life, no longer knew how to understand the words of his mother tongue … He looked at the door as if he did not know what it was for. Then suddenly he lowered his head, let out a shout, ran across the entrance way and the two long patios, and plunged into the kitchen. Without hesitating, he sank his arm into the blackened chimney and pulled out the little horn-handled knife he had hidden there as a boy. His eyes shone with joy and his parents wept because they had found their son.

The mother continued to believe that if she walked with the damaged young man, talked with him, caressed him enough, he would come back to her. But the truth was, Hudson wrote, that whenever she released him, he would make his escape:

He would go off to the quarters of the hired cattlemen and converse with them. They were his people, and he was one of them in soul in spite of his blue eyes, and like one of them he could lasso or break a horse and throw a bull and put a brand on him, and kill a cow and skin it, or roast it in its hide if it was wanted so; and he could do a hundred other things, though he couldn't read a book, and I daresay he found it a very misery to sit on a chair in the company of those who read in books and spoke a language that was strange to him – the tongue he had himself spoken as a child![19]

Borges' story came to an even more bleak finale:

Perhaps this recollection [discovering the horn-handled knife] was followed by others, but the Indian could not live within walls, and one day he went in search of his wilderness. I wonder what he felt in that dizzying moment when past and present became one. I wonder whether the lost son was reborn and died in that instant of ecstasy; and whether he ever managed to recognise, if only as an infant or a dog does, his parents and his home.[20]

I found the story deeply affecting, with its mythical, archetypal resonances. It reminded me of a legend of the Guaraní people of Paraguay about the *yasy-yateré*, a blue-eyed, white-haired boy who lives in the forest:

He could be heard and sometimes seen among the trees, especially at dusk. If you were a child he lured you into the *monte* with wild honey, making beautiful noises like a bird. But if you listened to the *yasy-yateré* you lost your wits and were never seen again.

Mary Gilmore had been intimately connected herself with the personal tragedy of a lost child. In the New Australia office in Sydney she had worked alongside Walter Head, editor of their journal and a former trade union leader. In February 1894 he was planning to depart for the Paraguay colony with his family. First, however, his wife Carrie took their three children to the Gippsland district of Victoria to say goodbye to relatives. On the third day of their visit, 4-year-old Rowland wandered into the bush and simply disappeared. Walter Head joined the exhaustive search, involving hundreds of volunteers, which went on for weeks. But the boy was never seen again and was presumed dead. Carrie Head did not recover from the shock and separated from her husband. Walter returned alone to Sydney, a broken man. It was Mary who consoled him as best she could, and took over the editorship of the *New Australia* journal.[22]

It is certain she would have been moved by the tale of the Gilmour child – so she must never have known of it, otherwise she could not have resisted repeating it. Perhaps that is the proof that her husband did not obtain his job at Estancia Los Yngleses through any family connection. On the other hand, although the story was generally renowned, Will might never have heard of it. The Gilmours, after sixty years in Argentina, could have lost their English as many had; Will had negligible Spanish himself and, as a hard-working practical man, may simply never have bothered listening to stories.

Over dinner I tried to untangle some stray threads in the history of the estancia. After Thomas Gibson's death in 1903 his land holdings were divided between his children. Ernesto, as the eldest, kept one-quarter of Los Yngleses land, with the main homestead and complex of outbuildings. He had no sons, so the property passed to his wife and two daughters.

A few years after Ernesto's death in 1919, his elder daughter Lorna fell madly in love with a man she met on board ship returning from England – Francisco (always called 'Paco') Boote. His grandfather had been a Savile Row tailor before coming to Argentina. His father and uncle were the most sought-after photographers in Buenos Aires and had become wealthy from the business.

Paco and Lorna were both third-generation Argentines of wholly British ancestry. 'He had just returned from the Grand Tour of Europe, which for him meant going from racecourse to racecourse,' said Minnie. 'He was dashing, handsome, charismatic and Lorna was more subdued, even though she had enjoyed a very society life.' However, the other Gibsons did not approve a suitor with a background 'in trade'. Nevertheless the couple wed in 1924 and Paco took over the management of Los Yngleses, which had deteriorated under leasehold to outsiders. It was a happy and successful marriage. John Boote, Paco and Lorna's only son, runs the property today, with shares also owned by his two sisters.

That was the simple story, I was told. Although I know that no family story is simple, least of all this one. John added that, despite his British blood, he rarely became involved with their social events. He identified almost completely as an Argentine, albeit one who had a soft spot for the British, with a portrait of Princess Diana on a side table and a framed thank-you note from Prince Charles after a visit to Argentina.

'This place is John's real passion,' said Minnie. 'I'm his wife, but Los Yngleses is his mistress.'

We talked late into the night about the desperate state of the country and the difficulties they had been experiencing since devaluation – having to buy machinery, spare parts, fertilisers and so on in dollars, but with the returns from the estancia in pesos. With all the country's volatility, they feared things would only get worse. Some of their friends were leaving for Uruguay or Costa Rica 'until there's a change for the better'. Others wanted the military back in power.

'They say they'd have them back in a minute,' said Minnie. 'In a flash!'

The Los Yngleses account books for 1900 and earlier have either been lost or sent to Edinburgh to be perused by an eagle eye. So I was unable to determine the exact dates of Will Gilmore's employment there. I estimated that it was for the whole month of October 1900, after which he rejoined his family in Buenos Aires in order to depart for Patagonia. He may have been sent for the job by the Salvation Army's own

Free Labour Bureau, but it most likely that Will was recommended to the Gibsons by Mary's Scottish-Chilean friend James McGregor Finland.

The man was still experiencing difficulties doing business at the time Will returned to the hostel. Tensions were on the rise between Argentina and Chile over the definition of their border in Patagonia. Owing to this state of affairs, McGregor Finland could get nothing done. Indeed, 'his life was not safe in the streets'. Chileans continued to be occasional victims of mob violence. Indeed, noting that 26,000 military conscripts were camped 'under canvas' on the outskirts of the city, Mary was glad that she and her family were leaving any day for the south.[23]

The consequence, she observed, of Finland's enforced inactivity was that his temper became atrocious: 'the flattened eye-bone, with the gleam of the white and the tawny iris under it, looked daily more and more vicious'.

'What will you do if war breaks out while you are here?' she asked him one evening in late October as they sat at dinner at the hostel. She realised it was a foolish question, 'but the tension of the times bred folly'.

He answered brutally, without looking at her: 'I will go out and cut Argentine throats till my own is cut.'

Mary's own resentment was drowned in a feeling of sympathy for his unlimited strength tied down. As he paced restlessly, he seemed to her like a caged panther. Suddenly he signalled her to be quiet, listening to something in the distance.

'There is a stir in the town,' he said at last, straightening his shoulders. And then more clearly, 'I must go out and see what it means.'

Just then Gilmore joined them, out of breath, having run from the city centre. He announced that the offices of the newspaper *La Prensa* had sent up a rocket. At that moment they heard an explosion. The rocket's flare illuminated Mary's and Will's anxious white faces. Finland was gone.

A second explosion and then a third.

The stress of the time throbbed out like heart beats … What terrible news had the great daily paper got hold of? … Was it the air that whispered '*War?*'

Shouting and tumult came from the city as hundreds of people, fearing the worst, poured out of doors. The Gilmores rushed out too.

As we stood, down the next street came the rattle and clatter of sabres, breaking out over the thunder of hoofs.

'*Los soldados!*' cried the multitude.

Through the Calle San Juan, citywards, they galloped, the crowd before them backing into patios and laneways, like chaff before the wind in its eagerness, closing in again behind the very hoofs of the horses … Trams shot by without stopping. Men sprang at them as they passed, and fell spinning back for want of an inch of foothold. And above it all was the infernal shriek of the sirens and the ghastly glare of the rockets as fresh information came in to the different newspaper offices.

However, it was not war – at least not officially.

As Mary packed their few possessions and Will made arrangements for their steamer passages, a harsh dry electrical wind was blowing in from the pampa, 'having a horrible effect on the nerves'. Their hosts told them that when it blew crimes of violence always occurred; that was why it was called *viento de los asesinos* – 'the assassins' wind'.

That day a mob in Buenos Aires attacked the Chilean consulate. 'You remember reading of it in the papers,' wrote Mary:

And Don Jaime – James McGregor Finland, of that ilk in Scotland, of the coalfields of Valdivia in Chile, and son of a *criolla*–Chilean mother – saw it, and, seeing, all Chile rose in his blood.

In the morning they found him in the morgue amongst a row of Argentines, found him with his throat cut, his fingers strings of bones from which the flesh hung in shreds, just as the knives he had fought with had left him.[24]

IV

SOUTH

As I packed for my flight the following morning, the day's events in Buenos Aires crashed into the hotel room via the television and the newspaper on the table. In the Plaza de Mayo protesters clenched fists for the cameras and ritually burned three American flags, flames rippling and blackening the Stars and Stripes. A judge indicted nine police officers on charges of 'aggravated torture and murder' of a teenage youth. A Cabinet minister solemnly assured the people of Argentina they were 'at the doors' of an aid agreement with the IMF. A petrol bomb set fire to the house of an investigative journalist in Corrientes. Shopkeepers' associations were organising a protest, calling on Argentines to 'blow horns and bang pots and pans to demand effective policies against crime'. Former president Carlos Menem, having completed six months' detention on charges of corruption and arms smuggling, was running second in the polls for the April 2003 presidential elections. The septuagenarian's face stretched in a taut, surgically enchanced smile as he expressed confidence in clinching the Peronist nomination. His blonde Chilean-born wife Cecilia Bolocco, a former Miss

Universe half his age, was practising an Evita-like piety: 'If I happen to be First Lady, I hope God gives me strength and wisdom to do my best in these times of hardship for Argentina'.[1]

I had spent the previous week in the Biblioteca Nacional, researching the two English-language newspapers for 1900-2, a turbulent time then with the looming possibility of war. There was a mention in the *Buenos Aires Herald* for 28 October 1900, just before the Gilmores' departure, of a 'fatal knife fight' in a city street, but no further details were given – killings were common enough and only cursorily reported. But assuming the Spanish-language newspapers were more intemperate than the genteel *Herald,* its editorial in the same issue indicates the prevailing mood which erupted in mob violence at the Chilean consulate with unfortunate result for Mary's friend. It was headed 'Bellicose Chilli' and did a good line in bellicosity itself:

> Chilli should understand that she cannot get ahead of this Republic in armaments. It is a ruinous policy, but if [she] is so mad as to keep it up there is nothing for us to do but to follow promptly in the same pathway ... Chilli is getting ready to suffer a thrashing, which will come in due time if her jingo element is not kept chained.[2]

But the newspaper had its lighter moments, and at the time was greatly diverted by reported sightings of a living Mylodon, or hairy giant sloth. Remains of this creature larger than a bull, incorrectly described as *Neomylodon Listai,* had been found in a Patagonian cave in 1893. It was generally believed to be extinct (and carbon dating later placed it on earth about 10, 000 years ago). But one Argentine scientist, impressed by news of the sightings, opined that a few were still alive somewhere in Patagonia. The *Herald* was delighted to report – in expectation of much fun to come – the arrival in Argentina of Mr Hesketh Prichard, sent by the London *Daily Express*, with a handsome expense account in expectation of a scoop. He was currently hiring assistants, purchasing forty horses and lavishly outfitting the expedition. He would then be heading south in search of the creature:

> Mr Pritchard [sic] has offered £5,000 reward for the death of the Mylodon. We do not know what the Mylodon has done to Mr Pritchard to cause this desire for his blood. A Welshman has reported that he fired three shots at the unfortunate Mylodon the other day. We wonder whether it was Scotch or Irish or Boca gin.[3]

At the beginning of November 1900 the Gilmores boarded a rusting tramp steamer, the *Santa Cruz,* for their own voyage south. There were thirty military conscripts on board – the garrison in Río Gallegos was being strengthened as a warning to Chile and conditions were cramped and primitive.

After two weeks of erratic crabbing down the coast, they passed the mouth of the Río Negro, the river recognised as the northern border of the vast territory of Patagonia. Two-thirds of the land mass of Argentina, it is neither a state nor a province but a geographical invention, shared between Argentina and Chile.

The Río Negro was William Henry Hudson's destination thirty years earlier, his final journey before leaving Argentina forever, a bird-watching expedition to Patagonia, a region he had longed to visit. In the 1970s Jorge Luis Borges, Argentina's literary *éminence grise* warned the travel writer Paul Theroux against an expedition south: 'You will find nothing there. There is nothing in Patagonia. That's why Hudson liked it. You will notice there are no people in his books.'[4]

Hudson, like the Gilmores, had a ghastly voyage on a steamer – perhaps it was the same unreliable *Santa Cruz*. He thought the ship 'as ugly to look at as it was said to be unsafe to voyage in'; the captain was ill and in fact died shortly afterwards, while the mate was asleep most of the time, 'leaving only the men to navigate the steamer on that perilous coast, and in the darkest hour of a tempestuous night'. Then, with 'a succession of bumps, accompanied by strange grating and grinding noises, and shuddering motions', the steamer ran on to some rocks.

Hudson heard the crew talk of abandoning ship in the one lifeboat, leaving the others to their fate.

My only thought was that at the last moment, when they would be unable to prevent it except by knocking me senseless, I would spring with them into the boat and save myself, or else perish with them in that awful white surf.

But the first engineer saved the day, stepping forward with a raised revolver to quietly announce that he would shoot the first man who continued with the mutiny. To the astonishment of all, the old captain, 'white and hollow-eyed from his death-bed, appeared like a ghost among us'. It was then that, 'by some lucky chance, the steamer got off the rocks and plunged on for a space through the seething, milky surf; then, very suddenly, passed out of it into black and comparatively calm water'.

The crisis was averted and land was just a stone's throw away. Hudson and some other passengers 'were lowered by means of ropes into the sea, and quickly waded to the shore'. He scrambled up sand dunes to confront the vision he had dreamed of:

> At last, Patagonia! There it lay full in sight before me – the unmarred desert that wakes strange feelings in us; the ancient habitation of giants, whose footprints seen on the seashore, amazed Magellan and his men, and won for it the name of Patagonia.

This pale, introverted, rather strange but endearing man, warned by his doctors to avoid any vigorous activity because of his weak heart, made epic and exhausting journeys in that desolate region, where the river carved a channel through sand and gravel and nothing grew 'except the barren things that Nature loves'. But birds lived there. He crouched, utterly entranced, to observe the feeding, mating and nesting habits of red-billed finches, brown gleaners, scissor-tailed tyrant birds, white-rumped swallows, grey-crested song-sparrows, red-breasted plant-cutters, thorn-birds, brown carrion-hawks and Patagonian mocking birds.

It was also my hope to find some new species, some bird as beautiful, let us say, as the wryneck or wheatear, and as old on the earth, but which had never been named and never ever seen by any appreciative human eye.[5]

Hudson had an accident, a gunshot wound below the knee cap, which laid him up for several weeks and forced him to adopt 'the habit of indolence, which was quite common among the people of Patagonia'. He lay immobilised during the long sultry summer days, listening to the buzzing of house flies, the conversation of other people in the house 'until it began to interest me'. He was helpless during the long cool nights, when a 'serpent with a cross' slithered close and he rejoiced to think that 'the secret deadly creature, after lying all night with me, warming its chilly blood with my warmth, went back unbruised to its den'. ('Mad old greenie!' said a friend of mine when he read this.)

It was this enforced period of passivity, of reflection and observation, which changed Hudson from mere ornithologist into a writer who could reach a wider public.

In the last few pages of *Idle Days in Patagonia*, published in London in 1893, Hudson wrote that the perfume of the evening primrose always brought back to him sharply his discovery of that frail bloom, 'growing on the barren sand not many yards from the sea', when he had first waded ashore from his wretched steamer, his 'first landing in Patagonia on a desert part of the coast'. And with the perfume 'many scenes and events of the past' came crowding in, and grief also 'for the loss of a vanished happiness', a wish once again to sleep under the stars of that great southern sky, more soundly than he had ever slept under a London roof.[6]

Seven years after that publication gave Patagonia-bound steamers a very bad name, the *Santa Cruz* was living up – or down – to their reputation. The Gilmores' voyage was agonisingly slow. At last the steamer entered the calm waters of a gulf protected by Peninsula Valdés – today a marine wildlife reserve – and was held up several days at Puerto Piramides, unloading rails for a train line to the nearby saltworks.

Mary sat on the deck and watched southern right whales come to the warm waters of the gulf to calve and mate, plunging and surfacing close to the ship. Along the stark grey cliffs, she saw hundreds of sea lions and seals, sunning themselves on rocky shelves:

> the whole surface was covered with walruses. The bulls reared up and made strange noises at us as we passed. There were hundreds of them, and the noises made by the mixture of young and old cries was a cross between pigs grunting, dogs barking and the long bleat of sheep … A little shooting was attempted, but a great deal more snap shotting, but with indifferent success.[7]

Next the steamer put in at Puerto Madryn on the southern side of the gulf, the port of the Welsh colony of the Chubut valley.

❦

Through my aircraft window, the wash of green across the earth leached to monochrome. Pampa became desert. We had flown over the Río Negro. The vast bare terrain of Patagonia was below, threaded by the lines of dry watercourses. The land seemed utterly unpopulated. Once it had been the hunting grounds of the scattered Araucanian, Mapuche and Tehuelche tribes. In the early nineteenth century, enraged at the advance of the Europeans, they had fought a war of resistance, burning crops, stealing sheep and cattle, raiding the huts of isolated settlers. But the Europeans struck back with a vengeance.

Charles Darwin, journeying through this territory as a sidetrip from his *Beagle* voyage of 1832, encountered troops of the bloodthirsty *caudillo* General Rosas, returned from an Indian hunt.

> The Indians, men, women and children, were about one hundred and ten in number, and they were nearly all taken and killed, for the soldiers sabre every man. The Indians are now so terrified that they offer no resistance in a body … but when overtaken, like wild animals, they fight against any number to the last moment … This is a dark picture; but how much more shocking is the unquestionable fact, that all the women who appear above twenty years old are massacred in cold blood.

When Darwin exclaimed to an officer that the lack of mercy to the women was inhuman, the man answered, 'Why, what can be done? They breed so!' Darwin was appalled by this gross attempt at unnatural selection. He did not doubt the perpetrators were a superior race, but, in the tradition of British liberalism, he believed that innate superiority brought obligations of decency with it. 'Everyone here is fully convinced', he wrote, 'that this is the most just war, because it is against barbarians. Who would believe in this age that such atrocities could be committed in a Christian civilised country?'

He learned that the plan of General Rosas was 'to kill all stragglers, and having driven the remainder to a common point, to attack them in a body in the summer, with the assistance of the Chilenos'. This operation was to be repeated for three successive years and Darwin made a bleak and prescient forecast:

> I think there will not, in another half-century, be a wild Indian northward of the Río Negro. The warfare is too bloody to last; the Christians killing every Indian, and the Indians doing the same by the Christians. It is melancholy to trace how the Indians have given way before the Spanish invaders.[8]

By the time W. H. Hudson made his own sojourn in the arid region of the Río Negro in 1870, he had certainly read Darwin's *Beagle* journal but had clearly paid more attention to the descriptions of birds and the plains of Patagonia than to Darwin's account of the systematic killing of the Indians. Hudson wrote that he picked up weapons, arrowheads and ornaments, and attempted to picture to himself 'something of the outer and inner life of the long-vanished inhabitants', who seemed to have died out of their own accord. He considered they might have been 'slowly progressing to a higher condition', but 'all efforts to know more, or to imagine more, ended in failure'. Contemplating the Indians 'had the effect of bringing a shadow, a something of melancholy' over his mind, especially when he came across an ancient Indian burial-place – or was it, I wonder, a massacre site? – 'where half an acre of earth was strewn thick with crumbling skeletons'.[9]

Hudson sentimentally mourned the inevitable passing of a race. However, in that year, 1870, the Indians were not all 'vanished', although they were desperately reduced in numbers by European armed reprisals, disease and the continuing encroachment on their traditional hunting grounds.

Less than a decade later, General Julio Roca, then minister of war, decided to make an end to the 'Indian problem'. In 1879, with a force of some 8,000 men in five columns, he rode south, fanning across the desert. 'For the Argentine Republic', he declared, 'there is no other frontier in the west and the south than the peaks of the Andes and the Ocean.'[10]

The Indians, most of them unarmed, riding their horses bareback, were overwhelmed by Gatling guns and the new Remington machine-guns. Except for the Indians of the far south and in the Andean slopes to the west, only about 2,000 survived the war of extermination. They were rounded up and shipped north to a reservation on the island of Martín García in the Plata delta, where they died of disease, their children taken as slaves.

The virtual genocide of the Indians was followed by a lavish distribution of land – some 4.5 million hectares – to officers, soldiers and those with influence with the government.[11]

I have noticed that many Argentine writers, even serious historians, seem to speak of the Indians with unremitting hatred, without acknowledging they were fighting a war of resistance, and without showing remorse for how they were slaughtered. Perhaps too few Indians have survived to be now demanding a re-evaluation of the standard 'white victor' history, as Aborigines have done and are doing in Australia.

But General Roca became a hero, swept into office as president. His 'Conquest of the Desert' entered the history books as a noble campaign that had rid the country of a troublesome people and made it possible for their European successors to occupy vast tracts. 'The handsomest man I ever saw,' wrote Mary Gilmore, with 'the beauty of strong just intent and mind'.[12]

A glimpse of grey ocean as the aircraft tilted, then nondescript heathland below. We were over 1,400 kilometres south of Buenos Aires, when we landed at Trelew, the airport for the former Welsh settlements. Wind whipped at poplars and willows at the edge of the strip.

In the terminal a huge mural celebrated the opening up of Patagonia by the pioneers from Wales: stern-faced men with vision in their blue eyes and modest women with lace ruffles at the high necks of their dark dresses. They presided over a triumphant pageant of progress: Model-T Fords in the street of a frontier town; a steam locomotive crossing a bridge, its plume of smoke drifting across grazing flocks. In the background the artist had painted in a group of Indians, dignified and passive, lost in awe, it seemed, at the miracles of the white man, grateful, apparently, to defer to such superior beings.

Trelew was named for Lewis Jones, a former Holyhead printer, one of two prospectors of the Welsh settlement in Patagonia, who became its first governor. The other was Captain Jones-Parry, the squire of Madryn Castle in Lyn, who won the naming rights for Puerto Madryn, the first landing place of the Welsh colonists in Patagonia.

I boarded a minibus bound for the port, joining some tourists from Buenos Aires and 200 fluffy yellow chickens, cheeping in open cardboard boxes. After a 65-kilometre drive across a monotonous plain of low thorn scrub, Puerto Madryn proved to be a dispiriting place, unconvincingly promoted as a seaside resort. A scattering of nondescript cement-block hotels looked towards an oil-drilling platform out in the sullen grey waters of the bay, at the bare brown encircling cliffs and the long pier of an aluminium smelter in the distance. The beach below the marine esplanade was flecked with seaweed and droplets of oil. But it had a cold eerie beauty, too: pale flatness of land meeting pale vastness of sky.

I walked along the esplanade, buffeted by winds rushing in from the Atlantic. Halfway along was a cement monument in the shape of a ship's prow. A plaque commemorated the arrival of the Welsh in 1865 and their establishment of *La Colonización Galesa*. On the sides of the monument, in bronze relief, there were those regal Indians again, extending their hands to Welsh farmers, while women in bonnets and long enveloping dresses looked suitably grim at the task ahead. Bruce Chatwin, visiting the same memorial for *In Patagonia,* described 'big-breasted girls with babies'.[13] I looked in vain for the babies. The chests of the stern women seemed innocent of any curve; in fact they looked to have finished with curves for ever.

The brig *Mimosa* put in to Puerto Madryn in July 1865 with 153 optimists from the mining valleys of Wales. Seeking a place on earth far from English domination, where they could exercise autonomy in their Methodist faith, Welsh language and culture, they had already considered emigration to the United States, Africa and Australia. But the Argentine government, recognising their value in opening up the Patagonian frontier and presenting a bulwark to Chile's claims, offered them haven. The settlers were an advance party; the terms of the colonisation agreement stipulated that between 300 and 500 families were to follow from Wales every year for ten years.

The land they were to occupy in the hinterland on the Chubut river – they called it *Y Wladfa,* the Colony – had been looked over by Lewis Jones, who conducted a lecture tour throughout Wales, promising: 'There is land to be pastured and farmed, wheat has been sown, one crop yielding 45 times the amount sown … Sheep weighing 300lbs are plentiful, their meat tasting like venison.'[14]

The reality proved different. The group from the *Mimosa* disembarked on a grey, windswept beach. One child had died on the voyage; soon after landing a man perished in search of water. While the men set off to their land grant in the interior, the women and children sheltered for six weeks in caves dug into the soft tosca cliffs around Puerto Madryn. Three small children died in the harsh winter conditions.[15]

Few of the Welsh were farmers and their experience was of the verdant vales of home. The Patagonian desert almost defeated them; starvation stalked the little colony. But they dug irrigation ditches and gradually their crops prospered, despite chronic drought and occasional floods. They did in fact establish good relations with the local Tehuelche people, the only such instance in Argentine history, and learned from them how to hunt the rhea – the South American ostrich – and the guanaco – a feral relative of the llama and alpaca – using the *boleadora,* a rope with three stones attached for flinging at the neck or legs of an animal on the run. The Welsh declined a more vicious form of hunting: when General Roca and his men swept through on their extermination drive, they refused to participate in the so-called Conquest of the Desert.

Other Welsh towns were established in the Chubut, but the large-scale immigration forecast in the colonisation agreement never came to pass. However, in 1896 David Lloyd George gave the colony British sentimental recognition by a visit to 'the little Wales across the sea'.[16]

Indian guanaco and ostrich hunt

Four years after Lloyd George, in November 1900, the
Gilmores' steamer was held up in the colony's port for a week
while more cargo was unloaded. Mary described 'a huge harbour, twenty six miles across' which gave safe anchorage, but
she, like me, found the township distinctly unimpressive:

Puerta Madryn presents a low line of sand and rock, rising in terraces away to the dreary interior. There are no trees, no grass, no birds to speak of except gulls and vultures, nothing but an everlasting unchanging hue of grey sand and sandstone. Half a dozen iron houses are thrown down haphazard on the beach, *galpones* or deposit stores, offices and barracks, a railway station, telegraph offices and trucking yards.

However, having recently lived in an experimental commune herself, Mary was eager to know more about the Welsh colony and was gratified that its own supply ship, the *Annie Morgan*, '500 tons burden', had recently come from Wales and was anchored in the bay. She made the acquaintance of some of the people on board. One of them pointed out to her 'the caves in the rocks where the stranger people found their first shelter' and described the hardships of the early days:

> There is a story told that after resting there, and reconnoitring the surrounding country, the settlers having chosen a location packed up their belongings and turning their faces inland to the rise of the pampa, left a woman and two sick children alone in the cave ... her children recovering, she drove her goats before her and followed to the village later.[17]

Although the early days were especially hard on the women, writer Jan Morris suggests that the little colony was arguably the first administration in the world to grant full womanhood suffrage – 'In theory the British Empire was staunchly feminist – the first women in the world to get the vote were those of the Isle of Man, the next were those of New Zealand' – but Morris, of Welsh stock herself and drawing a rather long bow, believes both claims were trounced by 'Y Wladfa', the Welsh settlement founded in Patagonia in 1865, where everyone over eighteen had a vote from the start. But that, as Kipling would say, is another story ...[18]

Mary learned that, other than the scrappy settlement at the port, the Welsh had three towns in the Chubut: Rawson (today the provincial capital), near the coast, named after Dr William Rawson who organised the immigration and Gaimán, a little further to the south-west. The third town of Trevelín, settled in 1885, was 'fourteen days' ride' away on the eastern slopes of the Andes, which she had heard, 'apart from the haulage question', had a situation which was perfect for the growing of wheat, apples, grapes and peaches.

The total population of the towns, Mary understood, was 'about seven thousand all told', a generous estimate, although she acknowledged that 'the half of these however are not *Welsh* but Argentines, who, attracted by the prosperity of the Welsh, came down and took up the unoccupied lands. This, in conjunction with government interference, the appointment of bad governors, etc. has led to the unrest among the Chubutans.'

She longed to visit at least the closer settlements of Rawson, and especially Gaimán, hearing that 'a train runs morning and evening to the nearest Welsh town, seven miles inland, the land within that distance to the sea being too arid for use. Either a telegraph or a telephone line follows the line of the train, terminating at the *Cuartel*, the barracks, and Government offices.' But presumably she found the logistics of making the journey too difficult and the departure time of her steamer too unreliable. It is as well she did not attempt it, for it would seem her vestigial Spanish failed her: Gaimán was more like seventy miles (112 kilometres) from the port. Still, Mary was envious of what she heard of the community's prosperity, comparisons with Colonia Cosme implicit in her astute description:

> The Argentine Government let the people alone for years. They tilled their farms, built houses, bred sheep and cattle and horses, made irrigation works and so prospered that today there is no person in poverty among them. They are neither socialist nor communist. Their only bond of union is the bond of race and of neighbourhood. Everyone has a farm, orchard, cattle and means to work their land, wheat and all European fruits and vegetables are grown. Water is easy to get, being only a few feet below the surface … They struggle under many difficulties. Beyond the radius of the river slopes, the land is useless. All land within is taken up and there is no room for expansion. Carriage of products, wheat and alfalfa, is very expensive; the freight, after it reaches the train, being almost prohibitive and there being no local factories, there is no local market. Everything goes either to Buenos Aires or to England … The Colony has its own newspaper, printed both in Welsh and Spanish, there are the ordinary

Chubut Intermediate School, Gaimán, 1908

schools in which latterly Spanish is compulsory, and each town has its co-operative store.[19]

Meanwhile, Mr Hesketh Prichard of the London *Daily Express* had arrived in the Chubut a month before the Gilmores, accompanied by all the expeditionary accoutrements a gentleman required to hunt a living Giant Sloth. The *Buenos Aires Herald* was not letting him out of its sights:

On Friday the English tourists in search of the mylodon set out from Trelew for Lake Buenos Aires. They have 40 horses and 7 peones who know the country. An infantry lieutenant at Chubut has seen and measured footprints and droppings of a mylodon … The correspondent of the London *Express* has offered the Welsh people at Chubut a large sum if they will find him one. He can see half a dozen of them if he will drink a little of genuine imported whiskey manufactured at the Boca, and if he will keep at it for a week he will see an entire menagerie of wonderful unknown monsters.[20]

At the time of the Gilmores' – and Hesketh Prichard's – brief visit to the region in late 1900, the Welsh colonists were locked in an argument with the Argentine government which had been going on for a year. Their original colonisation agreement had allowed them freedom from military service. But General Roca's government had rescinded it and had ordered that the men, as formal Argentine citizens, must serve fifteen days a year in the militia. Sunday was pronounced the appropriate day for military duties. With the border dispute with Chile intensifying, the Welsh were supposed to do their bit to defend Argentina's sovereignty. An expedition led by Colonel Fontana was laying claim to a contested area near Trevelín in the Andes, and a contingent of *Rifleros Galeses,* or Welsh Rifles, was expected to accompany him. The Sunday drill was mandatory.

The Welsh objected that they had left Britain in order to practise their religion in freedom, and attendance at Sunday chapel was crucial to them. The crisis – at its height in 1899 – had been much reported in the Buenos Aires English-language newspapers. Mary was aware of it and wrote about new developments learned from her Welsh acquaintances in Puerto Madryn:

When the Argentine Government issued conscription notices to the Chubutans, the Welsh evaded answering them,
by sending all sons of conscript age home to Wales and England, bringing them back the following year. Still there were
some who could not afford to do this, and their sons being
enrolled, parades and drills were ordered for Sunday. The
Welsh objected, local tyranny ordered the young men to
choose between drill and gaol. They went to gaol.

She noted that as the nation mobilised some of these unwill-
ing Welsh soldiers, were with them on the *Santa Cruz*. 'Of the
thirty conscripts who travelled in the same ship with us …
only one spoke English at all well, and not half a dozen spoke
anything else but Welsh.'

Mary was pessimistic about the future of a homogeneous
Welsh community that aimed to stay apart from the nation
to which it inevitably belonged, perhaps accepting that it had
been folly for the Australians to have attempted the same in
Paraguay:

I believe there were five hundred of the settlers who wished
to leave Argentina. Those represented the Welsh who would
not intermarry with the Argentines, who wished to remain
Welsh and bring their children up Welsh. One can understand the Argentines harassing these, for the South American is of all peoples the most intensely full of the sense of
nationality, and anyone being in his country and not na-
tionalised is a continual source of irritation and, owing to
fiery neighbours, possible danger.

She concluded that the Chubutans, as far as she could see, were 'a fine healthy people, obstinate if opposed, but quite law abiding among themselves, and full of obedience to law of their own making and just the kind to make good English colonists'. But she was convinced their only future lay with the more adaptable young, who were tending to be 'more Spanish' and would through intermarriage become more Argentine. 'In South America there is no middle course.'[21]

There were settlers of other nationalities in the region, and a Russian resident, the *Buenos Aires Herald* was pleased to report, was having some problems:

> A Russian gentleman who lives near Chubut tells us that he is plagued with mylodon hunters. They call every week and stay as long as the flour and *caña* hold out. The same gentlemen in the north are called 'Jemmy come lately'. In the West they are called sheep dip agents and travel in a sulky. In Australia they are called sundowners.[22]

In 1901, the Welsh of the Chubut once again appealed to Great Britain to protect their interests, claiming that the Argentine government was intervening unjustly in their affairs. The main Buenos Aires newspaper, *La Prensa,* carried an outraged editorial advising the government to make clear to London that Argentine sovereignty over Chubut was absolute. Another paper, *La Nación,* suggested that the Welsh should leave Argentina if they continued to appeal for British intervention.[23] But when a large defection of settlers left for

Canada and Australia in 1902, the papers actually expressed 'profound sadness' at their departure.[24]

The Welsh presence helped when Argentina's border dispute with Chile was finally sorted out in the same year. Both sides had agreed to the arbitration of a British boundary commission. It determined that with a Welsh settlement at Trevelín since 1888 and a contingent of *Rifleros Galeses* prepared to defend it, that region of the Andean *cordillera* should belong to Argentina. Once this was officially agreed, more Welsh settlers came up from the coast and founded the town of Esquel, which soon exceeded Trevelín in size and importance.

But not only the Welsh arrived. In 1902 some notorious gangsters on the run took up 6,000 hectares of land at nearby Cholila on the Andean slopes. They were Butch Cassidy and the Sundance Kid and the girlfriend they apparently shared, Etta Place.

In October 2002 I was unable to visit the inland 'Welsh' towns of the Chubut region. I had no time, if I was to catch my next flight south, just like Mary with her steamer about to depart.

But nine years earlier I had made the journey that she could not. I visited the dour town of Trelew, which seemed to me Welsh only in its street signs and the posters for an Eisteddfod held every October since 1890. From there by lumbering local bus I travelled the same route as the pioneers, through a landscape of sage bushes and thorn scrub to the village of Gaimán, seventeen kilometres to the west. It was then, and remains still, the most overtly Welsh of the settlements, made famous by Bruce Chatwin.

Over a rise a soft fertile valley opened out, poplars, willows and yellow broom bordering the river. 'How Green Was My Valley' seemed an absurd description for anywhere in Patagonia, but the miracle of irrigation had achieved it. The tidy streets of red-brick gabled houses were shaded by tamarisks, cherry trees and Chinese elms with pale luminous leaves.

The grassy plaza made its tribute, as most every plaza does, to the Argentine liberator General de San Martín with a bust on a plinth, but the churning water-wheel on an irrigation canal, shaded by willows, was picture-book Wales. Self-conscious Welshness was clearly the business of the village. The local optician was called Optica Williams, a cantina, a 'pub'. A craft shop window displayed dolls with embroidered aprons and high-crowned black hats, copper kettles, spinning wheels and tea-towels printed with verses from 'Men of Harlech'. In an attempt to cast wider the tourism net, there were also soft toys of whales, seals, penguins and, inscrutably, pandas.

Tea houses, impossibly exotic to Argentine visitors, competed to serve high tea. The most popular then, judging by the parked tour coaches, was the Plas y Coed Casa de Té, a neat bungalow by the river. Bees buzzed in drowsy ecstasy in a garden of roses and hollyhocks, snapdragons and delphiniums. The proprietor, Martha Rees, a tiny, bird-like woman, coped without fluster. She spoke English with a lilting Welsh accent but had never been to Wales. Her forebears, the Roberts and the Prices, she told me, came with the pioneers in 1865.

'My mother-in-law, Dilys Owen, opened the first tea house here fifty years ago. All the other ones got the idea from her. Well, there's room for us all, God willing.'

Across the road, outside a shop displaying straw brooms and plastic buckets on the pavement, an old man wearing a peaked cap, tartan shirt and rakish neckerchief mounted a bicycle. He grinned, blue eyes twinkling, as I delayed him with questions. (I wonder if that ingenuous friendliness exists now, with tour buses bringing people from all over South America to take advantage of the devalued peso.)

The old man's name, he told me in English, was Ache Herbert Johns and he was eighty-three years old. He had never been to Wales, but his grandmother, Anne Davis, had come with the first batch of pioneers. He propped up his bicycle and led me into the shop to meet his blue-eyed son Vivien, serving behind the counter. Vivien only spoke Spanish and seemed alarmed by mine. He called to someone in a back room who, he promised, spoke excellent Welsh. He assumed I was a visitor from Cardiff or Merthyr Tydfil.

His father-in-law, Oscar Arnold, came in, a man of some presence, with grey thinning hair and olive-dark eyes. He was a spokesman for the community of Welsh descendants, president of the Asociación de San David. He spoke no English either, but explained in Spanish that their main concern was to preserve the Welsh language and the tradition of choral singing.

In 1900 Mary Gilmore had predicted that the Welsh would find it both difficult and unwise to retain their sense of nationalism. It was true that in the former colony towns of Trelew and Rawson the Argentine character had become predominant. But a hundred years after her forecast, in the little village of Gaimán, people like Oscar Arnold, of mixed Welsh and Hispanic blood, were still fighting to preserve a Welsh identity: 'The number speaking Welsh here is actually expanding. You'd be surprised how many of our people, young and old, want to learn. Welsh tourists tell us the language spoken in Gaimán is purer in form than at home. This interests philologists and oral historians too. We get all sorts coming to visit us now.'

I suggested that the success of Chatwin's *In Patagonia*, which mourned the fading of the language in the Chubut, would have helped their cause.

'It was the interest in our centenary which did it,' Oscar Arnold answered, suddenly terse.

The tradition of choral singing had never been stronger, he told me with pride. Gaimán, with a population of just 3,500, had six Welsh choirs. Neighbouring Trelew, by comparison, with a population of 80,000, could manage only three. In 1991 Gaimán had competed, singing in Welsh, in an international choral competition in Germany and won third place.

There was just time to visit Gaimán's historical museum, presided over by Señora Tegai Roberts. A serene blue-eyed woman with grey hair pinned in a bun, she was the great-granddaughter of Lewis Jones, one of the founders of the

Chubut colony. Something about her gracious reserve forbade me from asking her age. She spoke perfect, very precise English (as impeccable, I understood from others, as her Spanish and Welsh). Cautiously she agreed to talk to me, 'although journalists and writers are dangerous'.

'Why do you say that?'

She smiled gently. 'They come here and then they go away and write strange things about us. What they say is not always true or even very kind. One book in particular. I'm sure you know the one I mean. Some of it was well written. Some of it was quite amusing. We quite liked what he said about other places in Patagonia, but we didn't like what he said about Gaimán. He rather made fun of us, I think … Oh well, he's dead now, poor man.'

A teenage boy, Carlos Alberto, arrived for his Welsh lesson. Though a student at Camwy College, he took extra coaching from Señora Roberts. 'Carlos takes his Welsh seriously', she smiled, 'and is a regular at Bethel chapel. Boys like him will take their place in the community and keep our traditions alive.'

As he walked me back to the bus stop Carlos Alberto confided that he would not be staying in the village. As soon as he could he would be off to Buenos Aires to join a dancing troupe. He dreamed that one day he would star in an Andrew Lloyd Webber musical.

In a hall across the plaza, the members of the choir were beginning their evening rehearsal as I boarded the bus. The full-throated voices, glorious in unison, seemed to reverberate around the storybook valley with its neat gabled houses, tea shops and willow-bordered river, as we wound back up to the bare Patagonian steppe.

Even at the time, my visit to Gaimán had the feeling of having found an unexpected colour fold-out in a child's picture book, after pages of print and line drawings. It still does.

V

GALLEGOS

The news of the massacre on the Indonesian island of Bali reached me as I was about to board my flight to Río Gallegos. Explosions had ripped through two nightclubs and, so CNN reported, up to 200 people were feared dead. I knew with a bleak certainty that very many would be Australians. It turned out that eighty-eight of them were. Friends had worried about my encountering 'dangers' in Argentina, to which I had replied that if it was a relaxing holiday I was after, I would go to Bali.

I was heading south to a region legendary for its desolation, incessant winds in summer, howling gales and winter blizzards, and for its geographic aloneness, projecting into icy seas towards Antarctica.

The Gilmores had expected their entire voyage on the *Santa Cruz* to take six or seven days; after all, they had heard that the big boats heading for the Pacific 'do it in two-and-a-half'. But for the whole month of November 1900 they were on that decrepit old steamer. The 1,200-kilometre trip further down the coast from Puerto Madryn was nightmarish. Mary suffered acute diarrhoea and young Billy was dangerously ill with measles and inflammation of the lungs:

The Doctor ... was kindness itself and used invariably to pray over my little one, but he dared not trust himself to do anything else beyond take his temperature. When I would beg of him, 'Doctor, is there *anything* can be done?' he would say, 'We can only wait, we can only pray'... *Yet* Billy lived.[1]

But as they entered Antarctic waters and headed towards the treacherous port of Río Gallegos, on the same latitude as the Falkland–Malvinas islands, Mary, despite her worries, was stirred by the drama of their destination. They were just a short sail from the Strait of Magellan. She had been reading about the great navigator, dreaming of 'the journeys of these old Spaniards without maps or encyclopaedias, believing in ghosts and magic and evil spirits, with no knowledge of roods and distance'.[2] She read how Magellan had discovered the narrow entrance to the waterway,

sailed through it and charted it, called and named the land on one side of it Tierra del Fuego, the Land of Fire, from the camp fires of the Indians along the shore – not from volcanoes as we were school taught – and named the land on the other side for the Patagones, the tribe of the Indians living there, the Tehuelches, who he said had big feet; probably they were skin-covered because of the cold.[3]

It was Antonio Pigafetta, one of the men sailing with Magellan around the world, who left the very first eyewitness account of a Patagonian 'giant'. In his journal Pigafetta described an incident in September 1521, when they were sailing past San Julian, just north of Río Gallegos:

> One day, without anyone expecting it, we saw a giant, who was on the shore of the sea, quite naked, and was dancing and leaping, and singing, and whilst singing he put the sand and dust on his head. Our captain sent one of his men towards him, whom he charged to sing and leap like the other to reassure him, and show him friendship. This he did, and immediately the sailor led this giant to a little island where the captain was waiting for him; and when he was before us he began to be astonished, and to be afraid, and he raised one finger on high, thinking that we came from heaven. He was so tall that the tallest of us only came up to his waist … The captain named this kind of people Pataghom – on account of their large feet – who have no houses, but have huts made of the skins of animals with which they clothe themselves, and go hither and thither with these huts of theirs, as the gypsies do; they live on raw meat, and eat a certain sweet root, which they call Capac. These two giants that we had in the ship ate a large basketful of biscuit, and rats without skinning them, and they drank half a bucket of water at each time.[4]

Charles Darwin, voyaging on the *Beagle* in 1832, also knew the stories about giants and was on the look-out for one when they stopped at Cape Gregory:

An encounter with 'Patagonian giants' from John Byron's A Voyage
Round the World *(1767)*

We had an interview ... with the famous so-called gigantic
Patagonians, who gave us a cordial reception. Their height
appears greater than it really is, from their large guanaco
mantles, their long flowing hair, and general figure: on an
average their height is about six feet, with some men taller

and only a few shorter; and the women are also tall; altogether they are certainly the tallest race which we anywhere saw.[5]

Land of mariners' myths, quests and escape, dreams and disaster; the very word 'Patagonia', said Bruce Chatwin, 'like Mandalay or Timbuctoo, lodged itself in the Western imagination as a metaphor for The Ultimate, the point beyond which one could not go'.[6]

Patagonia was to have a powerful impact on Mary Gilmore. From the moment of her arrival, in early December 1900, she was alert, intensely curious about everything around her. The bitter, complaining woman of Cosme seems to have disappeared altogether. As she stepped on to the jetty at Río Gallegos she was, like the main character in one of her unpublished stories, a well-read young woman called Marcella, wryly amused and prepared for whatever the strange new world might deliver:

> She was young. She had read all the new books as they came into the library ... consequently she thought she knew life, thought moreover that she had sampled the old world and the conventional till she knew the taste of everything and was weary of the whole lot. She was new to Gallegos and its ways and hoped much from what the hitherto unknown held for her. So she stood on the rotten timbers of the pier, with her hand bag in her hand, and watched the launch go puffing back to the far off ship ...[7]

As the young woman Marcella, Mary's *alter ego*, descended the rickety steps from the pier, she was introduced to a constant feature of Patagonia: 'Marcella clutched her skirts. Certainly she was new to Patagonia. Where the wind never ceases, people grow used to legs … when she held her skirts her hat blew over her nose, when she held her hat, her skirts inclined to do the same.' The discomfiture of her arrival did not bode well:

Her shoes were full of sand and she was watching and wondering with a little cold shrinking of the heart how long it would be before a cab would come. Besides, she was growing weary of the struggle with the wind … A mule cart came rattling down the slope, the chains clattering in the shafts, the driver shouting, his sombrero tied under his chin, his poncho streaming out behind, the fringe cracking in the wind.

'*Bruto, Chaucho, Sucis!*' he yelled. To Marcella it sounded much like ordinary horse talk and it seemed all right. By and by she learned Spanish and a dim glimmering of the kind of thing that delights the mind of the average *peon* came to her.

'*Carajo!*' he cried. 'If you don't gallop I'll cut your entrails out and feed them to your mother!'

He stared at the woman 'with the unconsciousness of a child', while she, with a growing sense of depression, watched the *peones*, with their rolled-up dirty corduroy trousers and bare legs, wade through the surf to the *chata* or cargo barge, back and forth bringing off cases and baggage, to fling them down in the sand. She resolved to learn Spanish as soon as possible, to get some top boots and shorter skirts with hems heavily weighted with shot, and that she would wear these 'all the time she remained in this infernal country'. And when she discovered to her disgust that there would *never* be a cab, that such luxuries were not available on this frontier, that in fact she was expected to perch on top of the luggage in the mule cart, she simply refused to arrive in the town that way:

'No, thank you,' she replied. 'I much prefer to walk.' She held her head very high and stepped out into the shingle. She wanted experience and dignity, not loss of it.

Mary's first impressions of the town were also very likely the same as her character's:

There was a sense of disheartenment in the endless vista of sand, shingle, *barranca,* and the monotony of a treeless landscape with a galvanised iron house fastened down to it here and there, while the wind was so utterly tiresome it would not let one rest a minute … Did it never drop or modify? She was fast coming to the conclusion that the ways of civilisation did not suit this place, and that being used to civilisation did not fit one for Patagonia.[8]

The port town of Río Gallegos is located on the southern shore of the turbulent river from which it takes its name, about ten kilometres from its mouth, and is the seat of government for the then territory, now province, of Santa Cruz. But it was never a reliable port, and boats at their moorings were sometimes seen 'dancing, hopping, snorting and plunging in an extraordinary fashion'.[9] Few visiting writers have given Río Gallegos a good press. John Bell Hatcher, an American palaeontologist from Princeton University who first came to the town just four years before the Gilmores, in April 1896, considered it little better than a village. It 'consisted of not more than twenty-five houses, for the most part small and miserably built of wood and galvanised iron, carelessly thrown together'. Hatcher, a wealthy man with impeccable connections, was relieved to be a guest of the governor, for, to add to his displeasure, 'there was not a comfortable hotel or lodging house in the place'.[10]

The Gilmores encountered the same difficulty, but no offers were forthcoming from Government House for them.

The family arrived in Río Gallegos at the beginning of December 1900. Will had wanted to have longer to settle Mary and Billy into suitable accommodation, but the extended voyage put paid to that. Will was contracted to start work immediately at Killik Aike, the sheep estancia owned by Herbert Felton who had employed him earlier that year. The property was just sixteen kilometres north-west across the wide and dangerous river, but almost fifty kilometres by road.

After two nights at the Hotel Inglés, Gilmore brought his wife and son to the cheaper boarding house of Philomena de González. Mary's initial impressions were not encouraging:

The house was a great oblong iron building set in the shelter of a slope. The front of it looked uphill and saw only the hilltop, the sky and a few scattered ridgings and stove pipes. The back watched the sea. In between it and the sea though, were the huddled houses of the lower town, the pigs, the dogs, the cast-out old broken stoves, the rivers of mud, the pools of liquid filth that made up the streets of the lower town, at least during the greater part of the year. It also overlooked Sophia's, where the fat, jolly-looking German woman advertised her calling by a red blind at every window of her big house, and had the name of being 'a real good old sort' because she was good to the poor.

At first Mary had not known what red blinds signified and assumed Sophia's 'girls' were her servants. When she later learned the truth she felt only disgust, 'which no amount of "she ain't so bad" could temper'.

Mary discovered her new landlady 'drooping' over a laundry tub, presenting broad hips and a froth of scarlet underwear. 'As one got the back view of her, one wondered which way (up and down or crossways) she measured most.' Philomena abruptly turned and looked up, 'a silk red hankerchief tied fisherwoman-wise over sleek black hair' and 'one saw a strong kindly keen Spanish face, dark and tanned with the weather. I had not expected this short petticoated, stout-legged woman to be the wealthy Philomena and when my husband called her by her name, my heart went down with a slump.' It seems the unease was reciprocated:

She came up and spoke to us in quite a guttural Spanish. I could not understand a word she said. Somehow I felt she did not feel cordial. Her eye had taken in every detail of my appearance and I instinctively felt she did not approve of women who were not strong. And when I saw her glance at Little Man in a half contemptuous way, Little Man over whom every Spanish woman up till now had gone into raptures, even to calling him, half in awe '*un angelilo – un Christo*', I felt literally frozen.[11]

Gilmore said his farewells to his wife and child and had to leave them, in time to catch a boat on the rising tide upriver to Killik Aike.

The landlady led Mary to her own bedroom while a guest room was prepared, and fired 'sharp short questions' at her. In answer Mary could only show her helplessness. After four and a half years in South America, she admitted to knowing only the Spanish words for water, whether hot or cold, a few items of food – bread, meat, salt, tea – and *sí, no* and *muchas gracias*.

Philomena did not hide her impatience. 'The more dumb and hopeless I was, the sharper became her tone. Till at last the storm burst in a torrent of scolding.' Weakened by illness and the strain of the voyage, Mary almost collapsed. 'Then Philomena became "good Philomena" from then till I left the house.'

The new arrival was settled in a chair with solicitude while the servant girl María, a child of no more than eight, brought her a glass of wine. Mary was introduced to

Philomena's 10-year-old son Luciano, who seemed friendly towards Billy. She also learned that an elder daughter, Eugenia, was boarding at a convent school in Punta Arenas, the main seaport of Chilean Patagonia, 300 kilometres to the south-west.

But the situation was deeply unsettling. 'I was left alone in a strange house and in a strange land without even a know-ledge of the language in which I was addressed.'[12]

Our aircraft circled over Río Gallegos, 2,600 kilometres from Buenos Aires, that is, further than London is from Moscow. Below, a great caramel river, smeared at its edges like finger streaks in wet plasticine, moved sluggishly across a brown plain where ponds glistened from the recent rains. As we descended, the mouth of the river came into view, its disgorgement of mud blurring far into the Atlantic. Huge treeless paddocks were marked out in grids, then scattered buildings of concrete and tin, streets of a town, all in grid pattern.

Some perverse impetus had made me want to come to Río Gallegos on my first trip to South America twenty years earlier. But that was May 1982 and the Falklands–Malvinas war had just erupted. It was during my flight from Australia that the cabin crew announced the news that the British had torpedoed the Argentine battlecruiser, *General Belgrano,* outside the declared 200-mile exclusion zone around the disputed islands. The newspapers, after I landed, were full of the atrocity and the loss of 668 Argentine lives.

Río Gallegos was a major garrison and transfer point for

Argentine troops, mostly raw young conscripts, heading to the war zone. Fighter and transport planes also left from there. Three British journalists, including Simon Winchester, had just been arrested further south, in Ushuaia. The Australian embassy advised me to stay well clear – unless I was prepared to take the consequences of heading south with my camera, tape recorder and a story about researching an Australian woman poet who had lived there a hundred years earlier. I should consider whether the Argentine commandant's response would be, '*Ah claro! Muy buen!*' or something less affable.

So it was not until 1993 that I eventually made my planned visit, and now I was returning with Luis. The vista was still not inviting, as our taxi from the airport sped across a plain of coarse grass and low scrub, through an industrial belt and a dormitory suburb. There were signs of much recent building activity, new apartment complexes going up; but most of the houses were still raffishly independent, rendered concrete and brick, dilapidated weatherboard, and the older ones, still standing from the Gilmores' time, of painted corrugated iron.

Banners strung across the main street, Avenida Roca, urged '*Kirchner por Presidente!*' The governor of Santa Cruz province, Néstor Carlos Kirchner, a Peronist, was running for Argentine president in the April 2003 elections. He had made himself popular locally with his massive programme of cheap public housing, but not with everyone. 'He's spending our money to get himself elected,' said the taxi driver in Spanish. 'But he's got a beautiful wife, intelligent too, like Señora Clinton. She might get him in.'

Río Gallegos was still a town of charmless architecture with a makeshift, reckless feel, music blaring from record shops, lots of people on the streets, and one or two new citified restaurants. The oil rig off the coast and natural gas plants had attracted many workers to the province and increased the town's population to 65,000. The main intersection was still dominated by a statue of General Julio Roca, the man who 'settled' the Indian problem. Some men of Indian descent, migrants from Chile, lounged on the cinema steps.

The driver pulled up at the Hotel Paris, down on its luck now, but once the second finest accommodation the town could offer (after the Hotel Argentino where the wealthy estancieros stayed). 'You're lucky with the weather,' he said as he thumped our bags on the pavement. 'We only ever get about six days a year like this.'

It was true: the notorious wind of Patagonia was taking a break. Not a zephyr stirred the air.

It was ten days before Mary sent a letter to Will, who was living in the single men's quarters at Killik Aike. He would have told her to take any letters to the wharf at the edge of town and leave them in the office for one of the estancia's own boats, the *Malvina* or the *Priscilla*. By the time she wrote, she had battled the winds to explore the rumbustious little town, had been scandalised to learn what went on behind Sophia's red blinds, had tried to interest Billy in the solitary sheep cropping the harsh brown grass in Philomena's yard, and had met a few of the other residents at the boarding house. Of most interest to her was Don Louis, a French travelling salesman who had been lodging with the señora for almost four years. 'He imports direct from France and goes up and down the coast from Punta Arenas to Port Deseado ... He offered to let me have dress stuff too and pay later on, so if you are not in soon I will accept his offer and get a skirt made up to go out decent in.'

The *Standard*, Buenos Aires' other English-language newspaper, gives an account of the town at the time, which suggests a rapid expansion since Hatcher's 1896 visit:

> Today Rió Gallegos boasts of two banks, barracks, a grease factory, several wholesale stores and about 700 houses. There is a telephone joining Gallegos, Sandy Point and several large estancias. This line progresses daily and proves of great convenience ... One can safely state that 5,000 inhabitants live in the town ...[13]

Although a telegraph line linked it to Buenos Aires, from 1898 the telephone line went by Punta Arenas in Chile, 'the nearest business and shipping centre, 186 miles away'.[14] This sheltered deepwater port, Mary wrote, as she gained some understanding of Patagonian politics, had once belonged to Argentina, 'and the dream of the Argentine is to get it back', for then 'trade with Europe would be unrestricted and easy. Without it Patagonia is like a man with his head cut off or in a bag'.[15]

The Braun & Blanchards' store in Río Gallegos displayed

a *capa* that Mary longed to purchase but could not afford. It was a cape made from the soft fur of the guanaco. Since ancient times the Tehuelche Indians had systematically hunted young guanaco in summer, November to December, after the females had given birth. They used the *bola*, stones (or, since contact with Europeans, lumps of lead), contained in swinging leather thongs. In the late nineteenth century the hard-pressed Tehuelche, dwindling in numbers, found that *capas* were among the few items they could trade with Europeans wanting to take a curio home. The cloaks, also known as *quillangos*, which were made by the women and often painted and decorated, were prized for their warmth and beauty. The soft fur of as many as fifteen young guanacos were needed to make just one cloak.

Mary was grateful when Philomena lent Billy her own warm *capa*. Although it was high summer, she, too, was feeling the cold and feared what was to come. She thought she would buy some warm socks from the salesman Don Louis and planned to make a petticoat of lambskins for the winter. Meanwhile, she informed her husband, she was wearing a pair of his old moleskin trousers, cut to the knees, over her underclothes.[16]

Despite her initial reservations, Mary now felt well disposed towards her landlady, who had also shown kindly concern for Billy's persistent bronchial cough and had recommended a local medication made from the 'powdered craw of ostrich', or rhea. This tall flightless bird, hunted for its meat and feathers, was classified by Darwin in 1832 as *Pterocnemia pennata*, but was known locally as the *ñandú*. Mary

Ship passengers buying painted skins in Patagonia, from Illustrated
London News, *July 1889*

thought the treatment had brought about a marked im-
provement in Billy, and wanted to continue with it, but wrote
to Will that 'I am afraid La Senora has no more':

> If you get a chance at all to get the food sack of an ostrich,
> get it, for I want to take it too. Get all you can. I have had
> and still have, another attack of that bad diarrhoea … I am
> so weak and weary. If I'm not better tomorrow I will see the
> doctor … I sometimes think I will never be strong again …
> Once I am free of this diarrhoea, I shall begin to feel myself
> again. It has been hanging about me for six months now,
> which is a long time.[17]

At the entrance of the Hotel Paris, a few oil-rig workers loi-
tered, on their fortnightly lay-off with nothing to do. The

exquisite ceramic tiles in the hotel's lobby were obscured by lurid carpeting, but the bedroom floors were of Canadian spruce, brought out on ships as ballast, along with sheets of corrugated iron. A soccer match was on television in the dining room, where three men and the receptionist played a regular poker game under the huge cedar-framed art nouveau mirror, imported a century ago from France.

The hotel looked straight across Avenida Roca at the modern glass-fronted Banco Sudameris. But the original building was the Banco Tarapacá y Argentina, opened in 1899, one of only two banks in town.

Just three years after the Gilmores' departure, the Banco Tarapacá y Argentina was the scene of a dramatic event. On 14 February 1905 it was robbed by bandits, said to be the notorious Butch Cassidy and the Sundance Kid – *alias* Robert Leroy Parker and Harry Longabaugh.

They and their girlfriend Etta Place were on the run and had been hiding out on a farm at Cholila in the Andean foothills of Welsh Patagonia. Their descriptions had been circulated by the chief of police in Buenos Aires, along with hundreds of copies of a picture taken of Butch and Sundance with their Wild Bunch, supplied by the famous American Pinkerton Detective Agency. The gang had posed for the portrait, 'just for kicks', at a studio in Fort Worth. I photographed a copy I found framed on the wall of an old log-cabin roadhouse on a mountain pass near San Martín de los Andes.

However, no one imagined the outlaws would come so far south.

The Fort Worth Five photographed 'just for kicks' by John Swartz in 1900 and circulated in Argentina by the Pinkerton Detective Agency. Left to right: Harry A. Longabaugh (The Sundance Kid), Will Carver, Ben Kilpatrick, Harvey Logan (Kid Curry) and Robert LeRoy Parker (Butch Cassidy)

At the bank in Río Gallegos they got away with 20,000 pesos and £280 sterling, or else, in another version, the sum of 430,000 pesos.[18] They left the assistant manager, Arthur Bishop, and the teller, Alexander Mackerrow, well set up with stories of surviving a dreadful fate. *El Antarctico*, a local weekly newspaper, reported five days later:

Bank Robbery
Last Tuesday this quiet town was surprised by the news that the Bank of Tarapacá had been assaulted by two persons

who after getting hold of the Treasury fled on horseback.
The robbers were two North Americans who arrived a
month and a half ago, saying they were cattlemen of the Río
Negro – and they had said that they wanted to buy large
spreads of land in this country ...[19]

Osvaldo Topcic, professor of History and Geography at
the University of Patagonia in Río Gallegos, told me more.
The subject of banditry on the frontier fascinated him and
he had written an article about the 1905 robbery for the US
Old West magazine. He said the bandits had arrived in town
six weeks earlier and had put up at the exclusive Hotel Argentino, saying they were partners in a powerful cattle company in the Río Negro and were interested in buying
extensive tracts of land. *El Antarctico* noted how they established their credibility:

> They mixed socially with the best people in town, including
> cashier Mackerrow ... The strangers made it clear they had
> plenty of money. They treated people to drinks and food
> and gave generous tips. They were invited to the Club Pro-
> greso, which the most distinguished residents patronised.
> They also implied to bank officials that more money could
> be shortly transferred from the United States, to be applied
> to the promised investments. All that created an atmos-
> phere of trust.[20]

Bishop and Mackerrow both testified that on 14 February
they were working in their office, as no customers were in the

bank, when two men armed with Colt revolvers burst in. The taller of the two gave orders, while the shorter man jumped on the counter, pointed his gun at the terrified bank employees, and threatened to kill them if they did not obey. Bishop was forced to open the safe and put all the money, including a tin box containing the pounds sterling, into a large white canvas bag. The bandits dashed out to their horses and 'galloped down the street'.

Their getaway was observed by Mary Keen, I was told later by her great-grandson, Pablo Beecher. She was making beds on the top floor of the White Elephant Hotel, which had a good view of the bank, when she saw the robbers galloping away in a cloud of dust. But she had seen them at the bank several times before, and they had always left on horseback at full steam. So she had no sense of alarm when they did the same on the day of the robbery.

The men had carefully planned their escape route, according to the professor's account in the *Old West* magazine:

> They turned and rode south-west into open land toward a ford where they could cross the Gallegos river at Gueraike and then travel north ... News of the robbery spread rapidly. In several minutes a police sergeant Rodriguez, two other policemen, and a few local residents mounted their horses to give chase ...[21]

At a property called Bajo de la Leona (Lioness Hollow), darkness forced the pursuing posse to stop. According to police records, they discovered that the outlaws had abandoned three tired horses there, and had stolen fresh mounts. A few days later a waggoner called Franciso Cuello found an empty tin box which had contained the pounds sterling, 'in a place known as Killik Aike Springs, in a hollow about 220 yards from the road'.

There was another story about the getaway that came from the local Smith family. On that 14 February 1905, Mrs Smith was having difficulty opening a gate at Estancia Coy Inlet when she was startled by two men on horseback. They stopped, insisted on opening it for her, then went on their way. She always remembered them because the one who spoke to her had an American accent and clear blue eyes.[22] However, Professor Topcic regretted that he had never found any evidence that specifically identified the two men as Butch and Sundance, rather than two other members of their gang.

But I was convinced – or wanted to be – by various suggestions that a young American woman had accompanied the two men to Río Gallegos. James Allsop, a North American salesman, testified he had 'occasion to meet the men' before the robbery. He encountered a woman with them, 'a tall, slender fair woman who led a loose life and was known as *La Americana*'. The journalist Diego León Meneses, writing for *El Antarctico,* described the woman who had arrived with the men to buy land, as 'truly charming'. Even the police evidence states that the fugitives had left *three* tired horses at La Leona after their escape.

Most conclusive of all, it seemed to me, a woman accompanying them was named in a Federal Police report as 'E. A. Place', who was 'slender, white-skinned with greenish eyes, about twenty-seven or twenty-eight years old, almost five-feet-five-inches tall, and who was apparently Longabaugh's wife'.[23] I was quite certain Etta would not have been in Río Gallegos without Butch and Sundance.

Professor Topcic was reserving his judgement. However, he showed me a news item from Buenos Aires of the following year, reporting that 'two men and a woman have been arrested in Neuquen' – the province adjoining the Welsh settlers – 'in the belief that they had been involved in the Río Gallegos robbery'.[24] After questioning they were released – so their luck held once again.

The outlaws' lives after the Río Gallegos bank robbery have been a matter of conjecture, but outside the admittedly sometimes vague limits of this particular story. They may have been joined at Cholila by Harvey Logan, one of the old Wild Bunch, and robbed one or two more banks. In one account Etta Place broke up the *ménage à trois* by becoming pregnant by an English neighbour.[25] In the version that went to film, the men died dramatically after a train hold-up in Bolivia. Bruce Chatwin had another story, that while 'the Sundance Kid was gunned down in South America', Butch Cassidy escaped, 'travelled with an Indian boy on a kind of Huck Finn idyll', and eventually returned to North America.[26]

❧

The book-keeper from Estancia Killik Aike, who 'seems to be a very nice man', Mary wrote to Will, called in to visit her while he was in town and gave her 'the good news that you were well and also the addition that you were making plenty of money'. She learned from him that the English governess employed by the Felton family was leaving shortly, and pinned her hopes on offering herself as a replacement. 'Everybody whom I have seen … seems to think that for us to go to Felton's is like going to Heaven. They talk about them having "everything" in almost a tone of awe …'[27]

Mary was missing her husband and continued to fret about Billy's health:

> I expect I will make you miserable often, dear, talking about Billy if he does not seem to improve, but you will try to bear with me, for he is so much to me … The man's life outside does not remind him of his child however much he may think of him. The woman lives surrounded by and in the midst of reminders that never can be lost sight of or forgotten.[28]

For the six weeks of her stay, she continued to regard her landlady with some affection and believed the feeling returned, but she felt hesitant about making herself too at home in the kitchen:

> I am still told to do and take as I like. But I seem to use such a lot of firing, for she burns nearly all yerba stuff and the minute she is done cooking the fire is out and I have to get in fresh stuff and fire up afresh. She always says '*No importe*,' but I feel uncomfortable. I fancy she rather wonders why I am staying so long, however it can't be helped.

She knew the tactful thing would be to accept Philomena's cooking, but complained to Will that she found it altogether too fatty. 'If I don't eat, the Señora is put out, and there the trouble is … There is no doubt about the Señora's kindness, but her ways and house are not our ways and house, however good they be, and however poor ours be.'[29]

Easy communication with Philomena remained a problem:

Philomena began one day to tell me about the trouble she had in getting the half breed Maria to go to school. I followed what she said fairly well, ejaculating, '*Que cosa*', 'Aha' and '*Sí*' at appropriate intervals. Philomena eyed me with suspicion. She did not believe a person with so little variety of comment or expression could understand. She began her tale again – from the beginning. I '*Que cosa*'ed, 'Aha'ed! and '*Sí*'-ed as before. She came to the end and a third time began it, but this time in a voice that continually rose in pitch and with a rapidity of language that left her breathless, winding up with 'You idiot, if you stand there staring at me any longer I'll give you a box in the ears.' It was meant as a joke … A shadow fell across the floor. We looked round. It was Luciano just come in. 'Why do you tease the woman?' he said.[30]

❧

I learned more about Luciano, Philomena's son, from a young journalist called Pablo Beecher, who wrote for the local paper *La Opinión Austral*. An intense 30-year-old with a thick crop of black hair and wire-rimmed glasses, he was from an old British–Argentine family in Río Gallegos; his forebears had owned the White Elephant Hotel and it was his great-grandmother, Mary Keen, who had observed the bank robbery.

Having gained a degree in communications at the University of Buenos Aires, Pablo had returned home to the town he loved; he had a passion for its local history. Luciano's surname, he told me, was Carrera – fathered by a husband previous to González – and he eventually became a man of great influence in the district. He began his working life breaking in horses, then started a transport company carting in wool from the estancias, using horse-drawn wagons which were faster than the bullock teams. The upwardly mobile young man then founded a farm, La Paloma, built the first stone house in the town in 1930 and married a girl from the landed Ríquez family. It seemed an inevitable progression when Luciano Carrera became mayor of Río Gallegos, a position he held for many years. He opened the town's first and, even today, only cinema, still called Cine Carrera.

We made the short stroll from the Hotel Paris to the Carrera, its name in neon tubing on the awning over the pavement, to find what was currently showing. There was a choice of *Camino a la Perdicion* (*Road to Perdition*) with Tom Hanks and Paul Newman or, at the late session, Cameron Diaz in *La Cosa Más Dulce* (*The Sweetest Thing*). I was amused to see a poster for the Harry Potter film in the foyer. I had had many sightings of Harry in Buenos Aires as well, and told Luis I was astonished by his popularity.

'But why not?'

'He's so English!'

'Yes, but people don't hate the English.'

'But the Falklands–Malvinas war …?'

'Yes, but that was mostly a problem for the military people on both sides,' said my friend. 'Anyway, we like the English much better than the Americans.'

On the last day of 1900, Mary managed to secure a consultation with the English Dr Victor Fenton. Her health was fragile – 'I am in a very weak state … Sometimes my heart scarcely beats' but she considered Fenton 'the most noncommittal doctor I ever saw … he said it was probably dysentery I had, and that I had brought the poison in my system from Paraguay … I am very weary to get into a place of my own, and I am counting the days till you come.'[31]

She had a new objective, the possibility of the governess position. She began to study Spanish in earnest. It may seem astonishing that Mary had never bothered to do this during her four years in Paraguay, but almost all that time had been lived within the confines of an essentially Anglo-Celtic enclave which discouraged fraternisation with the local people, so she had never felt the need to do so. She may have been helped in her study by one of the Englishmen in the town, for in her fragmentary short story set in Gallegos, her character Marcella is advised by an Englishman that she must decide what variety of Spanish to learn:

'There's camp Spanish and book Spanish, there's the Spanish you'll hear every day and the Spanish you must never use. There's Buenos Aires Spanish and Punta Arenas Spanish, and last but not least there's English Spanish.'

'Oh,' she ejaculated faintly.[32]

The book-keeper had apparently made a good report about Mary, for she now understood there was a real possibility of her becoming governess to the adolescent Emily Felton. It just needed a personal interview with the boss, Herbert Stanley Felton, to confirm it, and she considered the job as good as in the bag. Best of all, she understood her whole family had been offered a little house on the property. She had all kinds of practical instructions for Will:

> Be sure you measure the oven in the stove, and the diameter of the holes on top before you come in. Also lay in a stock of three kerosene tins for water and slops if possible. I hear we are only allowed salt, coal and mutton. If the coal is limited as it is nearly sure to be, the fit of dishes and saucepans is an important matter. We had better try to arrange to buy our stores from Mr Felton if we can.[33]

She could contain neither her excitement nor her propensity for list-making when she wrote on 5 January:

> I believe Mr Felton is expected here tomorrow or next day. I am going to speak to him about going out to the Estancia. I think it will be better both for Billy and for me … Of

course if Mr Felton arranges for me to go out, you will have to come in, as there are the things to buy – oatmeal, rice, yerba (it is cheaper than tea), tea, coffee, a broom, kerosene, candles, flour, sugar, two saucepans, frying pan, a baking tin, perhaps a kettle, milk for Billy and some condensed unsweetened milk for cooking puddings, rice or porridge. Matches, perhaps a little jam or treacle, soap ...[34]

Three days later she penned a rather histrionic letter. Now, with the expectation of preparing meals for her family in her own kitchen, the food at Philomena's suddenly became intolerable. It sounds like robust, flavoursome Spanish cooking to me, but Mary's culinary skills had been acquired in rural nineteenth-century Australia, an inheritance of the very worst of British cooking. Olive oil was an item which belonged in little bottles on apothecaries' shelves:

I think if I don't soon go out I will die ... The Senora offers plenty of good nourishing food, eggs, soup, mutton and fish, but the soup swims with oil, the fish is soaked with it and so on. I can't very well insult her by cooking for myself ... Of course, dear, I think seeing I had to stay in Gallegos, it has been great good fortune to get here, if only for the milk ... Also I find people do pay for what they get here, this being no ordinary accommodation house. It is a fine place for a strong healthy person, for there is salad and cream in the coffee, butter now and then and jam, with any amount of fat, mutton and greasy soup. But for a delicate person! ... I feel sure I will be better in my own place, for I can cook for one thing plenty of good strong soup, well strained and without fat. If we could only get a cow, so that I could have milk!

Mary had suffered another severe attack of dysentery, she told Will, and added – escalating the pressure – that she feared for their son if they stayed on at the boarding house:

> If I have to lay up (as indeed I should now) there is no hope for Billy as far as attention goes, for the Senora has neither the idea, the time nor the patience of feeding or caring for a delicate child. Mariá would be his care-taker and Mariá knows less than a pig, besides she is only 7 or 8 years of age. The only thing that makes staying here tolerable is the fresh milk but Billy wants mixed food now. He craves for bread and picks up scraps and dirty bits, hiding away in corners to eat them.

In case poor Gilmore had the slightest reluctance about bringing his family out to the estancia, it was suggested his son's very survival depended on it:

> There is another reason I would like to be on the Estancia and that is for warmth for Billy. This place is full of draughts for the cracks are not closed anywhere, there are openings in all directions and often I daren't strip Billy's chest to rub him because of the draughts coming through the cracks.

Mary was a woman of formidable strength of character

and could be implacable in achieving what she wanted. She was going out to that estancia and no one, certainly not her mild, good-natured husband, nor his employer, the dour Herbert Felton, was going to stop her.

> Write me a line to say when you think I may go out … I expect we will have to get a big advance from Felton to get ready for the winter … Though I feel so weak and all that, yet I feel sure I could do teaching for part of the day … Dearest one, I long to see you, to be with you. You help me and strengthen me.[35]

By mid January 1901 Mary and young Billy were on their way to Estancia Killik Aike, travelling not the long way round by road, but in the estancia's own boat, the *Malvina*, chugging upstream and across the great Gallegos river.

Now I too was planning to make a visit to Killik Aike. It would be my second. Nine years earlier, in 1993, I had made my first contact with John and Monica Blake, the couple who had bought the sheep property from the Feltons' son Carlos. At the time John Blake was also the manager of Estancia Condor, the largest sheep property in Argentina – and arguably the world – where Gilmore had also worked. Only *one* negotiation, I had exulted – until it occurred to me that a refusal also meant I could miss out on visiting both estancias.

I had put through a telephone call to Estancia Condor, almost 3,000 kilometres to the south. The voice that answered was very English, cultivated, cool and wary. 'We're not so sure about writers,' Monica Blake said. 'Some of our friends here have had an unhappy experience with writers.'

I told her I was researching a group of Australians who had settled in Paraguay, some of whom had ended up in Patagonia.

'Those socialists?'

'Yes, the group who went with a man called William Lane.'

'We've heard about them,' replied Monica Blake briskly, 'but we're very busy at the moment. It's unfortunate, but I'm sorry, I have to say …'

'I'm mainly interested in a woman called Mary Gilmore,' I persisted. 'A distinguished writer who became a Dame of the British Empire. In 1901 she was a governess on Killik Aike. Her husband also worked – '

' – on Condor, yes,' said Monica. 'In fact, we *are* rather interested in Mary Gilmore … How long were you planning to stay in Río Gallegos?'

'About three days,' I hazarded.

'Then ring us when you arrive. Perhaps we could put you up. We'd like to hear more about Mary Gilmore. We've become quite fond of her in a way …'

VI

KILLIK AIKE

A battered taxi was taking me the almost fifty kilometres to the estancia, and half of that, after we left the sealed road, would be heavy going after the recent rains. The driver, Joaquín Fernandez, balding, overweight and amiable, was willing to put himself out for the Blakes. He had known them – from a respectful distance – for thirty years, he told me in Spanish. In fact, from the days when he was driving an oil truck in the heavy snow and he came across an overturned Landrover far from town. He rescued Monica and her child trapped inside. It was 23 degrees below freezing, she told me later; they would have perished otherwise.

I was excited to be returning to Estancia Killik Aike (pronounced Killik I-key), the property established in 1890 by Herbert Stanley Felton. His son Carlos eventually sold it, with some very specific conditions, to the Blakes in 1980. Nine years ago I had been their guest there, and later at Estancia Condor, 100 kilometres to the south, where John was then manager: 'We normally manage to freeze writers out,' he had laughed, 'but you seem to have slipped under the net!'

The wide and turbulent Gallegos river was on the right as

we drove, its brown waters bringing melted snow from the Andes. On the far shore stood a line of gaunt cliffs with scarped edges carved by the flow – and somewhere beyond the cliffs lay Killik Aike. However, we needed to travel over twenty kilometres inland to where the river narrowed sufficiently for a bridge, then the same distance back east on the other side, to where the estancia looked across at the town.

'In the old days', John Blake had told me, 'people used to ride and drive carts three kilometres across the river at low tide when it's mostly a huge sandbank. But they always took a risk.' The river, he explained, exhibited some of the most prodigious tidal rises and falls in the world – the third greatest after the Bay of Fundy in Newfoundland and the Bristol Channel. Low and high levels could vary by up to fifteen metres. When the tide turned, it did so with ferocious speed. Many people had been caught and drowned.

To our left, barbed wire fences and power lines marched relentlessly across a blasted heath, the arid plain of Patagonia, its grit and shingle supporting only withered brown grass and dwarf shrubs, creasing occasionally into hard, flinty folds and rising to a line of old worn hills on the horizon.

On my previous visit I had thought it similar to the Australian outback, but lacking its vividness, as if photographed in sepia, the contours of the land in stark relief under a leaden sky. Paul Theroux deftly summed up 'the brown eroded landscape' as 'dust, withered bushes, blue sky, kitty litter'.[1] But it was hard not to be stirred by its majestic starkness, the enormous emptiness of the plain. Years after the voyage of the *Beagle*, Charles Darwin remained haunted:

In calling up images of the past, I find that the plains of Patagonia frequently cross before my eyes; yet these plains are pronounced by all wretched and useless. They can be described only by negative characters; without habitations, without water, without trees, without mountains, they support merely a few dwarf plants. Why, then, and the case is not peculiar to myself, have these arid wastes taken so firm a hold on my memory? I can scarcely analyse these feelings: but it must be partly owing to the free scope given to the imagination.[2]

But today there was a difference. The plains were not empty. Hundreds, thousands, perhaps millions of white flighty objects fluttered, flapped and danced across the steppe, clung and spun on the wires of the fences, like seagulls gone mad, like all the birds of Patagonia preparing to take off in some epic migration. Plastic bags.

'Yes,' agreed Joaquín Fernandez, accepting the sight as normal, 'people are very untidy.'

We crossed the substantial three-arched iron bridge across the river, left the sealed road which went on to the Chilean border and turned back east. We began the climb between bare undulating hills, winding up to the top of the escarpment, from where the plastic wastes far below looked like a meadow of pale wildflowers.

We passed gates and dirt roads leading away to other properties. Many of the landowners on the northern side of the river are of Scottish descent and had come to Patagonia by way of the Falkland–Malvinas islands.

That was the result of a policy devised in the late 1800s by President Julio Argentino Roca, whom John Blake considered a great statesman because of it. 'He could see that he wasn't going to get good settlers from Argentina. He could get people from Buenos Aires to go out and settle the provinces in the north – a nice Mediterranean climate, a pleasant comfortable life – but they wouldn't be willing to come down to the far south. But there was already a fairly flourishing farming community on the Falkland islands.'

Roca appointed Carlos María Moyano as governor of Santa Cruz, the huge southernmost territory (later province) of Argentine Patagonia, with a brief to recruit for the new frontier. Moyano set the pattern by travelling to the Falklands and marrying an English girl, Ethel Turner. He encouraged the island people to come across and establish farms in Santa Cruz. Most were Scots, shepherds and crofters from the western highlands and islands who had been financed under the British Land Order system to emigrate to the Falklands, because of their experience of sheep farming in harsh climatic conditions on poor peaty soil. With the invitation from Governor Moyano, a number of them seized the opportunity to better their positions.

They were a hard-handed, stoic lot, narrow in their views and strict in their religion, with a standard prescription at the end of a day's work, as Andrew Graham-Yooll observed:

The Scots settled, as they do anywhere, and ruled Patagonia and the Falkland (Malvinas) Islands, farming – with a copy of the Bible and a volume of Scott in one hand and a bottle of strong spirits in the other.[3]

These people established sheep properties around Río Gallegos. Soon thousands of bales of wool were being shipped to English mills. Although most of the great estancias in Patagonia today are run by Argentine conglomerates with interests in shipping and other branches of commerce, descendants of these Scots and English farmers remain.

On the plateau we sloughed through heavy mud, deeply riven by vehicle wheels, avoided bogging and passed a herd of the flighty red guanacos. And then there were sheep, handsome full-fleeced creatures, cropping the grassy slopes. We were on Killik Aike land.

The sheep were Cormo Argentino, the distinctive breed John Blake had developed over thirty years by crossing the Australian Merino, for its fine wool, with the Corriedale, for its meat and hardiness in cold and damp conditions. He had left the legacy of this breed for the new owner of Estancia Condor, Benetton, the huge Italian clothing company.

'I think Señor Blake knows more about sheep breeding', said Joaquín Fernandez, 'than anyone else in Patagonia.'

We went through a gate, passing some red-roofed outbuildings and the men's quarters, and pulled up under an avenue of pine trees, their branches interlocking. The red roof and chimneys of the main house loomed behind a high brick wall.

ॐ

Will Gilmore had worked for the Feltons at Killik Aike from December 1899 to June 1900. After the break in his employment when he had returned to Paraguay, he started again on 5 December, leaving his wife and son at Philomena's boarding house. As I discovered from the Killik Aike wages book 1896–1902, with its pages of double-entry book-keeping executed in spidery copperplate, Will's remuneration was £4 a month with accommodation provided in the men's quarters. His debits from the estancia store were modest: matches, tobacco, candles and soap. But suddenly, in mid-January 1901, he took time off work and made a flurry of purchases: potatoes, onions and beans; tins of butter, jam and milk; bags of sugar, salt and flour, tea and *yerba maté*; Lea & Perrins sauce; a bottle of 'Currie', half a ream of paper and a large order of Mellins' Baby Food. Will Gilmore had little use for the last two items – he was setting up house for his writer wife and child.[4]

Mary was full of optimism. After all, she was heading for a place viewed locally as 'like going to Heaven'.

When she arrived at the estancia in January 1901, she had achieved her aim of being appointed governess to the daughter Emily Felton. And when her family was offered a little house of their own, her satisfaction knew no bounds. But there is no record of her first impressions. I supposed that Mary spent a happy time settling in to a cottage so delightful and toy-like – a larger version of the dolls' house I had been given when I was a child in England – that I longed to camp in it myself.

ॐ

Double doors in the brick wall led, as if down a White Rabbit's hole, to a world unrelated to Patagonia. It was a very English garden: spreading oaks, silver birch and golden laburnum, lilac hedges and herbaceous borders, pathways edged with tulips, snowdrops, daffodils and hyacinths. It was a cosseted treasure, made possible by the windbreak of pines and poplars outside the wall, by the clanking windmills beyond bringing that rare Patagonian commodity, good underground water, and by Monica and a gardener providing the cosseting.

The Blakes welcomed me, the three of us assessing the difference nine years had made. John, tall, ruddy-complexioned, with thinning white hair, still exerted the considerable authority of manner acquired from his family background and from his experience over thirty years as boss of Estancia Condor. Monica remained a striking, grey-haired woman, tall and stately, her dark eyes and olive skin suggesting her part-Spanish heritage, but with a certain rigorous propriety, despite her soft speech and gentle manner, that left no doubt Imperial Britain was her birthright also.

Monica had told me previously about her upbringing in Montevideo, where her father was the local manager for Lloyds of London. It was a favoured, elegant life: polo, cocktail parties, balls and regular trips to England. On returning by boat to South America after a season in London, she had become acquainted with John Blake, who had just graduated from Cambridge. 'My family knew of his people, so it was deemed all right for us to continue talking.'

The interior of the house was as gracious as I remembered it. Many sitting areas, glass-protected, with chintz-covered chairs, looked out to the garden. A tinted photographic portrait showed a charming young girl in a white lace-trimmed dress smiling beneath a straw hat trailing pink ribbons – John's mother, Millicent Worsley, as a child. She was a favourite of a family friend, Charles Dodgson, the introverted mathematician who later became famous as Lewis Carroll. When she married and came to Patagonia in 1924, her mother-in-law advised her to 'bring your piano, know how to tune it, know how to cut your husband's hair, bring your music, your books and your paints'. A folio of delicate watercolours of the wildflowers of Patagonia was painted and annotated by Millicent as a young bride.

John was the third generation of sheep farmers in these climes. His grandfather, Robert Blake, from a well-connected Somerset family came to West Falkland island in 1873 and established a farm, Hill Cove. The early pioneering years were physically and psychologically punishing, with long periods of isolation, but the young man was soon recognised as one of the most capable farmers on those bleak windswept islands. According to the book *Falkland Heritage* he and a compatriot of similar social standing both longed to marry but discussed the importance of selecting the right wife: 'Romance, they felt, must be guided by sober reason, when it came to choosing a girl who would settle to life on a colonial sheep station.'[5]

When, on a visit back to England in 1878, Robert proposed to the 24-year-old Dora Herford, she was attracted to the strongly built, straightforward young man, a Unitarian like herself, but hesitated at first to 'go to the Wilds'. Dora was artistic, supported certain 'radical' ideas including Woman-hood Suffrage, and her sister was about to enter Newnham College, Cambridge. Her devoutly Unitarian family enjoyed the exchange of ideas and 'read widely, went to art galleries and the Hallé concerts'. The author and humanitarian Mrs Gaskell was a visitor at their house, while William Herford, Dora's father, 'corresponded with intellectuals in England and Germany'.[6]

When Dora at last agreed to become engaged to Robert Blake, she prepared herself for her new life by learning to cook and to sew and even how to lance abscesses. 'It takes nerve to face the hospital as you have done,' Robert wrote. 'I am sure that that sort of thing takes it out of you more than twelve hours in the saddle or a day's crutching alongside the dip.'[7]

After years of correspondence, through which they learned a great deal about each other, the couple married in July 1881 and travelled to the homestead at Hill Cove on West Falkland island. Just as Dora later passed on advice to her own daughter-in-law, Robert's favourite sister Florence gave some to her: 'Let nothing come amiss from the scouring of a saucepan in the kitchen to the entertaining of a bishop in the parlour.'[8]

Dora stoically adjusted to the isolated life, captured local scenes in her sketch book and did her best to establish a civilised lifestyle – despite her husband's protests, she banned smoking in the house. But her sketching and reading became infrequent after she gave birth to eight children in almost as many years. John's father, Arthur Locke Blake, was the seventh.

Robert remained obsessed with improving the quality of his sheep through careful breeding and was gratified by a letter from the London brokers: 'The flock now compares more favourably with the best fine qualities of New Zealand than any other from the Falkland islands.'[9] Later he leased, then purchased, a second sheep property at Puerto San Julian in Patagonia, installing a manager.

A neighbour on the adjoining West Falkland farm, Roy Cove, was of the Felton family. 'But there was never much socialising between my grandfather and the Feltons,' said John. 'They were not his kind of people at all.'

On hearing this, I was reminded of early nineteenth-century Boston, when 'the Lowells only spoke to the Cabots, and the Cabots only spoke to God'.

Herbert Felton Senior went out to the Falklands in 1849. 'He was a sergeant-major in the Lifeguards,' said John Blake, 'sent to the Falklands as second in command of a group of Chelsea Pensioners, who were ex-army people. Felton was second-in-command, the senior warrant officer, so obviously a very capable guy, but all warrant officers in that day were definitely regarded as rather lower deck.'

Many of the military pensioners brought families with them, and Felton came with some of his fourteen children. Herbert Stanley Felton, one of the younger sons, eventually married Emma Bartlett, an English girl born in the islands. While others in his family had become well established, he needed to find suitable land to start farming on his own. When Governor Moyano arrived on the islands offering favourable terms to settlers who chose to relocate on the mainland, Herbert saw his chance. 'When the governor turned up and said "Look, there's land over there!" he signed up,' reported Blake

Felton came over to Santa Cruz in 1886 with his wife and daughter Emily in a schooner, the *Rippling Wave,* which also transported 'provisions, farm supplies and 800 sheep'.[10] After a false start settling a farm at another location, south of Río Gallegos, Felton 'got bigger in his ideas' and moved over to the northern side of the river.

In 1890 he established the 33,000-hectare Killik Aike property, giving it the Tehuelche name for 'camping ground' or 'resting place'. He built a house and shipped fine furniture from Europe. Ten years later a son, Carlos, was born.

In mid-January 1901 Mary began teaching her pupil, Emily Felton, usually known as Millie. 'I think the most awful girl that ever lived,' Mary concluded later:

> She was 16; looked 18, and called herself 14. She knew every-thing ever known, and what I told her one day, told me back in a day or two as entirely her own. Among the items of her own peculiar knowledge was that 'she knew the woman who made *all* the lace for Queen Victoria's wedding'. Her

mother was a nice woman, her father a big man with a thin nose, a high voice, and a character and reputation to match.[11]

In an old album I found a fading sepia portrait of the Feltons, taken some years after the Gilmores' departure. In evening dress Herbert Stanley Felton, the estanciero, looks more like a Yorkshire mill-owner, portly and bewhiskered, peering down his long nose with the complacency of a self-made man. His wife Emma, in ruched brocade, her dark hair gathered in a curly top-knot, is elegant, fine-featured, even beautiful. But the lumpish blonde daughter Millie took after her father, a bovine sullenness seemingly undisguised by elaborate frills (though I admit I may have become party to Mary Gilmore's prejudice concerning her pupil). Another man, Henstock, Millie's husband, sports a calculating look and an elaborately waxed moustache. The child on the table, little Carlos Felton, with his golden curls and winsome smile, basks in the certainty of being forever adored, forever indulged.

After his father's death in the mid-1920s, Carlos inherited the property but left it in charge of a manager while he luxuriated in nightclubbing, womanising and gambling in Buenos Aires and Europe, thus reinforcing the saying 'as rich as an Argentine'. In 1980 he sold Killik Aike to the Blakes – on the condition that the Big House remained his during his lifetime. 'We spent most of the week living in the Big House at

Portrait of the Feltons a few years after they employed the Gilmores. Left to right: wife Emma (née Bartlett), son-in-law Henstock, young Carlos, Herbert Stanley Felton and daughter Millie.

Estancia Condor,' said Monica, 'so it was rather fun to come here and stay in a little cottage.'

Carlos, habitué of the gaming tables of Monte Carlo, was rarely in residence – 'he was fond of saying that in fifty years he'd never spent a winter anywhere' – but when he was, he proved to be an increasingly testy old man. An acrimonious issue was the burial place of his father. Herbert Felton's monumental grave was right in the middle of the flower garden. Monica found it depressing and asked Carlos to have it moved. The coffin was exhumed at last and, for a time, a frost colder than a Patagonian dawn settled between the Big House and the cottage.

Carlos died in 1988, was emphatically not buried in the flower garden, and the Blakes moved into the Big House. They had a sense of continuity with a property that had been established for 112 years. Everything to do with its history interested them, including the sojourn there of an obscure Australian shearer and his writer wife who became a Dame of the British Empire.

The Gilmores settled into a cottage Mary described as backing on to the Feltons' house.[12] On my previous visit, Monica had led me to the only building answering that description, just beyond the main garden: a neat two-storey gingerbread house, with walls clad in cream-painted corrugated iron, two bay windows and a red roof shaded by a pine tree. It was the right vintage. The Blakes used it as the estancia museum.

It smelled musty. Among the items on display in the diminutive living room was a warped fiddle that had done service playing reels and schottisches at dances on the property. There was a Baby Daisy vacuum cleaner, an 'Improved Magneto Electric Machine for Nervous Diseases', and a medicine kit with various numbered vials. Monica explained that

The cottage at the bottom of the Feltons' garden, Killik Aike

in the Gilmores' time the English Dr Victor Fenton prescribed for ailments over the telephone: 'For instance, for
stomach pains, take a spoonful of No. 4; for a cold, half a
spoon of No. 7. On the mantelpiece were a few cloth-bound
editions of Charles Dickens. Once there had been a complete
set. Argentine soldiers, billeted in the cottage during the 1982
Falklands–Malvinas war, had burned the others for fuel.
They had torn down the velvet curtains from the bay windows and set them alight, too.

'It wasn't exactly an easy time,' said Monica, 'but we don't
talk about it too much.'

The narrow bathroom of the cottage, though a luxury for
mere employees, was cold and dismal. The wind whistled
through a wide crack in the door. I tried to picture Mary
Gilmore lying naked in the claw-footed bath, but doubted
there had ever been much languishing. Bathing would have
been a hasty, unpleasant business, especially in winter. Mary

described how she kept a barrel of water outside the cottage door. In winter it burst, leaving a block of ice.[13]

Monica led me past the men's quarters and cookhouse. The Chilean cook sat on the steps, a fat tabby cat sidling against his legs. Across a paddock of low calafate bushes we came to the long, red-roofed shearing shed where Will had worked. Sunlight streamed through its windows, fell on worn floorboards hatched by shadows from the cross-beams, redolent of lanolin.

The Australian shearers had scorned the Spanish tied system, where the sheep's legs were first trussed by rouseabouts. Tom Hicks-Hall, one of the first Cosme men to shear in Patagonia, wrote: 'There was quite a gape of wonder and astonishment when I calmly untied my first sheep as a preliminary to shearing it, and I was conscious of many inquisitive eyes.'[14]

Mary must have visited the long shearing shed at Killik Aike and observed the men, for she wrote a detailed description of their work regime in Patagonia:

The shearing was done inside the *galpon* (shed or covered place). The order of the day was as follows: they began as soon as the sheep were dry enough; dew did not take long to dry off. At 8 a.m. they had half an hour for breakfast consisting of *yerba* (Paraguayan tea) and biscuit. Then they went on shearing in the *galpon;* the tyers got the sheep from the pens, tied their legs, and brought them to the shearers inside. Each man was given a *lata* (tag) for each sheep shorn. Later each *lata* was cashed for 11/2; the pay, therefore, for shearing a sheep. At 11.30 a.m. they knocked off work for 'the real breakfast and at this I think they had *yerba* and biscuit in addition to the regulation rice and meat. At 3.30 p.m. again there was half an hour for *maté* (*yerba*) and biscuit; and when at sunset, the day's work came to an end, they again had *maté*, rice and meat. Where and how they slept heaven only knows. I should say that the shearing was very rough in quality and not at all remarkable for quantity. These shearers are 'nowhere' as compared with New Zealanders or Australians.[15]

Never given to understatement, Mary claimed her husband was soon 'said to be the best shearer in Patagonia'.[16]

The early days at the estancia were clearly a happy time for Mary, except for school hours with the disagreeable Millie: 'This girl was so thick necked, narrow-browed, and arrogant that she was known as Queen Victoria.'[17]

Mary did not describe the interior of the Big House, where lessons were held. But the previous year J. B. Hatcher, on a second Princeton Expedition, was offered hospitality there by Wesley, the foreman, even though the owners were away at the time:

After a plain but substantial dinner I was invited by the foreman of the estancia to his room, where I spent the first really comfortable evening since our arrival in Patagonia. Mr Felton and his wife, though absent, were evidently people who believed in enjoying some of the comforts of life, even though they did live at the other end of the world.

There was an open grate in which glowed a cheerful fire of good English coal.

Perhaps coal from England was brought as ballast, a back-load on the ships transporting wool, otherwise its use would seem as extravagant as the rubber merchants of Brazil who sent their laundry to Lisbon. Hatcher admired the house's accoutrements of refined living, even though at an impossibly remote distance from anything reasonably regarded as civilisation:

> The house was well furnished with comfortable chairs, a piano, a well-selected library and numerous periodicals of the latest numbers, brought from England on the bi-monthly mail steamers ... Nor were our host and hostess unmindful of the inner man. There was an abundant supply of provisions and a choice selection of liquors, wines, beer, ale, stout, and mineral waters. Everything about the ranch bespoke comfort and consideration for the family, employees and guests.[18]

The Gilmores, of course, never expected or received such hospitality, for as mere workers they were separated by a great social divide. But once settled in the modest little corrugated iron cottage at the bottom of the Feltons' garden, they were content with their domestic arrangements. Beside the two new saucepans, the frying pan and the baking tin, Mary hung the battered tin pannikin which her father had always carried with him in the Australian bush until his death.

Killik Aike homestead in 1904

Money is money, and power is power,
But memory keeps for itself an hour,
When the gates swing open, the rails are down,
And youth like a king strides out of the town;
Then wealth and position are nothing at all,
O old tin pannikin, there on the wall![19]

Mary had a secret life of the imagination, the writer in her revelling in the spare, haunting beauty of this strange southern land. She loved to wake while all was still dark and her husband and child lay sleeping; she would pull on her woollen clothes and lambskin petticoat and tiptoe out the door. In a dim whitened world she would climb the hill to the headland overlooking the river, to her left a wide gulch that carved its way down to it. There she would sit to watch the sun rise:

Dawn. In a few hours the sky will whiten. Dawn comes stepping across the earth. Like a silver shield the sun will rise over the rim of the pampa. There is no warmth, there is as yet little wind, the frost continues unabated. In the east, the white changes to purple, the purple to indigo, the indigo to a wonderful blue, then the sun rides up, full fronted to the day. Life stirs and wakens, the great pampa shakes herself, and the sheep waken and follow the trail, while the fox sneaks out of his shelter and follows them.

At the bottom of the unsuspected *cañedon* that yawns suddenly at one's feet, the ostrich lifts his strong long legs and flying from the sight of man, loses himself in its windings. The guanacos call to one another across their camping ground and string out across the level pampa to feed. Riverwards the gulls cry and two carranchos circle and rise and fall, to where a lamb lies weak and helpless.

Thus is it day in the far far South.[20]

John Blake first heard about the Gilmores in the 1960s, early on in his time as manager of Estancia Condor, when a young Australian wool classer called Brian Turner told him about Mary and Will and their place in Australian history. When Carlos Felton returned to Killik Aike from one of his roisterings abroad, Blake asked him what he knew of the Australians. Carlos had heard of Mary, though he had been a baby at the time she was there, but said she was in a few of the old photographs.

John Blake took me down to the homestead's cavernous cellars. Under brick arches were shelves of pickles, preserved fruit, bottles of wine and a glorious clutter of Felton memo-rabilia: an Edwardian cane lounge with a folding leather hood, a Wimbledon croquet set, butterfly nets, fishing rods, saddles and sheepskins and matched sets of cabin trunks suitable for the Grand Tour.

John located a solid case containing a few hundred old glass negatives. All afternoon I held the gelatine-blotched plates to the light, straining to identify features in reverse image, especially those where the Felton family were with women employees. But one photograph was already printed, which Carlos had told John included the Gilmores. People dressed as if on their way to town posed in and around two wagonettes which were pulled up by the sheds near Killik Aike's jetty. Herbert Felton was seated in the wagonette on the right, his wife Emma nursed the baby Carlos in the back seat. Two people in white were possibly visitors (for surely the female was too old even for the precocious Millie, who was perhaps the photographer), but the man on the white horse looked the part for Wesley the foreman.

However, I was very unsure about it being the Gilmore family on the left. It seemed unlikely that they would be so-cialising with the Feltons, although their presence could have involved duties in town. Certainly, the man on horseback in the background bore a striking resemblance to Will – but the woman's face was shaded by her hat. And the swarthy youth standing by her wheel was never 3-year old Billy. I dismissed it – until later, when working on this book, I examined the image greatly magnified and discovered the small child, his profile barely visible, seated on Mary's right. I was convinced.

As dusk fell at Killik Aike, I walked down to the Gallegos river, through low thickets of calafate, the prickly berberry bush – *Berberis cuneata* – with a small dark fruit. Monica had told me of an old saying: 'Once you eat the fruit of the calafate, your bones will always return to Patagonia.' Mary Gilmore had obviously not eaten enough: 'I despised the calafate … The thorns tore one's hands to pieces, the seeds broke one's teeth and the skin produced stomach ache. It was a truly Patagonian combination.'[21]

The wide gulch opened out to a natural bay at the river, flanked by dramatically high cliffs called *barrancas*. Only a few corrugated iron storehouses, a blacksmith's forge, a clutter of rusting farm machinery and some wooden piles at the water's edge indicated a once bustling farm port. The estancia boats *Malvina* and *Priscilla* used to anchor at a long jetty to bring in supplies and take out wool bales. Most of the jetty had been washed away long before, while billeted soldiers during the Falklands–Malvinas war had used the remaining decking for firewood.

I walked along the rocky beach under the cliffs. The year before the Gilmores' arrival, Hatcher had made some of the richest fossil finds in Patagonia in the high rocky walls. He grieved that, as the action of the tides disintegrated the cliff face, 'nature's burial ground was now being desecrated by her own hand'.[22]

I picked up a flat stone with the tracery of a small mollusc and hurried back along the beach. The tide was rising with frightening rapidity. I climbed up on to the headland, to the grave of an employee, George Jeffries, who had been caught

Mary's favourite spot on the headland at Killik Aike, near the grave of George Jeffries who had drowned the previous year

by the tide and drowned in 1900. A convoy of upland geese rode on the swell. Far across the river, the lights of Río Gallegos glimmered, faint against the brilliance of stars appearing in the vaulting dark.

Mary had sometimes sat on the same headland in the evenings, too, savouring the peace of the Patagonian winter night, disturbed only by the cry of foxes and guanacos in the distance.

The winds have fallen for an hour, the incessant winds that sweep ever up from the frozen South, or from the icy summits of the Andean peaks, where ages of ice and snow lie piling upwards towards the Eternal. The air is clear and sharp. From miles across comes the sound of snapping ice, as the frost strengthens above the waters of Coy Aike. Breath comes easily and life grows vivid and strong. In the blood is a sense of joy, a sense of life and the joy of life. The mighty heavens are above us and the stars blaze upward from the South till the very horizon is a band star-studded, brilliant and wonderful.[23]

Once again there were tensions with Chile. The Buenos Aires *Standard* reported in July 1901 that the Chilean navy was purchasing two powerful warships despite the two nations' acceptance of Great Britain's offer to arbitrate their southern boundary. In response, the Argentine government was increasing its navy and had introduced compulsory military service for all adult males.[24]

The newspaper published a cartoon of a cockfight, with John Bull and Uncle Sam leaning into the ring to watch the feathers fly. A glum-looking John Bull declared: 'No, Sam. You see, I have money on each side.'[25]

The war rumblings must have seemed remote to Mary. She did not care for her employer, Herbert Felton, nor for Millie her pupil, but these were slight irritants. Her husband and son were with her, and she had begun to make friends.

Stephens, the cook at the men's quarters, drank hard but baked good bread and kept his kitchen clean. He had a brother in the peerage but never boasted of it. He lent Mary his treasured books, 'in a land where there were but few'.

In return I gave him a copy of the *Decameron* that had been given me by a friend who had not wished it to fall into the hands of certain lads he knew, yet being a book lover dared not burn. I had not wanted it, but took it as an act of charity and gave it away with the feeling of being a criminal.[26]

Mary was generous but possibly indiscreet in giving the man the *Decameron,* with its wild scenes of debauchery during the days of the Black Death in Florence.

She wrote, though, about another of the men who had known of finer things, Harry Marsdon. 'When Harry was English,' she noted, 'he was very proper, when he was Patagonian – which was most of the time – he wasn't. Also when he was English he had very definite ideas as to women, how they should speak, etc. When he was Patagonian he didn't mind.'

'Have a cushion, Harry,' I said, 'I know you like comfort.'

'That I do,' he replied, 'that's why I like you.'

'Thank you, sir,' I answered. 'Compliments fly when quality meet.'

'O I know,' he said, 'you needn't laugh. It is a comfort … to see a decent woman in this God forsaken place, especially one that will speak to a fellow.'

Harry was alarmed by Mary's interest in collecting Spanish oaths, research she had obviously used to advantage in her description of the cart driver at the port. 'Look here, little girl,' he told her, 'you leave this question of swearing alone. You're too fond of investigating and studying and looking for experience. You're an experience for us just as you are and we like it. We don't want you to do the things that we do or to know the things we know, and we want you to stay just as you are. These swine down here don't understand you, they don't know your kind.'

She had to understand, he told her, that women were the slaves of circumstances.

'In my country,' I said, 'they are the slaves of men.'

'Yes?' His tone was of polite interest. Harry was always polite. He took that from his English bringing-up.

'Yes,' I said stoutly, 'but they're working to get the vote and then they will be *free!*'

'Yes, but will that make any difference?'

I laughed. *'Olé,* as for that I don't know. I doubt it myself.'[27]

The Blakes were genuinely appalled when I told them these stories. 'Spanish oaths, erotic Italian books, talking with the men … *really!*' laughed Monica. 'No wonder the owners were against her! Even in our time we wouldn't put up with that! We've kicked a woman out because every single man who walked past her house used to stop – and so we told her husband she had to leave. If he wanted to leave as well, that was his look-out, but he had a job. But his wife was no longer welcome on the property.'

'One hundred years ago,' said John, 'these communities were much more self-enclosed. The sight of Mary talking to any man down at the cookhouse would be enough to justify asking her to go. She would immediately be branded as a trouble-maker by the boss.'

There was also a famously disreputable man whom Mary came to know, 'that old sinner' Bristol Tom, an ancient British ruin who cadged his way around the various sheep farms of the region and was viewed with exasperation and occasional grudging affection, while he 'cursed all the estancieros in it from San Julian down to Cape Virgins'. These wandering Britishers with mysterious pasts were something of an institution in Patagonia. Many were 'remittance men', receiving occasional payments from their families in England to stay away.

Mary despaired that Bristol Tom's unkempt appearance let down the side for his fellow kinsmen, 'for he wore the most battered, ragged old clothes that ever escaped falling to pieces, and it was only the dirt on him kept him warm'. He would complain bitterly to her that his only wish was to escape back to England. 'Thirty-seven years I bin tryin' to get away from this b—y country but they won't let me go!' he would tell her.

Mary wrote that Will would remonstrate with her for letting 'that old reptile' into the house. 'Didn't I think the ordinary risk of vermin sufficiently great?' But she actually liked the old rogue and her husband did too – 'Will was soft and Old Bristol got the nip he expected – as I knew he would.' One night, after some heavy-duty pleading, 'sure such kind friends wouldn't refuse an old man', Tom was granted permission to doss in their outhouse. Next morning all Mary's hens were missing. She commented ruefully:

Someone suggested that the *locos* in Felton's house at the

back of us had them, but I guess it was Old Bristol. Should anyone want to know anymore about the old fellow they can ask Will, for the rest of his story is too disreputable for my pen. I'm like Harry Marsdon – sometimes I feel Patagonian and sometimes I feel English. When I feel Patagonian I can tell things; when I feel English ... I'm at a loss.[28]

One special friendship Mary formed was with a young *peón*, a lowly odd-job boy aged about twelve called Jesús María. The Gilmores' Presbyterian notions found the name Jesús objectionable, so they called him José instead. By day he chopped wood, broke up coal and carted it indoors, sifted cinders, filled lamps, cleaned knives and polished boots. By night he slept on the remnant of a *capa,* a guanaco rug, in a corner of an empty room next to Stephens the cook.

José had come from Buenos Aires in search of work, because of a new government policy to encourage the urban unemployed to move to the provinces. He had never experienced a Patagonian winter.

From early May 1901, snow had been falling and the ground was icy. The ice clawed into a person's marrow. But no experience of childhood winters in Goulburn, considered one of the coldest districts in New South Wales, prepared Mary for this:

For many reasons I liked living in Patagonia, but the cold was too severe, not the degree of cold, but the cold combined with the wind. The wind gets in everywhere. I have been three days … trying to get the irons hot enough to iron, and burning English coal all the time; and water dropped on the floor in my kitchen froze at once. In the poorer houses the breath formed frost on the blankets, and I have had ice one-eighth of an inch thick day and night on the inside of my bedroom window.[29]

Even in the schoolroom of the Big House, her breath formed frost flowers on the window panes and she noted that the thermometer was sometimes 32 degrees below freezing, 'this, with a kerosene heater in the room'. She suffered desperately, despite her lambskin petticoat, heavy wood-soled clogs lined with wool and laced high up the leg. 'Even then I felt the frozen earth under my feet.'[30]

The other station hands donned snow boots, foxskin gloves and storm-collared ponchos. But young José shivered in thin dungarees. One day Mary noticed the boy's hands, 'like mutton hams from chaps and chillblains'. She asked him why he had not either brought warm clothes, purchased some from the estancia store, or had them advanced against his wages.

'I had no money, Señora,' he replied, 'and the *patrón*, the master, would not let me have any.'

'The brute!' I said under my breath. 'You wait and I will get Don Guillermo, my husband, to see about it.' I added to the boy, 'In the meantime, let me do something for your hands.'[31]

Mary bathed José's chapped hands and then mixed up honey, fat, white of egg and eucalyptus and gave him a pot of this unguent to apply every night. She was to discover that such solicitude towards a mere *peon* was most irregular.

In the Killik Aike wages book I found an entry for a Jesús Vasquez. Was this the boy, I wondered, whom Mary preferred to call José? Jesús Vasquez was listed among the ordinary labourers, the *peones*. He started work at the estancia in mid-1901. With some excitement I peered again at the magnified image of the wagonette party, particularly at the youth standing by the wheel of Mary's vehicle. He was poorly dressed (though not yet in need of the winter clothing), with a dark Hispanic complexion – almost certainly a farm labourer. So it is possible that he was Jesús – alias José – and was there to act as Mary's driver on whatever unlikely expedition the Gilmores were undertaking with the Feltons.

However, John Blake was sceptical about certain points in Mary's narrative: 'This story that the boy couldn't get warm clothes, couldn't get an advance ... I'm sorry, but that does *not* ring true. On all these Patagonian farms, this one included, the system was that all farms carried stock in the farm store of clothing and all sorts of things. Secondly, anybody could draw goods and things against their pay. I'm not defending Felton or the boss's absolute position or anything like that, but I see no reason for the boy to be going without warm clothes. And I don't know how Mary, without Spanish, would manage to converse with the boy. You know, I don't

Expedition party at Killik Aike, separated into two closer shots. Top (left to right): José the peón *(?), 3-year-old Billy in wagonette (profile just visible), Mary, Will Gilmore on horseback behind. Bottom (left to right): Possibly foreman Wesley on white horse, Mrs Felton nursing baby Carlos, Herbert Stanley Felton (wearing hat), unknown couple in white (visitors?), driver in cap*

want to spoil the story, but it does not quite ring true to me.'

Monica believed Mary had transgressed an implicit code: 'If she was talking to the men, she would be absolutely beyond the pale. The very idea of a woman in those days conversing with a *peón*, that would be enough to make her *persona non grata*. She would be seen as interfering with the working men. Women were expected to remain exclusively in the household. Mary as a governess was part of the household and she should never speak to the people down below.'

Whatever the basis for Mary's story, her concern for José's well-being would not have been merely an act of human kindness – although it was obviously that – but an industrial issue. With her socialist background and experience of trade unionism, she had an unshakable belief in even the lowliest labourer's right to decent and humane working conditions. The way Herbert Felton treated his workers would have been intolerable to her.

The rural *peones* of Patagonia had no trade union representation and, according to a recent Argentine study, on some properties they 'suffered barbaric levels of exploitation'. Many received no payment at all in money, only rations; they worked seven days a week, with no time off even to wash their clothes; and on some estancias they were required to work out of doors in the rain, sleet and snow.[32]

In Mary's account, she saw José again some days later, beaming, proud of the warm clothing Will had obtained for him. His hands were healing, but he had finished off the ointment. She made up some more and offered it to him next time he walked by her cottage. 'God and the Señora are good,' he told her; he was acquiring some 'early English', she noted, though mostly it was 'blasphemy' learned at the men's quarters.

They were observed by Herbert Felton. '*El patrón* came past, eyeing us out of the corner of his eye and whistling as he went … He went round to the store, waited half a minute then sent the book keeper to tell José he was wanted. José went at once.'

An hour later Will came home, shaking with rage. 'José's got the sack.' Wesley, the foreman, had ordered him off the property. Will believed that Felton had insisted on it from spite, resenting a mere *peón* talking to a white woman. José had done his work competently so there could be no complaint on that score. He was well liked and the men had made up a subscription of £3 but 'that won't last him long'.

In the morning the boy's departing tracks were erased by a fresh fall of snow. Mary watched the flakes come down with a deepening sense of gloom and hatred for the place, despairing that her husband could not break his contract.

At eleven o'clock Will returned for breakfast, but admitted his mind was plagued too: 'I can't do anything for thinking of him.' He drank his coffee hastily, deciding, 'I will go after him.'

My heart stopped. Yet what could I do? I put my arms round him and kissed him, of all men the most *lovable* and the most to be revered. He would do his duty though we were all, husband, wife and child, turned out for it.

I brought him his snow boots and a storm coat. He took an iron shod stick and started out …

As for me, I could do nothing but look out the window and dream of despair, and even Billy's chatter could not rouse me. The fire burned out, the room grew colder and colder, ice thickened on the window panes, the sun passed behind the hills … but my heart seemed darker and colder than anything inside or outside the room …

It seemed a very long time before Will returned. She rubbed his hands and removed his boots before letting him speak. She knew the great fact, and other things could wait.

At last I said 'You found him –'

'Yes,' replied Will softly, 'I found him.' Then he added 'His troubles are over.'

'I thought so,' I responded in the same tone.

I think I cried all night. Will slept from sheer exhaustion.

The following morning, Wesley the foreman ranted to anyone who would listen that since the Australian had been on the property he had had nothing but insolence and insubordination. Then he went up to the Feltons' house and got drunk. Later, he seemed subdued, even abject, when he met Gilmore. Mary believed 'he feared what the authorities might say if they got to know of things, and he knew we would not be afraid to speak. He told Will he had acted hastily and was sorry – as he probably was, for himself.'

Hurried arrangements were made for José's burial. Stephens the cook was ordered to 'take two men and dig a grave beyond the woolshed and say nothing about the occurrence'.[33]

❧

Mary's unpublished story, 'We Called Him José', was, I believe, essentially true. She did not fictionalise her husband and son's names, nor Herbert Felton's, and in all her subsequent references to the estanciero in her correspondence, her contempt for him never wavers.

I can find nothing but the events surrounding the *peón*'s death to explain her next move. The Gilmore family had a comfortable cottage at Killik Aike, Will was contracted through the summer and Mary had her governess job, albeit with an unpleasant pupil. But on 12 August 1901, still deep in the Patagonian winter, only four days before her thirty-sixth birthday and just over a week before Billy's third (surely both important family occasions), Mary and her son moved in to Río Gallegos and, with little money to pay for it, took a room at the Hotel Inglés. The Killik Aike wages book indicates that the following day Will Gilmore 'started food in cookhouse' and resumed board at the single men's quarters, purchasing a single mattress.[34]

Did Mary walk or was she pushed? Did she have words with Felton about José's death? Probably she would not have wished to jeopardise Will's job, but her dislike of the estancias owner may still have been too obvious for him to tolerate.

The entries in the accounts book for Jesús Vasquez the *peón* – my candidate as the boy José – abruptly end in August and never reappear. This would appear to confirm that he *was* the boy in question, and that he perished in the snow.

Except for one inconvenient fact. The last entry in the book for Jesús is 26 August 1901, and Mary left the property a fortnight earlier – so her departure could not have been in protest at his eviction and death. *Unless* there was a deliberate updating of it in the accounts book, making the failure to report to the coroner a less reprehensible delay.

There is a mystery here. *Something* happened to cause Mary to move into town in the middle of winter, an unaccountable action casting her into isolation and penury, but apparently never explained in letters to friends and family.

The Blakes saw not the slightest need to ruminate on reasons for Mary's departure. For them the wonder was that, given her own story of her relations on the estancia, she lasted eight months. John accepted that there could have been 'an apparently unfortunate death' on the farm and workers sent to bury the body without the coroner being informed. 'That is possible, because these things did happen. But you have to try to minimise the tensions in these tiny communities. About the time I was ready to take on this kind of career, to be in charge of a Patagonian sheep farm, my father said to me, "You will find that only 20 per cent of your problems will be the actual sheep. 50 per cent of your problems will be the women on the place. And the remaining percentage will be other things you would never dream were to do with farming!"'

Monica agreed. 'I have a rule now. I will not have a woman on the property. I don't want any more problems with them. They are always the first to make trouble.' She thought Mary had been particularly insensitive: 'Can you imagine a woman such as she was, an active radical, coming into such a very enclosed, stultified atmosphere and fitting in? There were bound to be some sources of friction, which she would not have agreed with. I don't think – perhaps this goes against some ideas you have – that the Feltons were quite as horrible as Mary made them out to be. They were very different to her, very different to her social convictions, they were Patagonian. And she didn't have enough knowledge of the Patagonian way of life, as to what made these people be as they were, and they were not interested in learning about her background or her thoughts, they were very self-sufficient people. They were here, they lived their way of life, and people either fitted in or didn't.'

Clearly the Blakes believed that Mary had failed to understand the Feltons' position. And they thought special concessions had been made for the Gilmores in terms of accommodation. 'Virtually no farm at that time had accommodation for men with their wives, or jobs for wives,' John said. His understanding was that the little corrugated iron cottage at the bottom of the garden had always been the home for the foreman. He thought that Wesley must have given up his own home, possibly reluctantly at the Feltons' insistence, when Mary arrived to be governess. If she had fallen out of favour with the owners, Wesley would have seen the opportunity to claim his home back.

John was not surprised that, if Gilmore was a good shearer, he was allowed to continue in the job. But Mary had to go. 'She had literally no alternative.'

Monica agreed: 'Look here, let's face it, anybody who took sides with a worker, would not be welcomed by the estancia people here. She would not be wanted. She would have been very different with her radical ideas – and in that period, a woman as well! Quite honestly, the owners in those days were virtual emperors, and if somebody fell out of favour with them, that was it!'

It could be that Mary's friendship with a mere *peón*, and the workers' offer to take up a subscription for José, had smelled too much like trade unionism, dangerously like sympathy with the socialists and anarchists who had been causing so much civil unrest with their protests and demonstrations in the capital.

It is very likely that the Gilmores' background – as participants in a socialist colony in Paraguay – had come to the attention of Herbert Felton, particularly with Mary having been so friendly with the workmen on the estancia. In those small communities, gossip spread rapidly. It would have been clear that she was more political than her husband, by her own account asserting the importance of women's franchise to Harry Marsdon. Gilmore may have worked quietly the previous season without mentioning a word of politics or the nature of the colony he had come from, but Mary was unlikely to have been silent on these matters.

Whatever the reason for her abrupt move, it was not marital discord; her loving, lonely, almost daily letters to her husband started immediately.

She brought her story of 'José' to an enigmatic ending:

> They say 'a bird in the air will carry a thing' and one could almost believe a bird had done it, only that no bird voice broke the frozen stillness of the pampa. Yet the fact of José's

death leaked out and got to town somehow, and right in the middle of July Wesley's new telephone rang him up and an official voice demanded why had not the death on the estancia been notified, and why had burial been performed without authority? And the end of it was that two men had to take picks and crowbars and break open a frozen grave to take a frozen body before the coroner.

If the story was true (the July date adds further confusion), Mary would have been suspected as the informant. The outcome was a great inconvenience for the estanciero. Wesley the foreman raged. Bullocks had to be taken from shelter, yoked up, and the dead body wrapped and put on to a *carreta*. Also some wine as a handy bribe. The team had to make the long journey, travelling far up where the river narrowed, to cross on the ice. Two bullocks slipped and broke their legs. The driver got drunk. It took a week to get into town.

And when they got in the coronial enquiry was only a matter of form to enable the official to draw his fee. His interest in the cause of José's death was nothing, and his liking for Wesley's wine much. Besides, what did a *peón* more or less matter, there were plenty more. So the little stiff body of the lad was taken out and by the aid of more picks and crowbars deposited under a foot of earth, where he made things decidedly unpleasant in the summer, poor little wayfarer from a warmer clime …

And such was the passing of José – and such also is life in Patagonia when the man in possession rules.[35]

VII

ENGLISH LESSONS

Just as Mary was coming down the gangplank from the rocking *Malvina* to the wharf at Río Gallegos, struggling with Billy and assorted bundles and bags, she bumped into Tom Hicks-Hall, one of the former Cosme colonists. He had been working at another sheep property, she wrote wistfully to Will, but told her he was taking a ship the next day, heading home to Australia.[1]

Mary's friend Louis, the French drapery salesman, was there to meet her and help with the luggage. She was expecting to stay at the old boarding house, but Louis must have given her some reason why this was impossible. It was only sometime later Mary learned that the voluptuous Philomena had taken a live-in lover, a much younger man. She was grateful that her respectability had not been compromised.

She went instead to the more expensive Hotel Inglés, although with no job prospects whatsoever, she wondered how she would afford it. May Hawkins, the wife of the English hotel manager, was pregnant and agreed Mary could stay 'until something turns up', in exchange for odds and ends of work at the hotel, sewing, and minding her children. The chance of some job just turning up in Patagonia for a genteel Anglo-Saxon mother in her mid-thirties with little Spanish was but a remote possibility. And by August 1901 the whole country was sliding into recession.

In that month in Buenos Aires, thousands of unemployed paraded through the avenues to the Plaza de Mayo, waving banners of protest. President Roca addressed the angry crowd from the balcony of the Casa Rosada, 'but his promises to study the problems were drowned out by whistles and jeers'.[2] The anarchists, who favoured active 'intervention in the class struggle', were soon commanding leadership of various unions, influencing others and rallying the unemployed to demonstrate. Industrial disputes were on the increase. Employers and government authorities were alarmed.[3]

Mary's thirty-sixth birthday, on 15 August, passed without her mentioning it. Two days later she wrote to Will that it was clear she would not be able to stay at the hotel for long:

> Mrs Hawkins has been very kind, but I do not suit. She really wants a person who can turn her hand to anything at a moment's notice ... She says, 'You have been used to better things than I have, and I really can't tell you to do things.'[4]

The young Hawkins brood, in Mary's jaundiced view, were 'something awful', so much so that they made her barefooted and irreverent pupils at Cosme seem like 'white angels'. She did not wonder that Mrs Hawkins remarked that she had never in her life seen 'such a well-behaved child as Billy. He eats so differently and is so considerate … neither swears nor uses dirty language.' But she fretted that this was about to change under the influence of the rowdy Hawkins children. Billy was learning 'low Spanish oaths' which he used, 'knowing no better', and they had shown him a boar and a sow copulating. 'But it isn't very nice, is it?'[5]

But May Hawkins, their mother, half Spanish and English, won Mary's respect for her stoicism:

Mrs Hawkins has been telling me about the hardships she had to go through before they began to make money. It is a wonder the woman is alive. She has told me of various others as well, I never heard of such awful hardships. It seems most of the women here have to be confined by their husbands – and when they won't undertake to it, they have to do for themselves. She says such things as butter, jam, condensed milk, sauces, etc., are never seen by the generality of the working people. Bread, mutton and *yerba* they live on, and a fire to be warm at is unknown. She says you must live like that to save – unless both are at work. She says she worked like a bullock to make a start and worked the same after to keep it going.[6]

Mary started making a habit of walking to the waterfront. She was struck by the fact that the birds and sea creatures 'were still unafraid as in the Indian times'. Schools of porpoises came in to frolic in the estuary. 'And they were so beautiful in the water in their movements as they chased one another that though used to them, the people of Gallegos would stand on the beach to watch them.' Sometimes the porpoises stranded themselves, their gleaming dark elastic hides heaving in the sand. One day she even saw a white drowned man, 'who lay for days like a patch of snow on the other side of the bay'.[7]

When schools of sardines shoaled in the shallows, the locals headed for the beach, carrying nets and buckets.

> The screaming of the gulls, the harsh notes of the caranchos, shags and cormorants called people to door and window. There the circling, dipping, diving, striking interlacing of wings gave the location of the fish. Those who had tubs filled them with sea water and poured in the silver catch to keep them alive for a second day's feast, or a cleaning and curing in oil. The small ones were fried crisp from end to end and so delicate they were they could be eaten bones, fins, heads and all. The larger ones were gutted, trimmed, salted and put away to keep.

But of all the birds of Patagonia, Mary wrote, the one she would never forget was the carancho, the crow-vulture, 'the old man of the sea,' reeling and soaring above the water all day, whose unceasing cry 'by its persistence and abomination of note bored into the brain. It was harsh, melancholy and without music of any kind in any part of it. It was just a cry, a cry that bit and tore the silence every time it was uttered.'[8]

There was eminent support for her dislike. Charles Darwin so detested the crow-vultures and their unpleasant habits – picking at sores on horses' backs and watching for sheep to give birth in order to attack the lambs – that the great naturalist became quite anthropomorphic in his description of them:

> A person will discover the necrophagous habits of the Carrancha (Caracara) by walking out on one of the desolate plains, and lying down to sleep. When he awakes he will see, on each surrounding hillock, one of these birds patiently watching him with an evil eye.[9]

Mary called to see her old friend Philomena, resisting the current gossip about her. This is a different person to the censorious woman of Cosme: 'Mrs Hawkins tells me ... that Philomena is living with that young fellow, Fernando, who stays there, and that she parted from her husband simply because he was too old for her. I felt very sorry to hear of it, but I feel too grateful to Philomena to let it make any difference.'[10]

Philomena came up with the idea that made it possible for Mary to stay on in Río Gallegos: she should open a school – 'an English class for adults, say from 8 to 9 in the evening'. John Hawkins at the Hotel Ingles also encouraged the idea:

> Mr Hawkins is of the opinion I could easily make $100 per month, but I am not over sanguine. He says charge not less than $10 per month. However, I will make enquiries and see how things go. If I get a class he will rent me a room and while I have it, I can see how things shape. There is no trade

at all here, so the Hawkins are going to give up the hotel in October – the end of their lease. They have scarcely paid more than light since they came in. [11]

She continued to write to her husband almost daily, then took a bundle of letters to the wharf for the *Malvina* skipper to deliver to Killik Aike. She was anxious to be 'settled at something', as 'Mrs H does not care for Billy, so you can guess I am not comfortable. Poor little man, he called me a "little devil" this morning. Of course he has no idea it was wrong.' But it was hard to forgive May Hawkins when she complained he was spiteful to her children and there was no celebration for the boy's third birthday on 21 August.[12]

Mary's need to escape the Hotel Inglés had become pressing and she resolved to explore Philomena's idea of teaching English. First she consulted the deputy governor, who encouraged her, despite Mary's own concern that her Spanish was so poor. 'Oh, but you are such a good English scholar,' he told her, 'you should do well at it.'[13] She found it an odd reply but was heartened to go ahead.

Soon she had her first pupil, Don Vicente Cane, the local manager of the Banco Argentina y Londres. 'The first month of teaching was dreadful. I felt such a fraud, for I hadn't the use of twenty words of the language, though with a dictionary I could read fairly well. As the lesson hour came round my knees used to shake with apprehension lest Don Vicente wouldn't come, and my stomach grow sick in dread of the lesson should he come. Whichever way it was awful.'[14]

But the word spread and she had expectations of other

pupils. By early September she was in a position to rent a small two-roomed house of her own.

༄

I wanted to find the house, so I asked my friend, the journalist Pablo Beecher, if he could help.

Mary described her new landlords and neighbours as a kindly English couple, the Lanes, who had converted their front room into a shop, from which Charles Lane ran his photography business. He made a modest living taking views of the town – houses blanketed in snow, Indian encampments – and sold them as postcards; he also offered studio portraits of bridal couples and members of the local estancia families.

Pablo considered him the first serious photographer in Río Gallegos. He was not sure of the exact location of the photographic shop, for it had long gone, but pointed me in its general direction, telling me there were still a couple of old houses down that way.

Luis and I took a taxi along the Costanera, the road beside the river, from where Mary had watched porpoises gambolling, sardines shoaling, a parliament of squabbling birds. It was a Sunday and I was astonished that we were caught in a traffic gridlock. It seemed all the vehicles of Río Gallegos – battered utility trucks, aggressive four-wheel-drives and saloons full of families hopeful of a picnic – were out on the road, horns blaring and honking at the irritating presence of others.

We edged past the heroic statue of a man on a winged

plinth, built in honour of airmen lost in action in the Malvinas war, went by the rusting skeleton of a coal loader and the old wooden wharf, its piles far out of the water to allow for the volatility of the Gallegos river.

'It's the fine weather,' said our driver in Spanish. 'We only get a few days like this every year, so everyone wants to be out by the river to take advantage.' A very beautiful young woman, she pushed her long dark hair into a heavy knot because of the unaccustomed heat. This weather made people *locos,* silly in the head, she told us. The previous night she had had a group of drunks who had been *muy difficil,* and she would be driving again all through the night.

'But isn't that dangerous?' I asked. Río Gallegos seemed to me still a frontier town, dominated by men, many of them itinerant workers from the oil rigs, gas fields and sheep properties.

'Yes, it is dangerous, *muy peligroso',* she replied calmly, matter of fact, 'but this is my job. I have two children to look after. I don't have a husband anymore.'

We turned away down a side street to look for some of the original houses of the town in the general area Pablo had suggested.

And there it was: a modest corrugated iron cottage answering Mary's description, on Calle Cordoba, just the right distance from the river. I photographed it from every angle, but have no way of proving it was the actual one.

ॐ

Mary's new house was tiny and, like most of the houses in the

*A pioneer's cottage in Río Gallegos which may have been Mary's –
being of the right vintage and approximate location*

town at the time, the iron cladding was lined inside with timber slats over which hessian or newspapers were pasted. It
had two rooms – the front one for cooking, living and con-
ducting her lessons, with a door on to the street, and the back
room, where she and Billy slept, opening on to a grassy yard.

Her neighbours, the Lanes, were soon being encouraged to
read the impenetrable prose of William Lane, their more im-
pressive namesake: 'I lent Mrs Lane *The Workingman's Paradise.* She is full of it, and is reading it now to her husband.' [15]

Mary wrote to her husband from the new address, 'c/o
Lane Fotografía', on 6 September 1901, the fifth anniversary
of their engagement:

We have had lots of worry since then, but it was all outside
worry, between you and me life has always been the same, so
that we grow nearer as the years go on ... If you were to
come in now you would come to the most comfortable

218

home we have ever had. If it were not for the money aspect I should feel in Heaven. The house is furnished with everything but bed linen and I had not needed to send for the things I did … There are three hens and a cock, I am to use the eggs … There is also the very latest sewing machine in the house, so new that the trouble is not to work too fast … The stove is the same make as the little one I had in Paraguay and about the same size. The walls and floor are of white American pine so there are no cracks or draughts, and there is a cupboard and shelves above … My teaching is as yet limited to one – Mr Cane from the Banco Argentine. He paid his $10 last lesson … Some of the storemen want lessons, but they can only take them at night, and I can't have men after hours.[16]

But within a week two storemen from Braun & Blanchards had agreed to come for lessons for an hour every Sunday, 'so that is the rent'. She decided she would specialise in adult pupils, though she confessed to Will that the teaching still terrified her. But if she acquired another one or two pupils she thought she could afford to buy a cow, or Philomena might lend one of hers, as 'with cow's milk I would not so much fear the winter'. The following cold season was a long way off but in the window of Jacobs' store she was eyeing a *capa* made of guanaco skins, 'Indian stained and only $20. I fancy I will buy it yet.'[17]

Mary had yet more entrepreneurial ideas: if she gained extra pupils she might poach Cynthy, the new English governess at Killik Aike who was rumoured to be unhappy there.

'If things go well financially I would like to get her on engagement. The amount of work she would have to do would
not be great. I would buy all the bread. I would pay her the
same as the Feltons pay, for a start and so much per cent on
all additional pupils after her coming.'[18]

Will was also given a money-making project, to occupy
whatever hours' respite he had from the spring estancia duties of crutching, lamb marking and dipping:

> I want you to send in, properly made up, your stockwhip. I
> can get it shewn in Lane's window (or possibly in the win-
> dow of the Hotel Argentino) and it is certain to bring in a
> few orders, in fact I have what is as good as an order for one
> for £1. The neck of the guanaco hide is said to be particu-
> larly good for plaiting …[19]

Mary detested the fact that her husband's every move was
still ruled by Herbert Stanley Felton, and wished he could
leave Killik Aike. When the English doctor mentioned a possible position on another estancia, she lost no time in writing: 'Can you shear with a machine? And can you instruct
others?' The job was to teach the use of the new Wolseley
shearing machines on Estancia Condor, a huge property bordering the Magellan Strait, eighty kilometres further south.
Dr Victor Fenton had inside information, having recently
married the wealthy widow who owned Monte Dinero, a
smaller adjoining property. He told Mary that Condor's English owners, Waldron and Woods, were 'putting up big works
for machine shearing and will want a Capataz'.

She wrote to Will, both cajoling and hectering: 'You would only just have to keep a jump ahead of the *peones* – pretend even if you're not confident … Besides, you will have Chilenos and Argentines to instruct and they will be ignorant enough to make almost anything excusable.'[20]

Next day, she wrote again, urging him to go to Condor in person, 'about seven hours' ride from here', but worth it to find out more about the machines.

> Now, my dear, think hard. I have tried to think of everything likely to help you. Is there anything else I can do or find out? … You must not be too self-distrustful in this matter. It will not be as hard for you as for me to face giving lessons in English to people to whom I have to explain everything in Spanish – I, whose Spanish is enough to make the furniture laugh.

In full schoolmarm flight she concluded, 'and mind you look after your grammar. All that sort of thing has counted in my making a start in good standing.'[21]

A few days later, Mary had three more pupils, making six in all, each paying $10 per month. Señora Blanco, wife of a doctor, was connected to the Menéndez family. Along with the Brauns, to whom they were related by blood and business, the Menéndez were royalty in the south, where they owned Estancia La Anita, the second biggest sheep ranch in Patagonia, other vast properties in Chile and Tierra del Fuego and a department store in Río Gallegos. Señora Blanco was the daughter of the store manager, and recruited two staff members as pupils as well: 'Her house is only across the Plaza from my house, and I go there from 2 p.m. to 3 p.m. to give her her lesson.'[22]

However, despite all Mary's pressing advice, Will had not done a thing about the job at Estancia Condor. Exasperating.

> Dear, a letter came today. As you say nothing of the Condor you apparently had not received my last letters. If you can get down there as Capataz for the shearing, and I can keep up with the teaching, we should have a little money saved after the season is over … I wish you had decent work here just now, as this is such a comfortable little home, the best I have ever had, for it has everything I need, even to a sewing machine. I think I will go and buy that *capa* tomorrow as we need extra blankets.[23]

Mary was often ill, still suffering the diarrhoea that had plagued her since Paraguay. Her loneliness could sometimes also be hard to bear. She was grateful to have an occasional visit from a new friend, Captain Eberhardt, a cultured man with an enquiring mind who owned a sheep estancia to the south of the town. Mary and her husband had met him by chance through one of his employees, an elderly English sheepworker called Wellburn. 'Captain Eberhardt comes into town tomorrow', Mary wrote on 13 September, 'and will call and see me.'

Captain Hermann Eberhardt was famous in his own right in Patagonia, largely because of the hairy giant sloth.

Captain Eberhardt and assistants at the cave at Last Hope Sound,
1893

His father had been a colonel in the Prussian army, but the young Hermann had deserted his military career. He was court-martialled and served eighteen months in a military prison, then wandered through the United States, China and the Aleutian islands, landed by no particular trajectory on the Falkland–Malvinas islands and worked as a harbour pilot in Port Stanley.[24] He came to Patagonia in 1884, responding to Governor Moyano's invitation to new settlers, and established Estancia Chymen Aike south of Río Gallegos.

In 1893 Eberhardt made the discovery which caused all the fuss. In a huge cave in a cliff at Ultima Esperanza (otherwise known as Last Hope Sound), seven kilometres from Puerto Consuelo in Chile, he found what a friend of his described as 'a most remarkable skin with small round bones embedded in the hide and covered by long coarse yellowish brown hair'. He took it back to his farm, where it lay about the place for over a year, 'nobody suspecting its immense scientific value – travellers cut off a piece as a souvenir', until a visiting scientist from Sweden took a piece home with him.

Soon there was an undignified rush of gentlemen and otherwise, scientific and otherwise, to the cave at Last Hope Sound. In 1899 Erland Nordenskjold from Sweden made some excavations there:

> A fine collection of bones and other remains of the big sloth, a *Glossotherium,* and many other animals, was brought together; in the upper strata he even found traces that a pre-historic human race had lived in the grotto. Close upon this Professor Hauthal of La Plata made an exploration of the great cavern.[25]

One of the travellers who cut off a piece of skin was a distant relative of Bruce Chatwin – his grandmother's cousin, Charley Milward the Sailor. In fact, according to the author, his relative was something of a palaeontological vandal, assisting a German prospector at the cave in 'dynamiting the stratigraphy to bits. Charley went up to help him and came away with yards of skin and piles of bones and claws' – which he sold off to the British Museum for £400.[26] A scrap of the brownish skin, embedded with bony nodules, described memorably by Chatwin as 'like hairy peanut brittle', had sat in his grandmother's glass-fronted cabinet when he was a child. He had thought it was a piece of brontosaurus. But it became the talisman, the call of the grail, that eventually pointed him in the direction of Patagonia and literary fame.

After some prodding from its fossil curator, Professor Hauthal, Captain Eberhardt donated his piece of skin to the Natural History Museum at La Plata. The professor speculated that the giant sloth, a creature larger than a bull, might have been contemporaneous with man in the Pleistocene era, perhaps even domesticated by him, arguing that the huge pile of dung in one corner of the cavern suggested its use as a stable.

I visited the great gloomy La Plata museum, where the attendants had not received any wages for three months and were on a go-slow, standing about in groups chatting, though still through either force of habit and conscientiousness keeping a wary eye on errant members of the public getting too familiar with the exhibits. In a crepuscular hall of looming dinosaur skeletons and stuffed birds, I found the sloth's rather mangy remnant in its glass case. Carbon dating had put it at 5,000 years old and the spongy brown balls of dung beside it, the size of coconuts, at twice that.

At the turn of the century the excitement really got going when a geographer, Dr Ramón Lista, declared he 'caught a glimpse of a living specimen disappearing in the forest'.[27] Cyril Arthur Pearson, proprietor of the London *Daily Express,* decided he could sell newspapers off the back of the sloth. In September 1900 he sent Hesketh Prichard off on what turned out to be a twelve-month search in Patagonia, the expedition comprising 'eight men, 60 horses, a wagon and a leaky boat'.[28] The *Buenos Aires Herald* had not forgotten its pursuit of Mr Prichard, although he had slipped from the paper's sight while he made a majestic progress, 'travelling 3,000 miles into the interior and the Andes, to Lake Buenos Aires and Lake Argentino'.

Prichard replied to his sniping critics with an article in the *New York Herald* which the Argentine paper had the grace to reprint. For a creature which had afforded him lavish travels for a year, he was exceedingly rude about the sloth:

> It was a short-legged, shapeless, ungainly brute, with four toes on each of its front feet and three toes on the hind feet … about as big as two large oxen.

After a year's exertions Prichard regretted he had no incontrovertible proof that the sloth was still about, although he insisted he had 'special information from an unimpeachable source that fresh tracks of great size have been seen within the last two years'. He was sticking to the belief that the giant sloth had been a domesticated animal:

> Exceedingly stupid and clumsy, it was so sluggish of movement that one might easily imagine a whole day expended leading it to the water of a nearby stream, and another day consumed in leading it back. It is probable however, that water as well as food was taken to its pen … Certainly it is impossible to conceive of a domesticated brute more uncouth and strange.[29]

Despite the great expense of the expedition, he had a placatory offering for his newspaper proprietor: he had 'discovered' a new lake and pronounced it Lago Pearson. The map of Patagonia today is innocent of such a name.

When Captain Eberhardt called on Mary on 13 September 1901, it was almost exactly a year to the day since Hesketh Prichard had arrived in Argentina on the expedition he was then dismantling. Mary does not mention whether Eberhardt made any reference to the whole charade, but certainly he had gained no money from his discovery.

Mary was in good spirits after sending off some new verse to the Sydney *Bulletin,* and wrote to Will, 'I find that the teaching I am doing now does not take nearly as much out of me as teaching Miss Felton did and as I can buy bread when I like and cook when I like, I get on very well indeed.'[30]

Herbert Felton was in town at the time, staying at the Hotel Inglés. Mary hoped that John Hawkins would not mention that Will was trying to leave Killik Aike, as the job at Condor was not yet secured. But she picked up some new gossip about Millie Felton:

> I was told the other day that 'she does things that give the impression that at times she is not responsible for her actions'. She has the line in her hand that is said to indicate weakness of intellect, and the fork at the end that is considered the sign of insanity. Bad breath is said to be allied to insanity – and she has a slight taint in hers, then, of course, there is the uncle. I, myself, had the impression that she was likely to develop mania.[31]

Mary still liked the girl's mother, though, and wrote to Will, 'You can tell Mrs Felton that Billy often talks about Carlito.'

Her son had to be with her during most lessons because she could not afford a nanny, and anyway she would not consider local candidates for the job, as 'only soldiers' wives were available, and they would only stay till they had pilfered all they wanted, in addition to which none of them could cook, and all were dirty and immoral'.[32]

She charted the child's growing independence for her husband:

> Billy has just got into a cart – the rocking chair – with a re-mark, '*Vamos* – goodbye!' I think I will teach him Spanish as far as I can. Indeed another language is an advantage to any-one, and one never knows when it will be a step to bettering one's position. The little boy's future is far ahead, but its roots are even farther back than the present.[33]

One day she found the time to write a poem, 'To Gallegos and the Gallegans', which she posted to the Buenos Aires *Standard:*

> Far down south, in wild Gallegos
> The folk all stand and stare
> When there ain't no wind a-blowin',
> An' the sun is shinin' fair.
>
> An' they swell with jubilation,
> An' almost bust with pride,

Till they seem to sad outsiders,
Like people glorified …

When the mud ain't in your boots, an'
The slush ain't past your knees,
An' the wind don't cut your eyes, an'
The cold don't more than freeze.

They smile with a smile most spacious,
And rub their hands and say,
With a joy that's something awful,
'How nice it is today!'[34]

At last, with Mary's prodding – or maybe despite it – Will made the journey over a hundred kilometres south to Estancia Condor. He saw the boss Arthur Waldron and secured the job of Capataz on the new machines – on the basis of living at the single men's quarters. However, he was not to start there until late November.

On his way back to Killik Aike he stayed a night with his wife and son in the new house in Río Gallegos. There were some unkind words. Perhaps Will resisted further advice or criticism. Mary would have been bitterly disappointed that there was no room for her on the estancia; it was galling after all the effort she had put in. The visit was a failure, and she knew it. She wrote immediately with apologies and blandishments:

I think you ought to take a week's holiday after leaving KA

and before going to Condor – if only to make the little boy happy … Indeed I have often thought that my irritability was enough to make you care less and less for me, and I have loved you for your patience and gentleness and felt over and over again how much I wanted to tell you so, only we can write so much more easily than we can speak …[35]

In October she was very unsettled, not sure whether she should wait out the winter in Paraguay or whether Will should do another summer's shearing in Patagonia, 'but that would make us too late for the Australian shearing in the north. When does NZ start?' She thought they could visit William Lane, by now a journalist on the *New Zealand Herald* in Auckland (he would later become its editor), and hoped he might help Will to get a shearing job there. If she were able to contribute more to their finances they could go home earlier, perhaps even do 'a ten-day tour in Europe for £10 everything found through Cooks Tourist Excursion Agency'. She had received news that a bank draft for £60 was being sent as a loan from Wallace Webster, her sister Rosie's husband. 'He writes for us to "come home at once", but of course it is impossible as it will take more than £60 – though we might get cheaper fares from London by the Shaw Savill Coy as immigrants to NZ.'[36]

Meanwhile, selling exotic curios seemed the most promising source of extra revenue. Mary had enquired about the prices for 'assorted snake skins, butterflies, armadillo shells, ocelot skins, etc. etc. … Then bless us and save us, I forgot the rugs! Why we will be millionaires in no time!' She gave Will a new project – to collect guanaco *capas,* their throat bones, ostrich claws, hawks' toe-nails and beaks, some dried foxes' feet, ponchos, a dozen *bombillas* and gourds for the drinking of *yerba maté,* native baskets or bags, snail shells, beetles, 'and all the Patagonian odds and ends we can get'.[37]

At the end of the letter she wrote that she had almost forgotten 'the very thing I most wanted to tell you'. When he got to Estancia Condor, where many Indians from Chile worked as station hands, Mary wanted Will to buy a gold nugget from them 'and make me a ring like this silver one' – her wedding ring, which Will had fashioned for her at Cosme by cutting the centre from an Australian shilling piece.

A week later Mary proposed an even more exotic curio for her collection. At her neighbours' place she had met an Englishman called Albert Mason who lived near Lake Argentino in the shadow of the Andes, where the Tehuelche Indians had their burial grounds: 'Mrs Lane is going to ask him to get me an Indian skull.'[38]

Punta Walichu is a sacred Tehuelche burial site, under a cliff bordering Lake Argentino, with the snow-capped cordillera in the distance. I visited the series of caves and walked among great clusters of ritually arranged stones. Rock paintings, including ochre hand stencils similar to those of the Australian Aborigines but also to those found at Lascaux in France, were estimated to be 4,000 years old. The Tehuelche bodies had been mummified, painted red and ceremonially wrapped in the skins of the South American ostrich. Food, weapons and personal effects were placed next to a corpse to aid the soul on its journey to its reincarnation as a star. But the caves have been systematically raided over the last hundred years and most of the human remains have been stolen. By Europeans. By museum collectors. And by nice people like Mary Gilmore.

Her insensitivity is puzzling, not for the times, but given her own background and her respect for her father, who befriended Aborigines and 'could make himself understood in several native dialects and spoke one well'.[39] I assume the lingering influence of William Lane's racism. However, back in Australia, from the 1950s Mary transcended these attitudes with her crusade for Aboriginal rights.

The Indian encampments around Río Gallegos reminded Mary of the Aboriginal fringe camps in Australia, although she knew there was a darker comparison. Much later, back in Sydney in the 1940s, she observed: 'The history of the extermination of the Indians of Tierra del Fuego was the same as that of the black in Australia.' In both cases these people had received terrible retribution for pilfering the occasional sheep, although 'the land being taken from them, they had to eat something'. She repeated hearsay that certain farmers of Tierra del Fuego 'set a bounty on dead Indians, and two men who shall be nameless – they were English, I was told – set out to make a living by bringing in the ears of the victims ... they shot and massacred'. She concluded with a shocking statement: 'as here I have seen a wheat bag nearly full of blacks' ears'.[40]

That would be hundreds, maybe thousands, of ears. No. Such a reckless claim can be given little credence, if it is com-

Tehuelche Indians at Río Gallegos, 1901

pared to the difficult work of historians uncovering the actual stories of 'rencontres' (the usual euphemism) in the Australian colonial period, where 28 Aborigines were slaughtered at one place, 83 at another, and up to 300 at a site called Waterloo Creek, forming a cumulative litany of horror.[41]

Mary was writing wrong history – for right reasons of outrage, from a wish to jolt European Australians out of complacency or ignorance about an ugly past. But wrong history it still was.

More latitude is possible in poetry. A powerful poem, 'The Hunter of the Black', from Mary's later body of work, concluded:

> Tomahawk in belt, as only adults needed shot,
> No man knew how many notches totalled up his lot;
> But old stockmen striking tallies, rough and ready made,
> Reckoned on at least a thousand, naming camps decayed.

Time passed on, and years forgotten whitened with the dust;
He whose hands were red with slaughter sat among the just,
Kissed the children of his children, honoured in his place,
Turned and laid him down in quiet, asking God his grace.[42]

Charles Darwin's first impression of the 'wild' Indians of Tierra del Fuego, on Christmas Day 1832, could hardly have been more negative:

> They were the most abject and miserable creatures I anywhere beheld … These poor wretches were stunted in their growth, their hideous faces bedaubed with white paint, their skins filthy and greasy, their hair entangled, their voices discordant, and their gestures violent. Viewing such men, one can hardly make oneself believe that they are fellow-creatures, and inhabitants of the same world …[43]

With those few words Darwin imposed on the Yaghan – by his estimate, 3,000 of them – a stigma that lasted until they died out as a race. It was yet another insult from the pink people of the north, who had already plundered their seal colonies, kidnapped their young people and, in exchange, brought but three gifts: cheap Bibles, influenza and venereal disease.

At the time of his encounter, Darwin was already acquainted with three Yaghan Indians from Tierra del Fuego who had been offered the benefits of 'civilisation'. They had been given the names Jemmy Button, Fuegia Basket and York

Minster. Captain FitzRoy had picked them up on the previous voyage of the *Beagle* and invited them to come to England. They had no idea to what strange place they were going, nor the gravity of the audience they were granted with King William and Queen Adelaide.

After a year, their hair cut and with the acquisition of some European clothes, a basic competence in English and the impression that God and the Bible were not subjects to be trifled with, they were returned to their icy homeland on the same voyage as Darwin. Captain FitzRoy was convinced he had done well, and that they 'would be able to impart the divine light' to their wilder brethren. Darwin had never approved of FitzRoy's experiment, believing it had simply made the three Fuegians unfit to live among their own people again. When they were dumped ashore, he had a vivid memory of Jemmy Button in his English suit, warily circled by his relatives. He had all but forgotten his own language. 'It was laughable, but almost pitiable, to hear him speak to his wild brother in English, and then ask him in Spanish whether he did not understand him.'[44]

When the *Beagle* returned a year later, Jemmy was barely recognisable through his thick matted hair: 'Instead of the clean, well-dressed stout lad we left,' Darwin wrote, as if surprised at the absence of barbers and tailors, 'we found him a naked thin squalid savage.'[45] Some twenty years later Jemmy was implicated – one can speculate on his fury – in a massacre of Anglican missionaries on Navarin island.

∾

The story has always moved me because of a more intimate comparison that I have had to live with in not so distant times. In New Guinea in the late 1940s, when it was a UN Trust Territory, my own father was the engineer on a little boat owned by the Bulolo Gold Dredging Company. The skipper was known for good reason as Shanghai Brown. They made long voyages up the mighty Sepik river, stopping at every village to sign up the strongest, finest men, offering them the chance to earn riches working in a remote place called 'the goldfields'. It was too tempting for many of the men and they signed the indenture papers. They were spirited away by the boat and then by aeroplane to the Bulolo mines in the highlands, 300 kilometres away, with no possible way of returning until they completed their two years of indentured labour. Many never made it back.

In October 2002 I visited Tierra del Fuego and Argentina's southernmost town of Ushuaia, snowcapped mountains rearing above it. I was on a boat, buffeted by icy winds, on the Beagle channel and gazed at the rocky shores of Navarin island, close enough to observe the sea lions flopped in huddles, pestered by aggressive skua birds. In the 1920s the remaining Yaghan – reduced to about fifty – had subsisted on a reserve there. But I learned that, by the late 1990s, only three Yaghan speakers, of mixed Chilean blood, remained.[46]

There was no question of my going ashore. Since another dispute between Argentina and Chile over some islands in the channel, so fraught that the Pope had intervened, I was told it was far too complicated to visit. It would require bureaucratic negotiations, special papers and a chartered boat.

VIII

ILL WINDS

We passed through the entrance gates of Estancia Condor. I imagined my host composing the opening line for a book: 'I had a farm in Patagonia, at the foot of the Convent Hills ...'

At 2,000 square kilometres, it is the largest sheep ranch in Argentina, indeed in the world, said John Blake, if defined as 'run under one single administration all in one block'. With another 360 square kilometres of summer grazing land to the north-west, it matches the area of Oxfordshire, is approximately the same size as Luxembourg or the Australian Capital Territory and is over twice the size of Hong Kong including Kowloon and the New Territories. John managed this vast estate for thirty-five years, master of its 100,000 sheep, its seasonal 50,000 fat lambs, 1,500 head of cattle, 400 horses, a permanent staff of 80 and 28 extra contract workers for shearing.

Now that Condor is owned by Benetton, visitors are not welcome. 'The place is hermetically sealed,' Pablo Beecher told me. 'You just can't get in there.'

But nine years ago I stayed there with the Blakes. After spending two nights at Killik Aike, their home at weekends, we drove over 100 kilometres south to Condor. John was effectively returning to the office for the start of the working week. Two rheas – South American ostriches – sprinted across the road in front of us, followed at a coltish trot, by four guanacos, stones flying under their hooves.

It was quite an office. Like a medieval kingdom, it seemed guarded by stone forts: to the left the rocky Frailes hills, named after the friars of St Ignatius Loyola, rising abruptly from the brown *stipa* grass plain, matched forty kilometres away towards Chile by the flat-topped mesas of the Convent Hills. The property had sixty-five kilometres of Atlantic coastline, John's litany went, and ran for sixty-two kilometres parallel to, and in sight of, the Strait of Magellan. Once it had run to the strait, but Chile won a corridor in the Boundary Arbitration of 1902.

Estancia Condor was established as an enterprise by two English families, the Waldrons and the Woods, who leased enormous sheep runs in Chile. In 1881, with the opening up of Argentine Patagonia, they seized the chance of acquiring freehold land. Nine of the ten family shareholders remained in England, while the capable Arthur Waldron was appointed general manager at Condor. The property fell within the area of the border dispute between Argentina and Chile, and, taking that into account, the original title deed, was, in John Blake's view, 'a marvellous piece of legal dexterity'.

The sheep drifted in grey flocks across the brown plain. They were John's Cormo Argentino, the only registered new breed created solely within Argentina.

We could have passed through a small European country

by the time we reached the main settlement, one of four on the property. The Big House was surrounded by the red-roofed buildings of a village, a school, the mammoth shearing shed and the single men's quarters close by, where Gilmore had lived.

'Of course Mary couldn't have stayed here,' said Monica. 'The men would have been very rough. She was in an impossible situation really. Not quite a lady and yet not a domestic either. Her only chance was to be a governess, and apparently the people managing Condor didn't have children of the right age. She was in a most difficult position.'

Will Gilmore finished up at Killik Aike on 16 October 1901, collecting his wages of £9. 13s. ½d. He was able to enjoy a month with Mary and Billy in the little house in Río Gallegos before he travelled south to Estancia Condor to supervise the use of the new Wolseley shearing machines.

Having delighted in his company, Mary was fretful after her husband left on 23 November to start the new job. She had no alternative but to continue with the English lessons and battle the west wind, at its most malevolent in spring and summer, especially for women, whose long skirts almost sent them into flight:

> I have been half an hour going 100 yards, and holding on to fences all the way, and I have seen men – who wear no skirts – have to put their hands to the ground to maintain their balance.[1]

The main settlement at Estancia Condor, shearing shed at left

A visit from Stuart and Walker, two British workers from Killik Aike, was a welcome diversion. Mary even overlooked their insobriety – in mitigation, they had at least considered their unsteady condition: 'Walker remarking that they had better leave calling on me till their heads were clearer. However they concluded that if they left it till later, their heads would be worse instead of better.' She heard from them 'of the awful roughness of living down at Condor. So I am sending a couple of old forks which will be no loss if lost.'[2]

Mary had a new concern more serious than her isolation and the wind. In mid-October 1901 the smouldering border dispute between Argentina and Chile flared up again. 'AL-LEGED CHILIAN AGGRESSION!' headlined the Buenos Aires *Standard* on 16 October. The disputed terrain along the Strait of Magellan, much of it occupied by Estancia Condor, was only eighty kilometres from town. Chileans were regarded as enemies and were arrested in the streets. Mary had

deep misgivings when she was told that all aliens were suspect and 'that unless we had our passports Will would be imprisoned. He was away and I was alone.'[3] She adopted some
of the prevailing hysteria: 'I bought a chain and lock for the
fowl house. That old Chileno came for water before you had
been an hour gone. So I think I only got it in time to save the
daily eggs.' She resolved she would 'buy a cheap revolver next
month'.

> Dear old kind Will,
> I feel horribly lonely without you, and sad to think of you as
> so far away, but it is better than when I was in Paraguay … I
> have told you all my news, but feel I want to keep on writ-
> ing. Goodnight my dearest. I know how you love me and
> think of me and it makes me love you more and more.[4]

Back at the Hotel Paris, my friend Luis had been reading
Mary's letters and had taken a set against her husband: 'He
was a failure as a husband. He didn't support his wife prop-
erly and he left her exposed to danger!'

But poor Gilmore didn't have much option, I countered;
they didn't have the money to get away. And Mary wasn't a
wilting violet. She was a brave and resourceful woman.

But Luis would hear no excuses for him. An *Argentine
man,* he stoutly insisted, would have found a way of protect-
ing her, even if it meant taking a menial job in Río Gallegos.
'Here she was, all alone with a child in this town – it would
have been very rough. It's rough enough now! And where

was her husband? He was a shadow, just a shadow! She had no protection. It wasn't right!'

∾

Troops were being mobilized on both sides of the border and soldiers were drilling daily at the back and front of Mary's house, beginning at 2 a.m. as 'the days were long and there was little darkness at night'.[5] Rumours abounded.

The British, with large investments at stake if hostilities broke out – worth £125 million according to *The Times* of London[6] – had offered to mediate and, having been accepted by both sides, their Boundary Survey Commission was on its way south to arbitrate on the disputed border.

One advantage of the situation for Mary was that an army physician, Dr Facio, was now based at the local *cuartel*, or garrison. She went to see him about the diarrhoea that had plagued her for over a year. An English resident, Mrs Turner, accompanied her to translate. The consultation was very confrontational: 'I had to almost strip for the examination he gave me … He punched, pounded, poked and squeezed me all over and sounded both heart and lungs as well.' The doctor, whom Mary decided to trust, wrote out some fearsome prescriptions – subnitrate of bismuth, Benzo naphthol and opium.

A big Argentine man-o'-war, the *Buenos Aires*, anchored in the river as a warning to Chile, and two other warships were said to be beyond the point, out of sight. The military doctor had admitted to Mary that hostilities could break out any time.

It will be a serious matter for all the English, as there is no British Consul here and consequently no safety. No woman will be safe and all the men whom they can lay hands on will be forced to bear arms … However there may be British intervention in any case as Britain holds such big mortgages over Argentina. The presence of the man o' war and the rumours afloat are making many grave faces in Gallegos.[7]

The members of the Boundary Commission arrived in Patagonia, led by a veteran of boundary arbitrations in Afghanistan and India, Colonel Sir Thomas Hungerford Holdich. Taking advantage of the summer, they began the arduous survey of the precipitous border region between the two countries and the shores and islands of the Beagle channel. Mary expected the Commission's presence to put a brake on hostilities, but was only partly reassured by a discussion she had with the town mayor. He told her the recent trouble was caused by 'some officious Gallegos official' planting the Argentine flag over the boundary.[8] Her suspect as provocateur was the Comisario, or police chief, whom she soon came to despise for his brutal treatment of Chilean residents.

'Our hope was,' she remembered later,

that negotiations would go on till snow fell in the Andes, when the passes – there were only two – would be closed, and in the meantime we might get a man-o'-war from the Falklands. Remember we were living amongst people only semi-civilised, and among whom three parts were of Indian extraction. I never kept a revolver in the town, though I had one offered me. It is an awful thing to kill a man, and down there unless you kill it is useless shooting, and I wouldn't dare to kill.[9]

There were some shady characters about, she wrote to Will, and she had experienced an alarm only the previous night. One of her evening students, as he was leaving, warned her to be careful as thieves had been breaking into houses in her neighbourhood:

> As he finished I opened the door to let him out and at the instant a voice at the door said, '*Quiere vd. Naranjas.*' It gave me such a start for it was a queer hour to be hawking oranges … I can tell you I slept nervously after it, and this morning went and asked Lane about a revolver. He says that I can hardly get one that will fire without risk of bursting under $40. I can't afford that so I bought a whistle like Hawkins bought for the same purpose, i.e. alarm, and got Mr Lane to bring over the pup. The latter is in the spare room just now. I will keep him inside at night for he will at least bark. Mr Lane will get me a barrel for him to go into by day.[10]

She had heard that there had been big riots in Buenos Aires over the Chilean question and new taxes imposed to raise loans for a war. The banks had had a run on withdrawals. She was hardly consoled by the assurances of the English bank officials at the Banco Londres y Tarapacá,[11] who promised to defend British women with everything they had if the Chileans invaded. The cellar of the bank was provisioned for an emergency and officials had been issued with revolvers and just two bullets each: one 'to save a lady from a fate worse than death'; the other to use on themselves.[12]

At the end of the month she wrote that the latest she had heard 'about war matters' was that a request had been sent to Chile by the Boundary Commission asking why roads had been built on the disputed territory.

> So far Chile has not chosen to answer. That the question of war depends entirely upon the answer. Also that we shall probably know on Tuesday whether or not there is to be war. At present the carrier pigeons are being actively trained and excitement is calming into a waiting suspense.[13]

The reason for the carrier pigeons was that the lines for telephone and telegraph communication went via Punta Arenas in Chile and, as Mary recalled later, 'when Chile chose that we should get news of the progress of negotiations she opened the lines, when she didn't choose she closed them'.[14]

Mary slept with an axe, carving knives and the whistle under her pillow and the pup in the house: 'The dog is not so bad. He heard a noise last night, and barked at once, and this morning frightened the milkman who leaves the milk at the back before I get up.'[15] Her pupils impressed upon her 'never to open my door at night should a knock come till I knew who was outside and indeed I was thought to be a phenomenal woman to live alone'.[16]

Mary was concerned that the many Chilenos in the region – up to 20,000 in the early 1900s[17] – were being arrested in the streets of Río Gallegos and subjected to rough treatment on the orders of the police chief. She heard that Manuel, the well-liked driver who took the mail to and from Estancia Condor, 'was very anxious – all Chileans must be, for if war breaks out they have the choice of going back to Chile to become soldiers – if they can get back – or being forced into the Argentine army, and of being made prisoners or shot as spies'.

And all the while, if the rain was not teeming down, she had to battle the howling westerly wind, which put her in a mood 'either to swear or cry'. It was all too much. 'I really think that unless things look very bright after shearing,' she wrote to Will in November 1901, 'we had better move out of the country.'

But, meanwhile, the writer in her recognised that the explosive situation presented an opportunity. She sent a letter to the editors of the *Standard* in Buenos Aires 'asking if they want a correspondent for Gallegos, and offering to act as one provided they pay. If they put me on they will pay. The work will not be much, and it will give me a standing and a right to apply for information from people who can give it.'[18]

This was a good entrepreneurial idea. But the *Standard* did not take up Mary's offer, just as they had chosen not to publish the poem she submitted. The editors may have believed a woman could not do the job – this was a country where women did not achieve the vote until 1947. Or they may have suspected she was not a very stable person.

Much later – in 1947 – Mary stated that with her submission to the *Standard* she enclosed a report for the Argentine president concerning the harassment of Chileans in Gallegos. And about this she made an absurdly grandiloquent claim:

> In a small way I helped stop the last threatened war between Chile and Argentina (when we were in Patagonia) by sending a letter through the Mulhalls (on the Buenos Aires *Standard*) to President Roca, telling him how the Comisario of Police for Patagonia was having Chileans imprisoned and threatening to flog those he could not shoot. I took my life in my hand in doing this, as my letter might have been stopped in the post.[19]

The editors may have considered her report – if she ever really sent one – too emotional for someone proposing herself as a reliable correspondent. And there are curious discrepancies. The *Standard*'s proprietors, the Mulhall brothers, were both dead by then.[20]

She went on to make an even more colourful assertion about her time in Patagonia:

> British estancieros asked me to start a movement for the annexation of Patagonia (then a territory of Argentina) by Great Britain. As I knew it was no use raising a flag without an Army I wrote to Lady Jersey and told her to send out people for interpenetration.[21]

This all seems like elderly self-delusion. It is possible Mary may have met Lady Jersey, wife of the seventh Earl of Jersey who had been Governor of New South Wales from 1890 to 1893, and she may even have sent her some sort of letter along these lines. Lady Jersey had written a nationalist Federation poem, 'One People, One Destiny', for the Sydney *Bulletin* in 1891 and could have met some of its radical writers. But once back in England, though undoubtedly influential, she was known for her conservatism and opposition to women's suffrage, not for her sympathy towards Australian socialists.

As for British estancieros asking Mary to head the vanguard for an annexation movement, the only ones she had become acquainted with in Patagonia were the Feltons of Killik Aike – and the only movement they asked her to organise was her own speedy exit from their land.

She never met Arthur Waldron – the leading estanciero in the south – nor ever visited Estancia Condor, and she asked Will for information: 'How does Condor compare with an Australian shed of the same size and condition?'[22]

When I lingered in Estancia Condor's vast shearing shed, furnished with eighteen stands, the Wolseley shearing machines had long since been updated.

Monica was reluctant to show me the men's quarters, where Gilmore had stayed. It was off limits to women, too far 'down below'. Instead, she took me to the schoolhouse which, like most of the buildings on the property, was constructed out of cream-painted corrugated iron with a red roof. Monica founded it in 1964 for the children of thirty families who were employed full-time. We agreed that running it would have been an ideal situation for Mary, but over sixty years too late. The children and their teachers in crisp white dustcoats stood to attention to sing the national anthem as the blue and white national flag whipped in the wind.

We continued on past the office where a military campaign seemed in progress, pins and small pennants positioned on a map to indicate Condor's four settlements, what sheep breeds were where, the location of the Hereford cattle, and the paddocks being rested. Meanwhile another campaign was in progress on the soccer field – estancia workers training for a match against Río Gallegos.

Back at the Big House a border collie romped across manicured sloping lawns. Beyond the lavender beds, cypresses, yew hedges and drooping golden laburnum, the bald hills loomed. The house, with its weatherboard walls and a conservatory of potted geraniums, pelargoniums and ferns, had the homely feel of a farmhouse that had simply kept growing. But the drawing room verged on the baronial, with a vast fireplace dominating one end and a billiard table the other. An elderly cook brought tea on a trolley and hobbled back down the long hall to prepare a dinner of roast lamb and creamed broccoli, to be followed by lemon flummery. She had been with the family for forty-six years.

'It's the kind of loyalty you don't get anymore,' said John. 'Not with all this Peronism nonsense.'

I said I had noticed the strident graffiti on a building as we passed through Río Gallegos – '*Volver de Perón* – Bring back Perón.'

John drily agreed that the town was a strong centre for the

movement – which was impossible to understand for anyone who was not Argentine. 'For that matter, it's pretty well impossible for anyone who is. Peronism means everything and nothing. It appeals to the poor and the dispossessed but it's not about socialism. Quite the opposite. It's about looking after the rich, but making the poor feel good about it.'

He had heard the rumours that a film about Evita would be shot on location in Argentina and Madonna was touted for the role. He thought it would mean more romantic mythologising of a silly spoilt woman. 'Various film companies keep asking us to let them use this place for a set,' he said, waving his arm at the grand lamplit billiard table, 'but we're not interested.'

'All sorts of people try to inveigle their way in here,' said Monica. 'That writer, Bruce Chatwin, simply arrived, unannounced and uninvited, cool as you please, when we had the Archdeacon to tea. We sent him away with a flea in his ear.' But apparently with some copy:

And you can find, nestling behind windbreaks: herbaceous borders, lawnsprayers, fruit-cages, conservatories, cucumber sandwiches, bound sets of *Country Life* and, perhaps, the visiting Archdeacon.[23]

'It's absolute nonsense that we had cucumber sandwiches,' said John.

Mary was having a hard time of it in Río Gallegos, fighting

the westerlies, illness and depression. She had been back to the garrison to see Dr Facio, who gave her an even more thorough overhauling:

> I am positively stiff and sore all across back and front of the waist from the squeezing and poking and jamming he gave me. The result of it was that he found that I had one kidney loose, but he says only slightly, and that it is a common thing with women who have had children. On account of this I must always wear a bandage.

To add to her trials there was something dead and foul-smelling at the bottom of the well in her backyard, so she had to carry water in from the Lanes' shop next door. A soldier called in while she was there 'and mentioned among other things that though the war talk is over they have orders to sleep under arms. Each man is supplied with 100 cartridges. A sentry deserted after the order came out. If war had been declared at the time he would have been shot.' As it was, 'he has Life on Ushuaia', the grim prison on Tierra del Fuego.[24]

She worried about the vulnerability of their own position, 'for we have no passports, not even our certificates of birth. Anyone without papers can be forced to serve or to be shot as a deserter. I feel very uneasy especially as communication with you is so uncertain.'

With so much of his mother's time given over to teaching, young Billy was becoming a problem, fretful when she left him with Mrs Lane. With Christmas approaching she was at a loss as to what to buy him with her limited funds: 'I think some lollies, biscuits and fruit', though he yearned for toys from the local store windows. Mary wondered if Will could make a whip for the child and send it in with Manuel, the driver, but she hoped against hope 'for the little man's sake' and for her own that Will would be able to join them at Christmas: 'I would count the hours till you came and grudge every one that passed before you went.'[25]

The day after she wrote this letter, 12 December, Mary was too ill to teach, wanted to leave Patagonia as soon as possible, and wrote to Will in utter misery, begging him to come and meet her if he could. She had cancelled all her classes and wished to leave immediately for Buenos Aires, where she could be admitted to the British Hospital. While she was being treated, she suggested, her husband and the boy could stay once again at the Salvation Army hostel. 'Dear old Will, I know you will nearly despair when you get this letter. Come in for a day at least, by that time I will either be better or worse.'

That evening she added a postscript. She had seen the doctor again who prescribed new medication, and she had even felt well enough to enquire about the cost of their boat fares: at $72.50 each they should soon become affordable. 'So after all you need not come in in such a hurry, and it will be a great thing for us if you can finish out the shearing.'

But, for most of December 1901, Mary seemed in a morbid state – driven mad by what was obviously a severe case of amoebic dysentery, and by the wind which either penetrated every crack in the house or savaged her when she ventured out. 'Oh! the wind of the last few days! I don't wonder that people down here swear and drink, the play upon the nerves is so terrible.'

Mary kept changing her ideas about leaving or waiting. She knew her letters would distress her husband, but hoped he would understand that she needed to confide in him:

> It is terrible to be always alone – and sick. Not a friend to turn to to say 'Send someone to stay with me' or 'Let me stay with you'. No one but a child to speak to all day and all night – except as regards lessons. It is no wonder I grow low spirited and depressed. And I am not strong enough to keep from writing letters that I know will make you miserable. Yet I am your loving wife, Mary Gilmore.[26]

Though she had hoped the possibility of war had been shelved, at least until the arbitration of the British Survey Commission, there was worrying news of anti-Argentine riots in Chile. In Río Gallegos the soldiers were again on full alert.

Mary had heard that horses were being shipped by the British from South America to South Africa for the war against the Boers, so thought they might get a passage on a horse boat. 'I wish we were away … If you have any more dealings, see you are paid in English money, not South American. Waldron pays English money.'[27]

A few days later, she was quite cheerful on a number of counts. The war scare was said to be over, Chile having agreed to abide by the arbitration: 'It is said she was afraid as 40,000 Italian troops and their general are reported to have been offered to Argentina.' She had received a swag of family mail, including 'the nicest and kindest letter in the world' from Will's farmer parents in Victoria, whom she had never met, 'bidding us come "home" – you can read them for yourself. I was so touched by them that I slept with them under my pillow.' She had a letter from her sister, and her eldest brother Hugh had dispatched £20 to Buenos Aires towards their return fares.[28] There was also a note from Jack Cameron, her war correspondent brother in South Africa, saying he and his wife hoped they might all meet up in London.

Mary urged Will to ask Arthur Waldron at Condor to at least allow him a short break in town for the festive season: 'Billy's little heart will rejoice on Xmas morning. I went out and bought him a cart and horse, top, jack-in-the-box, pop gun, fiddle and bugle. Won't his eyes shine and won't his tongue go?'

Mary's rare good spirits were not even dampened by having almost collided with Herbert Felton at her neighbours' house: 'I had hardly gone out when, I believe, Mr F. came in. I was so glad to have missed him.'[29] The estanciero would have been just as reluctant to meet Mary, no doubt still suspecting her of bringing about the coroner's inquiry.

The Feltons were on good personal terms with the Lanes, but they also had a business relationship. Ever since their son Carlos was a baby he had been taken to the photographic studio to have his winsomeness recorded for posterity. At Killik Aike the boxes of Felton photographs in the cellar documented a literal Rake's Progress: from crimped curls and

Rio Gallgos.   C. Lane,   Argentine Rep

A Charles Lane study of young Carlos

cherubic smile in a white lace christening dress, through art-
ful pose in kilt, sporran, Highland shawl and feathered cap,

to complacent schoolboy in a Burberry, culminating in a study of a handsome young man with impeccable suit, neat brush moustache and permanent leer. After that Carlos clearly had no more need of the photographic services of Charles Lane – a series of candid snaps from his own camera recorded his polo games, picnics and parties, his new motor vehicles, shipboard holidays and glamorous female partners. 'The Man of 100 Summers' who for fifty years avoided winter anywhere, was said to have had one mistress in Buenos Aires, another in London, and a third in Europe.

In the boxes of photographs I sifted through there was only one studio portrait of his decidedly plain, much older sister Millie. If the girl was unloved by her parents, she had recently received another slight: Cynthy, her governess, was leaving to marry Walker, one of the English workers at Killik Aike and Mary's friend.

But even news of this did not cheer Mary for long; her next letter conveyed black despair. The local pharmacist had taken it upon himself to offer a diagnosis of her condition, and certainly his proposed remedy (if any of this nonsense *really* came from him) was exactly what she wanted to hear:

The chemist says he thinks I am suffering from Neurasthenia, it is a disease of the nerves, caused by poor food and loneliness. The cure is rest of all kinds, mental and physical, cheerful company, plenty of change, the best of wine and food and nerve strengtheners. The disease is almost purely mental, the mind acting on the body. In it the spinal marrow does its work imperfectly and the whole system suffers gradual, continual and almost imperceptible decay till it becomes too weak to rally. One either just fades away or becomes paralysed. I have the symptoms of it in full.

Mary's situation was genuinely wretched, and she seems to have succumbed to clinical depression. It is hard not to feel compassion for her, but I feel that too for the gentle Will Gilmore, for when Mary was at her lowest ebb, her sense of survival, her will to overcome, made her powerfully manipulative:

> The chemist says it is always in countries like this that the disease is most common, as there is no society, no scenery, no change, no variety. It is all loneliness and work. Don't you remember how I used to ask you to stay in the house and talk to me? I being extremely sensitive to surroundings, and highly nervous of course, am a most likely subject.[30]

She added next day that the draft for £20 from her brother Hugh had arrived at the British Consulate in Buenos Aires. 'I take it as a good omen, and perhaps I'll get better after all.'[31]

Manuel the driver arrived on Christmas Eve and Mary penned a final few lines while he waited:

> My dear old Will,
> You will feel very sad by the time you come to this page. I wonder how soon we can get away? ... Billy is well, but so cross and irritable ... Poor little man, he has his sock ready hanging up for Santa Claus. I expect Johnny Hawkins will smash most of his things, for the poor little fellow isn't of

the kind to want to play with them in secret. He must have company. It is as necessary for a child's health as for an adult's. By the bye, the women on the colony who went in for 'lovers' had the best health, the women who didn't had the worst, because the former always had some fresh interest, the latter not … Now I will leave this doleful letter.

This is virtual blackmail, from a lonely, desperate and sexually frustrated woman. Gilmore was granted time off to come into Gallegos for Christmas Day. After receiving such a letter, how could he not?

No doubt he and Mary tried to make it a joyous occasion for young Billy, but when Will travelled back to Condor on Boxing Day another gloomy letter followed him: 'I think I am a bit better today. But the war scare has started up again worse than ever. It is said (the news only came an hour ago) that it is almost certain war.' Mary had heard that all shipping would be stopped if hostilities broke out and they would be trapped in the south. 'If there is war and a message can be sent I will telegraph to you – if it seems any use. Whatever you do, don't change English cheques for Argentine money … If there is war we will lose the £20 in BA.'[32]

After almost a week's silence, Mary wrote again on the first day of 1902:

Dear old Will.
Today is New Year's day and I write you a line because I love you and you love me and because of the day. We have only once begun the New Year together since we were married

and it seems very sad to think of it. But I mustn't be sad. I am still feeling very ill indeed and unless I get better it will be as much as I can do to hold out till we get to B. Aires – if I do that.

Dr Facio gave Mary a referral to the British Hospital in Buenos Aires. He could be forgiven if he breathed a sigh of relief as he returned to treating Argentine soldiers drilling for war.

Mary had heard that the German ship, the *Chubut,* which had sailed from the Chilean port of Punta Arenas, was already two days overdue: 'last time it came to Gallegos its launch was smashed and the men in her drowned – he may be afraid to put in in such awful weather'.[33] She had been packing up and the saratoga trunk was almost full. She had written to Cynthy, who was about to leave governessing to marry, and offered her 'the clock, fowls, corn and kerosene, about $30 worth for $15. I told her that if she did not buy them and no one else did I would leave them for her in any case. All the other things I will leave for her except the rocking chair. That we must take.'

With the draft from her brother and if Will's accounts were made up, the Gilmores now had enough for their passages, but still Will lingered in a maddening way. Mary either experienced an appallingly sudden decline in health or else the last words of her letter were calculated to assure their immediate departure. She assigned all her worldly goods in what was effectively her final will and testament:

Dear old Will,

If I have to go away from you only remember how I loved you; keep all my papers and such things to take to Australia. My clothes can go to the soldiers' wives here. Don't ever give away my ring or Billy's … I give Billy to you and you to Billy. My music is at Mrs Lane's and one book at Mrs Hawkins. It is all to go to my sister. The music I wrote myself is to be kept with my papers, perhaps some day something might be done with it. But everything I have is yours, even as I am yours. Keep the ring I wear. Carry it on a chain round your neck. It was yours and is mine and because it is my only wedding ring the thing most mine and the one I most care for … If only I can get to B.A. and into the hospital I'll be all right. The terrible time is now.

Dear, dear Will, always your loving wife, Mary Gilmore. 1.1.1902[34]

The letter had its effect. Gilmore rushed to Mary's side and stayed for almost a fortnight. He arranged their passages to Buenos Aires on the *Comodoro Rivadavia,* a Hamburg–American coastal liner doing its first run on the route and expected in Gallegos within the month.[35] On 12 January he returned to Estancia Condor to pack and collect his wages, riding his horse through torrential rains. Mary wrote the next day: 'I do hope you got out to the Estancia safely last night. But what a night! People tell me there has never before been such a night in Gallegos. The streets are full of lakes. I am better today than yesterday and am going on nicely I think.'[36]

She had recovered so nicely in fact that she had managed to write a poem, 'Patagonia in the South', dated 12 January. It was both an elegiac farewell to that windswept, wintry land and her turbulent time there and an affirmation of her love for her husband:

God set our souls to one full tone
And sent us, sep'rate, in our sev'ral ways.
I heard the music of ten thousand souls
Re-echo, splendid, to eternal days;
Yet, to my waiting heart, though this was sweet,
Though that was deep and strong, and this one beat
With throbbing melody divine,
And, yet another, with a sweet control
Half called me, yearning, thitherward,
None blent with mine in true accord
Till you, Beloved, turned your eyes to mine.
God set our souls to one full tone
And sent us, sep'rate, in our sev'ral ways,
God sent us two, unknowing and unknown,
To find each other after many days.[37]

She had arrived in Paraguay a single woman, wishing for marriage, 'even though it be rye bread'. She was returning with a beloved family and, because of the verse she had posted to magazines from South America, she had a reputation as a poet.

Mary's last letter from Río Gallegos to her husband was written on Thursday, 16 January 1902. She expected him in on Saturday when the *Comodoro Rivadavia* would be berthed at the wharf, 'but I am in the Doctor's hands and he will decide whether I go by her or not'.

Mary was later to recount the story of her final adventure in Patagonia. She maintained that the letter she had sent to President Roca, via the Buenos Aires *Standard,* complaining about the police Comisario in Río Gallegos and his brutality towards Chilean residents, had resulted in an official investigation of the man. The Comisario hurriedly left town, she wrote, but she discovered to her horror that he was boarding the *Comodoro Rivadavia* at the same time as themselves:

He fled – hiding on the same ship in which we left Patagonia. My husband saw him hiding from him behind a bulkhead. When we reached Buenos Aires, I asked Will to wait till everyone was off the boat; as I did not want anyone behind me in case of a knife in my back. I came off with the calves of my legs trying to walk in front.[38]

IX

HOMECOMING

Will and Billy lodged at the Salvation Army hostel in Buenos Aires while Mary was admitted to the British Hospital to have all her ailments checked out. After a few days she was pronounced well enough to travel.

The family took a ferry across the Río de la Plata to Montevideo, from where their ship would sail for England. It was carnival time and Mary was struck by the extraordinary mixture of colour among people in the streets, 'ranging from ordinary European white to the jet-black of the Brazilian Negro, who is black enough for anything'; the 'invariably picturesque' costumes of the dancers; and the fashionable beauties who wore too much rouge and powder, were 'gloveless, bareheaded or wearing a mantilla', but had 'a deportment anyone might envy – a carriage that belongs to a people guiltless of corsets and high heels'.[1]

In early March 1902 the Gilmores boarded a P&O ship bound for Liverpool, its first port of call Río de Janeiro. Like many before and after her, Mary was spellbound by the city's harbour, the panorama from the funicular railway up Corcovado, 'and behind, above and beyond it all the blue sierras piercing the horizon of the sky. Such beauty! Such colour! Such light!'[2]

Crossing the Atlantic from Río in a third-class cabin, the family all went down with influenza. Billy's case worsened to pneumonia and the ship's doctor feared he would die. Mary, ill herself, tried to nurse her husband and son:

> A few hours before reaching Liverpool, Billy passed the crisis. 'He will live – with care,' the Doctor said. We came into Liverpool in a drizzling rain and biting wind ...[3]

They booked into a temperance hotel, but that proved too expensive. Two days later they moved into 'a furnished room with some Salvation Army people'. Mary sent word of their arrival to her old friend Henry Lawson, now living in London with his wife Bertha at Princes Mansions, Liverpool Road.

While they waited, Mary was offered an access key to the small fenced square of garden opposite their boarding house, 'being deemed respectable enough to be allowed there'. She commented wryly, 'Only *nice* people had the privilege. The bare ground and stunted growths made me wonder where the privilege came in, especially after the splendour of the Paraguayan forests and the spaces of Patagonia.'[4]

But Billy was on the mend and outings in the pale sun did him good. Then a message arrived from Lawson: 'Bed's made, and cot's ready for the little fellow. Come at once, am simply mad for the sight of an Australian face.'[5]

With South America and the frontier world where they had met behind them, in London the social and intellectual disparity between Mary and Will became more apparent.

Her writing began to insert a small wedge between them. She was gratified to discover that, in the milieu to which Henry had at least a degree of access, a few people recognised her as a poet. She was invited to take tea with the critic Edward Garnett, a central figure in the London literary world. But it *was* only tea, not one of his famous Thursday luncheons at the Mont Blanc restaurant in Gerrard Street, sometimes attended by Joseph Conrad and even sometimes the reclusive W. H. Hudson.[6]

Lawson also took Mary and her husband to meet William Ernest Henley, physically disabled but a formidable writer, critic and editor of the *National Observer* and the *London Magazine*. Henley could be a blustering bully – he was known to be the model for the fierce, one-legged pirate Long John Silver in his friend Robert Louis Stevenson's novel *Treasure Island* – but he could also be 'generous in his promotion and encouragement of unknown talents and … launched many better writers than himself on their way to fame'.[7] Lawson must have hoped Mary might become one of his protégées, but it was not to be. She remembered the encounter with Henley, 'huge in his wheeled chair', as awkward:

> There was only one chair for visitors. I sat, my husband stood on my side, on the other Henry Lawson who had brought us … Henry asked me to write him something for

Blackwood's. But I was too conscious of my own inferiority and too shy to send him even a line. I think at times what a fool I was. But mostly know I was right.[8]

These literary meetings must have been an ordeal for Will Gilmore and, with his broad Australian accent and lack of social graces, he was no doubt received in London as an oddity, an embarrassment. He was aware, too, that his famous host had once been Mary's suitor. To add to his discomfort, Henry and Bertha had violent arguments in front of their guests in the tiny flat. 'Within half an hour she was telling us how unhappy she was and how badly he was treating her,' Mary later wrote in a very partisan account of the visit. 'That night Will said to me – "If that woman were my wife I would wring her neck! She isn't fit to be any man's wife."'[9]

They were relieved to board the Sydney-bound *Karlsruhe* on 30 April but appalled when, just before sailing, Henry sent Bertha with them as a quarrelsome travelling companion.

∾

The six-year adventure in South America was over.

A few months after the Gilmores' departure from Patagonia, the British Survey Commission reached a satisfactory boundary settlement and war between Chile and Argentina was averted. Chile gained half of the island of Tierra del Fuego and a wedge of southern Patagonia which blocked Estancia Condor from access to the Magellan Strait. To celebrate the 'perpetual accord', a heroic statue of the Christ of the Andes was erected on the pass above Mendoza, in the shadow of Aconagua, the continent's highest peak. Later an inscription was added to its base: 'Sooner shall these mountains crumble to dust than Argentines and Chileans break the peace sworn to at the feet of Christ the Redeemer.'[10] Mary considered it 'the noblest statue in the world'.[11]

After they returned to Australia, the Gilmore family moved to rural Victoria, to a slab hut where Mary and Billy were alone for long periods, while Will gained itinerant work where he could find it. Later Mary remembered those isolated years as 'the dark night of the soul'. A year after the publication of her first volume of poetry, *Marri'd and Other Verses*, in 1910, Mary moved to Sydney. She had been offered the job of editing a new women's page for a trade union paper, the New South Wales *Worker*. The marriage, in any real sense, was at an end. However, Mary preserved a bond at long distance with Will on the farm where he settled in Queensland, and wrote a chiding, confiding, loving and sometimes merely dutiful letter to him almost every week for the next thirty-four years. But the rest of her very long life was devoted to her writing and to campaigns for just causes. One acquaintance remarked: 'One almost senses an invisible *army* behind Mary Gilmore when her sense of justice is aroused.'[12]

Her life was remarkable in its complexity and paradox: she was made a Dame of the British Empire in 1937, in recognition of her achievements in literature and social reform; fifteen years later, she began writing a regular column for the communist newspaper *Tribune*, in protest at the Menzies government's attempt to ban the party, which she never

William and Mary Gilmore and 12-year-old Billy in 1910

joined; the former racist of Paraguay became one of the early
European campaigners for Aboriginal rights. She encouraged aspiring writers and was a favourite of journalists for
her feisty opinions on almost any subject: industrial arbitration, prison reform, the planting of native trees, freedom of

the press, old age pensions, assistance for working mothers, pocket handkerchiefs for women in gaol, a statue to honour Henry Lawson (who died in 1922), a memorial for working dogs.

But apart from some verses in school primers, Mary Gilmore's poetry was little read by the wider public until the Second World War. Then her patriotic poem 'No Foe Shall Gather Our Harvest' became a battle-cry for the nation – displayed in shop windows, read on the radio, set to music, published in magazines and on Christmas cards. In another poem, 'Singapore', she condemned the British for their failure to defend the island stronghold, abandoning thousands of Australian soldiers to capture by the Japanese and exposing the continent to invasion. In 1944 William Dobell's prize-winning portrait caused a controversy for its idiosyncratic representation of her – looming like an aged Queen Elizabeth I bereft of the red wig. But she saw its originality, breaking down 'the usual plain two purl three' of conventional portraits.

By 1945, the year the war ended, Mary had become the most famous woman in Australia, a Grand Old Lady revered as virtual matriarch of the nation. But a desperately sad one. In February she heard news from Queensland of the death of her husband from septicaemia, and, just five months later, of her son Billy from alcoholic poisoning.

> Never admit the pain,
> Bury it deep;
> Only the weak complain,
> Complaint is cheap.[13]

Mary lived on for another seventeen years, her fame ever increasing, not without considerable help from her own regular pronouncements in the press. When she led the workers' procession through Sydney as 'Queen of the May' in the year before her death, it was, she said with a glint of amusement, 'my last glorification'. She was 97 years old when she died on 3 December 1962. She had asked when she was gone to be remembered not by the 'mighty ones' but by 'the little folk'.[14] When she was honoured with a state funeral in Sydney, so many dignitaries filled St Stephens Presbyterian church that few 'little folk' could find a place. Later her portrait graced the Australian $10 note, as it still does.

If the utopian William Lane had been one of Mary's first heroes, the Russian cosmonaut Yuri Gagarin was her last. She had spanned a century of unprecedented change:

> I began, myself, with a slush lamp, went to the tallow candle … the imported stearine candle, to kerosene lamps, from kerosene lamps to gas, from gas to electric light, and now we have ahead of us the atomic power to cover every mortal thing we can think of.[15]

But the period 1900–1902 in Patagonia stands out as extraordinary, even in the rich context of her life. It was the most testing time in one of the harshest places on earth, exposing her to extremes of emotional and physical stress, concentrating her protective energies on two great loves, her husband and her child, with the conflicting knowledge that her third passion, her writing, must be held in abeyance.

Old habits linger: Mary in her nineties drinking yerba maté

Despite her lapses into frailty, it was her bravery that shone through, and her sense of humanity that endured.

There is one poem in *Marri'd and Other Verses* in which Mary expresses everything that was good and hard-won and to be treasured in those early years of her marriage, motherhood and coming of age in South America:

Yea! I have lived -
Have felt the husband-kiss upon my lips,
Have felt my child's mouth pull upon my breast;
Have foughten Death, have toiled and taken rest,
Have sinned most human sins, have felt the whips
Where conscience struck; have drunk of life
In laughter and in song, in tears that burned,
In Hope that sang, in peace, in plenitude of strife
That germined strength; have lost, and gained, and
    learned …[16]

AFTERWARDS

Before leaving Río Gallegos to make my own way back to Australia, I paid a final visit to the gabled British Club at 900 Avenida Roca. Luis and I had roast lamb for lunch with Pablo Beecher in a dining room with wood-panelling, regency-striped wallpaper and Stubbs' horse prints.

Pablo said he valued his British heritage but identified as an Argentine. As a child he went to two schools in Río Gallegos, the local public school in the morning and the English-language school in the afternoon. This was never a problem for him until the Falklands–Malvinas war of 1982. He was ten. The British children were ostracised at the morning school, which hurt him as his sympathies were with Argentina.

It was worse at the British Club, which his parents frequented. Windows were broken and graffiti daubed on the walls: '*Club cipayo* – This club is a lap dog' was the least of it. Two portraits used to hang in equal pride of place – Queen Elizabeth and General José de San Martín. After the sinking of the battle cruiser *General Belgrano*, with the loss of over 600 Argentine lives, Queen Elizabeth was quietly removed to a back room 'where she was put with the sacks of potatoes and onions'.

I had another interest in the club: it was the venue for a grotesque celebration in 1922, re-enacted in the 1974 film *La Patagonia Rebelde,* directed by Hector Olivera.

Pablo introduced me to the manager, Miguel Campos-Davidson, who admitted the club had been used as a location, 'but we didn't realise what they were doing till they put the film together. It was a story better not talked about ...'

The Gilmores never knew, for the story was long suppressed, that just twenty years after their departure, a strike by sheep-workers in Patagonia, some of those involved once known to them as young *peones,* was savagely put down.

They and other Australian socialists who followed William Lane to South America had abandoned their own country because of a series of strikes in which, despite bombastic rhetoric on both sides, little blood was spilled. They left because of the inequities of a social system that favoured the wealthy landowning class over the worker. But they came to a continent where class structures were inflexibly entrenched. In Argentina the power and wealth of the oligarchy was beyond their imagining, backed up with force beyond their worst fears. Any notion of rights for workers was implacably resisted.

The 1917 Russian Revolution inspired socialist ambitions in some Argentine workers, just as it instilled unease, fear and a determination to be on their mettle in the upper and middle classes. Anarchists, favouring direct action and the general

Workers' demonstration in Buenos Aires, 1919

strike, instigated a number of violent demonstrations in the capital. In 1919, the authorities moved decisively to staunch the wave of radicalism, mobilising the army against striking unionists – a grim new theme for Argentina. The socialist press reported 'the final toll was 700 dead and 4,000 injured'.[1]

However, there had been little political activity in Patagonia or progress for rural workers. In Santa Cruz, 20 million hectares were held by just 600 landowners. A fall in international wool prices after the First World War and increased competition from Australia and New Zealand threw the regional economy into crisis. The landholders passed on their losses in the form of reduced wages and conditions.[2]

In November 1920, the local workers' organisations around Río Gallegos called a general strike in protest at the 'barbaric levels of exploitation' suffered by *peones* and sheep-workers on the estancias. Their demands included the men's right to be paid in money not in kind and a free afternoon a week to wash their clothes, concessions won long before by Australian workers. But, like the shearers in Queensland in 1891, they also insisted on clean living quarters, free candle-lighting, the right not to work outdoors in the rain and, above all, to be able to form trade unions and be represented by workplace delegates. In an unprecedented spirit of rebellion, whipped up by city-based organisers, horsemounted posses of *peones* rode around the district 'collecting provisions, horses and arms',[3] or, more like, looting and intimidating property owners with their demands.

President Hipólito Yrigoyen advised the governor of Santa Cruz to 'settle the matter'. The governor, after hearing all sides of the issue, ruled in favour of the workers. But the estancieros refused to concede the recommended conditions.

Another general strike was called in October 1921. An anarchist trade union organiser, Antonio Soto, urged the sheepworkers – frontline troops for his ideological fervour – to stand their ground:

> You are workers! Carry on with the strike, to triumph definitively, to shape a new society where there are neither poor nor rich, where there are no weapons, where there are no uniforms or uniformed, where there is happiness, respect for the human being, where no one needs to bend the knee to a priest's cassock or before any boss.[4]

The British Embassy in Buenos Aires sent a firm note to

President Yrigoyen.[5] The powerful pastoral corporations of the south, including Braun-Menéndez of La Anita and the Waldron–Woods-controlled Patagonian Sheep Farming Company of Condor, put pressure on him to act. Yrigoyen had no wish to alienate any of them, and he also suspected Chilean interference in supplying the strikers with arms. He sent a heavy contingent, the 10th Argentine Calvalry, to 're-establish order'. They were joined by young Patriotic League volunteers, looking for a fight. This combined force, led by Lieutenant-Colonel Héctor Benigno Varela, whose instructions were to use 'extreme measures', pursued and summarily dispatched the illiterate, isolated and mostly unarmed rural workers and *peones*. Reports of summary executions, with corpses heaped on bonfires of thornscrub, began to leak out.[6]

On 6 December 1921, Antonio Soto and a few hundred strikers took the manager and his staff hostage in the homestead of Estancia La Anita, the second largest sheep property in Patagonia. They were cheered on by the estancia workers, but they had blundered in causing trouble for the most powerful Argentine dynasty in the south. The rebels were overwhelmed when Varela and his troops arrived. Soto managed to escape in the confusion and fled to Chile.

I visited Estancia La Anita, near Lake Argentino, on the way to see the great Perito Moreno glacier. With a little encouragement, our driver swung through the gates and right into the property. It was now owned by a company, La Anonima, but the original families were still principal shareholders. I climbed out to photograph the shearing shed. It seemed

La Anita shearing shed: a crime scene

too spick and span, sparkling with new green and white paint, to be the site of a massacre.

The *peones* were mostly of Chilean origin, but also Spaniards, Scots and Croatians who had fled from the Balkans' strife. Only a handful were Argentine. These men desired better wages and conditions but few were driven by ideology. With Soto's departure, they promptly surrendered to the military and raised a white flag. Almost 300 of them were locked up overnight in the vast shed with its bright green roof. 'They are enemies of the state in which they live,' pronounced Varela. Other local landowners came to witness the drama.

Next morning a contingent of captives was ordered to dig a deep trench beyond the La Anita sheep dip. When it was completed, the *peones* were brought out a few at a time; if an estanciero wished to retain a good worker, he spoke up for him and the man was judged innocent and released. The unwanted ones were led away in groups to the open grave beyond.

After the first shots were fired, the men held captive in the shed knew what was to happen to them. But no amount of crying, screaming, soiling themselves, beating and clawing at the timber walls stayed their fate. According to various sources, between 120 and 250 men were executed and buried in the mass grave there. Some old hands in Patagonia put the figure much higher.[7]

As I took photographs, two Andean condors, rarely sighted, soared above on the thermals. An old horseman ambled by, a sheepskin under his saddle, and paused to watch as a vehicle roared down from the homestead. The four-wheel-drive pulled up in a spray of dust and the manager gave us the benefit of a few short sharp words.

However, beyond the estancia's jurisdiction, on the dusty verge of the public road outside the gates, was a semicircular monument surmounted by a cross. It had been raised by subscription among sheepworkers and trade unionists 'in memory of the hundreds of workers – *trabajadores* – who died at this place in 1921 for a just cause'.

No grave has ever been exhumed. According to Osvaldo Bayer, 1,500 men – strike leaders and ordinary workers – were killed in Santa Cruz territory by 1922.[8] However, without more evidence, that figure does seem excessive, with less than one fifth of it accounted for by the most notorious massacre at La Anita. Andrew Graham-Yooll argues that the numbers cannot be known, as 'neither army nor church – the two institutions which kept records of the incident – have released to date the full details of the death toll of that strike'.[9]

With the workers' federation destroyed, the *peones'* wages

were further reduced. The local *Magellan Times* applauded Colonel Varela's 'splendid courage, running about the firing line as though on parade ... Patagonians should take their hats off to the 10th Argentine Cavalry, these very gallant gentlemen.'

The region had been 'satisfactorily' pacified and for years little word of the massacres surfaced. In the National Congress a deputy called de Tomaso spoke of 'immoral brutality' in Santa Cruz and demanded an official inquiry, but without success. The terrible stories which circulated in trade union and radical journals seemed too unbelievable, perhaps even for Mary Gilmore, if any filtered through to her as she worked on a trade union paper in Sydney. (She had expressed outrage at the harsh existence and needless death of one young labourer in Patagonia. Only the treatment of Aborigines in colonial Australia could have prepared her for the knowledge of a cold-blooded extermination of hundreds.)

It was in 1972, ten years after Mary's death, that the Argentine writer and historian Osvaldo Bayer produced the first two volumes of a monumental work, *Los Vengadores de la Patagonia Trágica (The Avengers of the Patagonian Tragedy)*. He tracked the story of the strikes and their aftermath, with testimonies from survivors, letters, pamphlets, union records and newspaper accounts.

He described how, after the last of the 'troublemakers' had been killed in 1922, the English and Scottish landowners organised a reception at the British Club in Río Gallegos in Colonel Varela's honour. They cheered him and sang 'For He's a Jolly Good Fellow'. The following year Varela was killed in Buenos Aires by a bomb hurled by Kurt Wilckens, a German anarchist who declared 'I have avenged my brothers!'. Varela was buried in the Chacarita necropolis, with a plaque on his tomb provided by 'the British residents in the territory of Santa Cruz – In memory of Lieutenant Colonel Varela, an example of honour and discipline in the fulfilment of his duty'.

The third volume of Bayer's history, and Hector Olivera's film based upon it, *La Patagonia Rebelde,* were both released in 1974. Both were promptly banned by the Argentine Ministry of Defence and Bayer's work was removed from bookstores by soldiers and loaded on to army trucks. After receiving death threats, he fled the country and published his fourth volume in exile in Germany.

The army had been the real source of power in Argentina since 1930 when it overthrew an elected government. It traded favours with the traditional oligarchy, while the poor of the rural areas and the ever more crowded capital were left further behind. Political protests became more violent. After a series of kidnappings, the army intervened again in 1976, replacing the puppet presidency of General Perón's widow, Isabel, with a military junta. The state repression of the Dirty War, the apologist Alfonsín, the playboy Carlos Menem and a clutch of five presidents in 2001–2 were to follow.

My departing aircraft circled over Buenos Aires and the engorged Río de la Plata flowing out over the land, its brown waters swallowing the shanty settlements which had sought precarious tenure on its banks. A flight attendant handed me the *Buenos Aires Herald.* It reported that 1,000 people had been moved from their homes because of the floods and more were to be relocated.

In this country famed for its beef and wheat, many people were starving. In the north-western province of Salta a group of more than 400 native Indians were threatening to 'burn their women and children if their requests for more land and welfare programmes' were not met.[10]

A financial journalist predicted that 'a deal, albeit a modest one' with the IMF was imminent. But he was disturbed by the results of a survey which indicated a familiar Argentine deferment to authority:

> Many people are looking for the benevolent boss-type leader who will dole out the benefits and save them from having to do much of anything except suck up to the right people to get their share ... In a society that has endured four years of recession – the last of which qualifies as a depression – and that has half its population under the poverty line and nearly a quarter of its workforce unemployed, these results are understandable. But they are still disturbing ...This is just one way Argentina is repeating the past.[11]

In the race for the April 2003 elections, Adolfo Saá, a Peronist with a dubious past, was still leading, but Carlos Menem, another Peronist released from detention on corruption charges, was gaining ground.

Some advertised events relied on tradition. The Oxford

and Cambridge Annual Dinner invited the attendance of graduates, with an address by Sir Robin Christopher KBE, CMG. Saint Andrew's Society of the River Plate, which was holding its 114th anniversary banquet, 'request Highland dress, black tie, dark suit'. The Alcoholics Anonymous English-speaking group was meeting as usual. Escort Susan was available: 'Only foreign visitors. Hotels, interviews, calls.'

Australians got a mention, for storming past Pakistan in the cricket and for the Bali bombing. The *Herald* reported:

> The final death toll is not yet known, but … Australia (with about one-fifteenth of the US population) has suffered a loss of life of roughly the same order as the United States did on 11 September 2001.[12]

I knew I was returning to a sadder nation, one which might never be quite as carefree again. But still almost every Argentine I met made desultory enquiries about emigration there, just as they would have done – even more pressingly – if I had been North American, Spanish, Italian, Canadian or British.

The lights of Buenos Aires glimmered and receded. I was leaving this tragic and beautiful country behind, so rich in natural resources, so poor in leadership. It could have had, and should have had, a very different trajectory. As we veered south to cross Patagonia, my emotions were in turmoil – feeling relief to have come through, a sense of loss that I might never return, and a certain niggling doubt that I, like Mary and Will Gilmore exactly one hundred years earlier, was able to exercise personal choice in the matter of leaving.

NOTES

ML = Mitchell Library of State Library of New South Wales
NLA = National Library of Australia
USL = University of Sydney Library
All 'Mary to Will' correspondence quoted below from 'Letters from Mary to Will Gilmore in Patagonia 23-9-1899 to 26-12-1901' (typescripts loaned by Dr George Mackaness), ML microfilm copy FM4/2280.

1. Waterways

1   Maude Kearney-Morgan, a pupil of Mary's at Stanmore public school, letter of 15 July 1945, ML Papers of Dame Mary Gilmore, ML MSS 123.

2   Mary Gilmore, Verse Notebook, ML Papers of Dame Mary Gilmore, ML MSS 123 box 3.

3   Maude Kearney-Morgan letter, as above *n.* 1.

4   '"The most dangerous man in Queensland," W. T. Stead said of him. "In Australia," a Victorian Cabinet minister corrected.' Quoted in Vance Palmer, *The Legend of the Nineties* (Melbourne, 1954, 1980), p. 83.

5   Mary Gilmore, 'Henry Lawson: Personal History – Henry Lawson and I', written Goulburn, October–November 1922, Diary vol. 41, ML Papers of Dame Mary Gilmore A3292.

6   As above.

7   Henry Lawson, 'The Rejection', *Bulletin,* 21 October 1893.

8   Henry Lawson, 'Freedom on the Wallaby', Queensland *Worker,* 16 May 1891.

9   'Sister Jacey' [M.J.C. – Mary Jean Cameron], 'The Why and the Wherefore', *New Australia* (The Journal of the New Australia Co-operative Settlement Association), 28 January 1893.

10 William Lane (under pseudonym 'John Miller'), *The Workingman's Paradise* (Sydney, 1892, 1980), p. 10.

11 Sydney *Bulletin*, 2 June 1894.

12 Gilmore, Verse Notebook.

13 Mary Gilmore, 'Henry Lawson and I', Diary vol. 41; Jack Jones writes of Lawson nearly stowing away on the boat in *Henry Lawson – By His Mates* (Sydney, 1931) p.33.

14 Gilmore, Verse Notebook.

15 Mary Gilmore, 'Paraguay and Elsewhere in South America', 'Prose 1902–04', ML Papers of Dame Mary Gilmore, ML MSS 123 box 8.

16 As above.

17 Mary Gilmore, 'By the Gleneig', *Marri'd and Other Verses* (Melbourne & Sydney, 1910), p. 6.

18 Mary Gilmore, 'Recollections of Colonia Cosme', 'Prose 1902–04', ML Papers of Dame Mary Gilmore, ML MSS 123 box 8.

19 Hilda Lane in letter to Gavin Souter, 23 May 1965, Cosme Colony Collection, Rare Books Library, USL.

20 Mary Gilmore article, 'Life in Cosme, Part 1', *The New Idea*, June 1904.

21 Eric Lane, son of John, in Anne Whitehead, *Paradise Mislaid: In Search of the Australian Tribe of Paraguay* (St Lucia, Qld, 1997), p. 280.

22 W. H. Wilde, *Courage a Grace: A Biography of Dame Mary Gilmore* (Melbourne, 1988), pp. 99–100.

23 Dave Stevenson's notebook, Cosme Colony Collection, Rare Books Library, USL.

24 Walter Alan Woods (formerly named Walter Head), letter to Mary Gilmore, 9 October 1924, recalling Mary as he knew her in the 1890s, *Letters of Mary Gilmore*, W. H. Wilde & T. Inglis Moore, eds. (Melbourne 1980).

25 Mary Gilmore, poem 'The Linen for Pillow', of which only the first of its three verses is quoted, from Dymphna Cusack, T. Inglis Moore & Barrie Ovenden, eds., *Mary Gilmore: A Tribute* (Sydney 1965), p. 153.

26 Mary Cameron, letter to W. G. Spence, n.d., approx. March–April 1896, W. G. Spence papers, ML A 1562/2, CY 931.

27 Mary Cameron, postcard to Henry Lawson, 5 August 1896, Henry Lawson correspondence, ML AL 29/23.

28 Harry Taylor, quoted in Gavin Souter, *A Peculiar People: The Australians in Paraguay* (Sydney, 1968, 1981; St Lucia, Qld, 1991), p. 175.

29 Hilda Lane in letter to Gavin Souter, 23 May 1965, Cosme Colony Collection, Rare Books Collection, USL.

30 Mary Cameron, letter to W. G. Spence.

31 Tom Hicks-Hall letter, quoted in Souter, p. 175.

32 Mary Gilmore, 'Wedded', *Cosme Monthly,* January 1898.

33 Mary Gilmore, letter to W. A. Woods, 11 June 1903, Wilde & Moore, p. 18.

34 Whitehead, *Paradise Mislaid.* For the most complete history of Lane's Paraguay experiment, see Souter, *n.* 28.

35 Mary to Will, 20 October 1899; 10 January 1900.

36 Mary to Will, 2 December 1899. Walter Stone notes in *Mary Gilmore: A Tribute*, p. 219: 'The promised selection of her poetry in the *Bulletin Booklets* never appeared, Louise Mack being the one woman represented in the series of five between 1899 and 1903.'

37 Mary to Will, 2 November & 9 December 1899.

38 Mary to Will, 15 December 1899.

39 Mary to Will, 17 & 25 December 1899.

40 Mary to Will, 22 April 1900.

41 Mary to Will, 27 May & 9 June 1900.

42 Mary Gilmore, letter to W. A. Woods, p.19.

43 Mary to Will, 18 June 1900.

2. **Tango**

1 Mary Gilmore, 'Paraguay', 'Prose 1902–04', ML Papers of Dame Mary Gilmore, ML MSS 123 box 8.

2 Elizabeth Love, 'Kidnapping Rife in Crippled Argentina', *Guardian,* 29 August 2002.

3 *Buenos Aires Herald,* 21 July 2002.

4 Mary Gilmore, 'El Ejercito Salvacion: Buenos Aires', 'Prose 1902–04', ML Papers of Dame Mary Gilmore, ML MSS 123 box 8.

5 Reference from Agar, Cross & Co, Calle Defensa 124 y 136, Buenos Aires, 30 September 1899, Cosme Colony Collection, Rare Books Library, USL.

6 Letter to Will Gilmore from Jack Black, 7 October 1899, Cosme Colony Collection, Rare Books Library, USL.

7 Pete McCarthy, *McCarthy's Bar* (London, 2002).

8 *Buenos Aires Herald,* 29 & 30 September 2002.

9 Carl Solberg, *Immigration and Nationalism: Argentina and Chile 1890–1914* (Austin, 1970) pp. 5–6.

10   Mary Gilmore on Buenos Aires in 'Paraguay', 'Prose 1902–04', ML Papers of Dame Mary Gilmore, ML MSS 123 box 8.

11   Mary Gilmore, 'General Roca', 'Prose 1902–04', ML Papers of Dame Mary Gilmore, ML MSS 123 box 8.

12   Ronaldo Munck, with Ricardo Falcon & Bernardo Galitelli, *Argentina: From Anarchism to Peronism* (London, 1987), p. 39. (The Socialist Party was founded in 1896 by Juan B. Justo, but the anarchists became more influential in the labour unions.)

13   James R. Scobie, *Buenos Aires: Plaza to Suburb 1870–1910* (New York, 1974), p. 140.

14   *Buenos Aires Herald,* 4 & 8 September 1900.

15   Mary to Will, 25 February 1900.

16   Quoted in Joyce Hollyday, 'Strength through the Ages: The Parallel Stories of Biblical and Contemporary Women', *Sojourners* magazine, November 1994.

17   Hebe de Bonafini addressing Sydney Latin-American Solidarity Gathering, UTS Sydney, 29 June 2002.

18   As above.

19   Michael Radu, 'Know Thy Enemy', *National Review Online,* 3 December 2001.

20   Reported as Bonafini's statement on a Buenos Aires TV programme '*Detrás de las noticias' (Behind The News),* on 10 October 2001, with interviewer Jorge Lanata. Cited by Radu.

21   'Pickets and Peasants Join for Land Reform', *Buenos Aires Herald,* 11 October 2002.

22   Mary Gilmore, Verse Notebook, ML Papers of Dame Mary Gilmore, ML MSS 123 box 3.

23   Mary Gilmore, 'El Ejercito Salvacion: Buenos Aires', 'Prose 1902–04', ML Papers of Dame Mary Gilmore, ML MSS 123 box 8.

24   *Buenos Aires Herald,* 6 & 27 September 1900.

25   Gertjan Dijkink, 'Peripheral Dignity and Pain: Argentina' in *National Identity and Geopolitical Visions* (London, 1996), p. 72.

26   President Alvear, quoted in James Bruce, *Those Perplexing Argentines* (London, 1954), p. 7.

27   Film documentary *Cry For Argentina*, directed & produced by Angus Macqueen, October Films and BBC, 2002.

28   W. H. Wilde, *Courage a Grace: A Biography of Dame Mary Gilmore* (Melbourne, 1988), p. 119.

29   Mary Gilmore, 'In Buenos Aires', 'Prose 1902–04', ML Papers of Dame
     Mary Gilmore, ML MSS 123 box 8.

30   Gilmore, 'In Buenos Aires', as above.

31   *Buenos Aires Herald*, 13, 18 & 19 October 1900.

32   W. B. Gurney, *The Trial of Lieutenant-General Whitelocke*, (London,
     1808), pp. 509–10, quoted in George Pendle, *A History of Latin
     America*, (Harmondsworth, 1963), p. 91.

33   H. S. Ferns, *Britain and Argentina in the Nineteenth Century* (New
     York, 1977), p. 43.

34   Deirdre Ball, ed., *Insight Guide – Argentina* (Hong Kong, 1988), p. 116.

35   National Vigilance Association, *Congress of the White Slave Traffic*
     (London, 1899), p. 86, quoted in Donna J. Guy, *Sex and Danger in
     Buenos Aires: Prostitution, Family and Nation in Argentina* (Lincoln &
     London, 1991), p. 6.

36   Mary Gilmore, 'El Ejercito Salvacion: Buenos Aires', 'Prose 1902–04',
     ML Papers of Dame Mary Gilmore, ML MSS 123 box 8.

37   Guy, pp. 76, 83–4.

38   For this information I am indebted to Guy, pp. 8–10, 16–17, 44, 111.

39   M. Savigliano, *Tango and the Political Economy of Passion* (Boulder,
     1995), p. 110, quoted in Eduardo P. Archetti, *Maculinities: Football,
     Polo and the Tango in Argentina* (Oxford, 1999), p.122.

40   Ezequiel Martínez Estrada, quoted in Jason Wilson, *Buenos Aires: A
     Cultural and Literary Companion* (Oxford, 1999), p. 196.

41   Gardel *canción*, 'Tomo y obligo', quoted in translation in Simon
     Collier, *The Life, Music & Times of Carlos Gardel*, (Pittsburgh, 1986),
     p. 262.

42   Jorge Luis Borges, 'Evaristo Carriego', quoted in translation in
     Archetti, p. 142.

43   Guy, pp.143–56; Miranda France, 'Cry for Me, Argentina', *Spectator*,
     reprinted in Australian *Good Weekend*, 3 August 1996.

44   Homero Manzi, tango song 'Malena', quoted in Manuel Puig,
     Heartbreak Tango: A Serial, translated by Jill Levine (London, 1987),
     p. 76.

45   *Buenos Aires Herald*, quoted in Andrew Graham-Yooll, *The Forgotten
     Colony: A History of the English-speaking Communities in Argentina*,
     (London, 1981), p. 231.

3. Grasslands

1   Archibald Macleish, quoted in James Bruce, *Those Perplexing Argentines* (London, 1954), p. 123.

2   Mary Gilmore, 'The Gaucho', 'Prose 1902–04', ML Papers of Dame Mary Gilmore, ML MSS 123 box 8.

3   Charles Darwin, *Journal of the Voyage of the 'Beagle'* (London, 1845; Geneva, 1968), p. 42.

4   Gilmore, 'The Gaucho', as above, *n.*2.

5   James R. Scobie, *Argentina: A City and a Nation* (New York, 1971), p. 120.

6   Letter from Mary Gilmore to John Lane, October 1900, John Lane papers, Cosme Colony Collection, Rare Books Library, USL.

7   Mary to Will, 31 December 1899.

8   Juan Pablo Queiroz & Tomás de Elia, eds., text by César Aira, *Argentina: The Great Estancias* (New York, 1995).

9   As above, p. 178.

10   J. Monteith Drysdale, 'Argentina's Debt to Scottish Pioneers', *Daily Telegraph,* 3 September 1937.

11   Undated copy (but *c.* 1870s) of letter from Thomas to Herbert Gibson, in possession of John and Minnie Boote.

12   W. H. Hudson, quoted in Richard E. Haymaker, *From Pampas to Hedgerows and Downs: A Study of W. H. Hudson* (New York, 1954), p. 20.

13   Haymaker, p. 32.

14   W. H. Hudson, *Far Away and Long Ago: A Childhood in Argentina* (London, 1918, 1985), p. 78.

15   Quoted in Haymaker, p. 33.

16   Richard Curle, introduction to W. H. Hudson, *Adventures Among Birds* (London, 1951), p. vi.

17   Letter from Thomas Gibson in Edinburgh to his sons Herbert and Ernest at Estancia Los Yngleses, 10 August 1903. Possession of John and Minnie Boote.

18   Jorge Luis Borges, 'The Captive', *Dreamtigers*, translated by Mildred Boyer & Harold Morland (New York 1964, 1970). I am also indebted to unpublished ms., 'Memoirs of Robert Nathaniel Greene', edited and annotated by Susan Wilkinson, copy held by John and Minnie Boote.

19   W. H. Hudson, 'A Second Story of Two Brothers', *A Traveller in Little Things* (London, 1923).

20 Borges, as above, *n.* 18.

21 Whitehead, *Paradise Mislaid: In Search of the Australian Tribe of Paraguay* (St Lucia, Qld, 1997), p. 341.

22 I am indebted for details of the tragedy of the lost son of Walter Head to Gavin Souter, *A Peculiar People: The Australians in Paraguay* (Sydney, 1968, 1981; St Lucia, Qld, 1991), p. 101, and W.H. Wilde, *Courage a Grace: A Biography of Dame Mary Gilmore* (Melbourne, 1988), pp. 93-4.

23 Mary Gilmore, 'The Welsh Colony at Chubut, Patagonia', 'Prose 1902-04', ML Papers of Dame Mary Gilmore, ML MSS 123 box 8.

24 Mary Gilmore, 'In Buenos Aires', 'Prose 1902–04', ML Papers of Dame Mary Gilmore, ML MSS 123 box 8.

4. South

1 *Buenos Aires Herald* and América TV channel, Buenos Aires, both 8 October 2002.

2 Editorial 'Bellicose Chilli', *Buenos Aires Herald*, 28 October 1900.

3 *Buenos Aires Herald*, 20 September 1900.

4 Paul Theroux in Bruce Chatwin & Paul Theroux, *Patagonia Revisited* (London, 1985, 1992), p. 18.

5 William Henry Hudson, *Idle Days in Patagonia* (London, 1893; Berkeley, 1979), pp. 1–6.

6 As above, pp. 232–7.

7 Mary Gilmore, 'America. The Sea Lions', NLA Papers of Dame Mary Gilmore, National Library of Australia, MS8766/5/1; also Mary's letter to W. A. Woods, 11 June 1903, W. H. Wilde & T. Inglis Moore, eds., *Letters of Mary Gilmore* (Melbourne, 1980).

8 Charles Darwin, *Journal of the Voyage of the 'Beagle'* (London, 1845; Geneva, 1968), pp. 101–4.

9 W. H. Hudson, *Idle Days in Patagonia* (London, 1893), pp. 38–41.

10 Quoted in Hubert Herring, *A History of Latin America: From the Beginnings to the Present* (London, 1954), p. 622.

11 David Rock, *Argentina 1515–1982: From Spanish Colonization to the Falklands War* (London, 1986), p. 179.

12 Mary Gilmore, 'General Roca', 'Prose 1902–04', ML Papes of Dame Mary Gilmore, ML MSS 123 box 8.

13 Bruce Chatwin, *In Patagonia* (London, 1977), p. 24.

14 Lewis Jones, 17 June 1863, quoted in Glyn Williams, *The Desert and*

the Dream: A Study of Welsh Colonization in the Chubut 1865–1915
(Cardiff, 1975), p.34.

15 For further detail of deaths among first Welsh settlers, see Andrew Graham-Yooll, *The Forgotten Colony: A History of the English-speaking Communities in Argentina* (London, 1981), pp. 173–4.

16 As above, p. 179.

17 Mary Gilmore, 'The Welsh Colony at Chubut, Patagonia', 'Prose 1902–04', ML Papers of Dame Mary Gilmore, ML MSS 123 box 8.

18 Jan Morris, *Farewell the Trumpets: An Imperial Retreat* (London, 1978), p. 400.

19 Gilmore, 'The Welsh Colony at Chubut, Patagonia'.

20 *Buenos Aires Herald*, 8, 22 & 25 September 1900.

21 Gilmore, 'The Welsh Colony at Chubut, Patagonia'.

22 *Buenos Aires Herald*, 26 September 1900.

23 *La Prensa*, 26 February 1899; *La Nación*, 19 October 1901.

24 *La Nación*, 15 May 1902.

5. **Gallegos**

1 Mary Gilmore to W. A. Woods, 11 June 1903 in W. H. Wilde & T. Inglis Moore, eds., *Letters of Mary Gilmore* (Melbourne, 1980), p. 19.

2 Mary Gilmore, 'Cortes', NLA Papers of Dame Mary Gilmore, MS 8766/5/1.

3 Mary Gilmore, 'Magellan', NLA, Papers of Dame Mary Gilmore, MS 8766/5/1.

4 Paul Theroux, quoting Antonio Pigafetta, *The First Voyage round the World, by Magellan, translated from the accounts of Pigafetta, and other contemporary writers* (London, 1874), quoted in Bruce Chatwin & Paul Theroux, *Patagonia Revisited* (London, 1985), pp. 30–31.

5 Charles Darwin, *Journal of the Voyage of the 'Beagle'* (London, 1845; Geneva, 1968), quoted in Chatwin & Theroux, p. 7.

6 Bruce Chatwin in Chatwin and Theroux, p. 7.

7 Mary Gilmore, 'Patagonia in the South', NLA Papers of Dame Mary Gilmore, MS 8766/14/3.

8 As above.

9 J. M. 'Trip to the South by Sea', V, Buenos Aires *Standard*, 3 October 2001.

10 J. B. Hatcher, *Bonehunters in Patagonia: Narrative of the Expedition* (Woodbridge, Conn., 1901).

11 Mary Gilmore, untitled essay about Philomena de González, 'Prose 1902–04', ML Papers of Dame Mary Gilmore, MSS 123 box 8.

12 Gilmore, untitled essay about Philomena de González, as above.

13 Buenos Aires *Standard*, 3 October 1901.

14 Information from Osvaldo Topcic, 'Butch Cassidy and the Sundance Kid and the Río Gallegos Bank Robbery', *Old West* (Fall, 1993), p. 30.

15 Gilmore, untitled essay about Philomena de González, as above, *n.* 11.

16 Mary to Will, 16 December 1900.

17 As above.

18 Figures from Bruce Chatwin, *In Patagonia* (London, 1977), p. 94; Topcic, p. 37.

19 *El Antarctico*, report in English, 19 February 1905.

20 Osvaldo Topcic, quoting *El Antarctico*, above, and the testimony of Río Gallegos Police Chief Dámaso Lachaga.

21 Topcic, p. 37.

22 As above.

23 Noted in *El Antarctico*, above, *n.* 19, and testimony of Police Chief Dámaso Lachaga.

24 Topcic, p. 39.

25 Andrew Graham-Yooll, *The Forgotten Colony: A History of the English-speaking Communities in Argentina* (London, 1981), pp. 217–19.

26 Chatwin, *In Patagonia*, p. 65.

27 Mary to Will, 18 December 1900.

28 Mary to Will, 5 January 1901.

29 Mary to Will, 18 December 1900; 5 January 1901.

30 Gilmore, untitled essay about Philomena de González.

31 Mary to Will, 5 January 1901.

32 Mary Gilmore, 'Patagonia in the South', NLA Papers of Dame Mary Gilmore, MS 8766/14/3.

33 Mary to Will, 18 December 1900.

34 Mary to Will, 5 January 1901.

35 Mary to Will, 8 January 1901.

6. Killik Aike

1 Paul Theroux, *The Old Patagonian Express: By Train Through the Americas* (London, 1979), p. 325.

2 Charles Darwin, *Journal of the Voyage of the 'Beagle'* (London, 1845; Geneva, 1968), pp. 503–4.

3   Andrew Graham-Yooll, *The Forgotten Colony: A History of the English-speaking communities in Argentina* (London, 1981), p. 15.

4   Killik Aike wages book, 1896–1902, debits for Will Gilmore in January 1901. Possession of John Blake, Estancia Killik Aike.

5   Mary Trehearne, *Falkland Heritage: A Record of Pioneer Settlement* (Ilfracombe, 1978), p. 76.

6   Trehearne, pp. 77–8.

7   Trehearne, p. 84.

8   Quoted in Trehearne, p. 82.

9   Broker's letter 1894, quoted in Trehearne, p. 82.

10 From booklet, *Patagonia Argentina,* no identifiable author or date, Carlos Felton's papers, in possession of John Blake.

11 Mary Gilmore, letter to W. A. Woods, 11 June 1903, in W. H. Wilde & T. Inglis Moore, eds., *Letters of Mary Gilmore* (Melbourne, 1980).

12 Mary writes in 'Patagonia in the South' of 'the *locos* in Feltons' house at the back of us'. NLA Papers of Dame Mary Gilmore, MS 8766/14/3.

13 Mary recalls the barrel of water at her kitchen door in Patagonia; the barrel would burst and leave the water standing solid: Diary, vol. 3, 7 March 1942, ML Papers of Dame Mary Gilmore, A3254.

14 Tom Hicks-Hall, quoted in Gavin Souter, *A Peculiar People: The Australians in Paraguay* (Sydney, 1968, 1981: St Lucia, Qld, 1991), p. 185.

15 Mary Gilmore, 'America', 'Prose 1902–04', ML Papers of Dame Mary Gilmore, ML MSS 123, box 8 – her notes reviewing *Argentine Plains and Andine Glaciers* (1911) by Walter Larden, brother of Larden the owner of Estancia Santa Isabel.

16 Mary to Will, 25 August 1901.

17 Mary Gilmore, 'Notes for Patagonia', NLA Papers of Dame Mary Gilmore, MS 8766/14/3.

18 J. B. Hatcher, *Bonehunters in Patagonia: Narrative of the Princeton University Expeditions to Patagonia – March 1896 to September 1899* (Woodbridge, Conn., 1901), p. 55.

19 Mary Gilmore, poem 'The Tin Pannikin', and annotation in *The Passionate Heart and Other Poems by Mary Gilmore,* (Sydney, 1948, 1969, 1979), pp. 280–81, 316.

20 Mary Gilmore, 'Patagonia. Night', 'Prose 1902–04', ML Papers of Dame Mary Gilmore, ML MSS 123 box 8.

21 Mary Gilmore, 'Patagonia in the South', NLA Papers of Dame Mary Gilmore, MS 8766/14/3.

22 Hatcher, p.53.

23 Gilmore, 'Patagonia. Night'.

24 Buenos Aires *Standard,* 24 July 1901.

25 Buenos Aires *Standard,* 19 July 1901.

26 Mary Gilmore, 'We Called Him José', 'Prose 1902–04', ML Papers of Dame Mary Gilmore, ML MSS 123 box 8.

27 Gilmore, 'Patagonia in the South', NLA Papers of Dame Mary Gilmore, MS 8766/14/3. (I have supplied words after 'when I feel English …' because of a gap in the original manuscript.)

28 Gilmore, 'Patagonia in the South', as above.

29 Mary Gilmore to W. A. Woods, 11 June 1903.

30 Mary Gilmore, *Old Days: Old Ways: A Book of Recollections* (Sydney, 1934), p. 62.

31 Mary Gilmore, 'We Called Him José', 'Prose 1902–04', ML Papers of Dame Mary Gilmore, ML MSS 123 box 8.

32 Ronaldo Munck, with Ricardo Falcon & Bernardo Galitelli, *Argentina: From Anarchism to Peronism* (London, 1987), pp. 88–9.

33 Mary Gilmore, 'We Called Him José'.

34 Killik Aike wages book 1896–1902, in the possession of John Blake, Estancia Killik Aike.

35 Mary Gilmore, 'We Called Him José'.

7. English Lessons

1 Mary to Will, 13 August 1901.

2 James R. Scobie, *Buenos Aires: Plaza to Suburb 1870–1910* (New York, 1974), p. 140.

3 Ronaldo Munck, Ricardo Falcon & Bernardo Galitelli, *Argentina: From Anarchism to Peronism* (London, 1987), pp. 49–50.

4 Mary to Will, 17 August 1901.

5 As above.

6 Mary to Will, 18 August 1901.

7 Mary Gilmore, 'Mary Gilmore – achievements', written 1946–7, NLA Papers of Dame Mary Gilmore, MS 876615/2.

8 As above.

9 Charles Darwin, *Journal of the Voyage on the 'Beagle'* (London, 1845; Geneva, 1968), quoted in Alan Moorehead, *Darwin and the Beagle* (London, 1969), pp. 110–11.

10 Mary to Will, 17 August 1901.

11   Mary to Will, 18 August 1901.

12   Mary to Will, 19 & 25 August 1901.

13   Mary to Will, 13 & 14 September 1901.

14   Mary Gilmore to W. A. Woods, 11 June 1903, W. H. Wilde & T. Inglis Moore, eds., *Letters of Mary Gilmore* (Melbourne, 1980).

15   Mary to Will, 16 October 1901.

16   Mary to Will, 6 September 1901.

17   Mary to Will, 13, 14 & 17 September 1901.

18   Mary to Will, 14 September 1901.

19   Mary to Will, 12 September 1901.

20   Mary to Will, 12 and 14 September 1901.

21   Mary to Will, 13 September 1901.

22   Mary to Will, 17 September 1901.

23   As above.

24   Some details re. Eberhardt from Bruce Chatwin, *In Patagonia* (London, 1977), p. 175.

25   Carl Skottsberg, *The Wilds of Patagonia: A Narrative of the Swedish Expedition to Patagonia, Tierra del Fuego and the Falkland Islands in 1907–1909* (London, 1911), pp. 289–90.

26   Chatwin, pp. 179–80.

27   Hesketh Prichard, 'Search for the Giant Sloth', New York *Sunday Herald,* reprinted *Buenos Aires Herald,* 20 September 1900.

28   Charlie Jacoby, London *Daily Express,* internet, n.d., *c.*2000.

29   Prichard, as above, *n.* 27.

30   Mary to Will, 20 September 1901.

31   Mary to Will, 6 & 13 October 1901.

32   Gilmore to Woods, as above, *n.* 14.

33   Mary to Will, 6 October 1901.

34   Mary Gilmore, poem 'To Gallegos and the Gallegans', written on 21 September 1901 and posted to the Buenos Aires *Standard* and also to the *Buenos Aires Herald,* which published it. ML Papers of Dame Mary Gilmore, ML MSS 123 box 4. I thank Dr Jennifer Strauss for bringing this poem to my attention. (The poem goes on for another five verses.)

35   Mary to Will, 6 October 1901.

36   Mary to Will, 15 October 1901.

37   Mary to Will, 7 October 1901.

38   Mary to Will, 12 October 1901.

39 Mary Gilmore, 'Flora', in Dymphna Cusack, T. Inglis Moore & Barrie Ovenden, eds., *Mary Gilmore: A Tribute* (Sydney, 1965), p. 129.

40 Mary Gilmore, 'South American', NLA Papers of Dame Mary Gilmore, MS 8766/5/1.

41 See Roger Milliss, *Waterloo Creek: The Australia Day Massacre of 1838* (Ringwood, 1992); Henry Reynolds, *The Other Side of the Frontier: Aboriginal Resistance to the European Invasion of Australia* (Ringwood, 1982) and other works.

42 Mary Gilmore, poem 'The Hunter of the Black', from *The Wild Swan*, reprinted in *The Passionate Heart and Other Poems by Mary Gilmore* (Sydney, 1948, 1969, 1979), pp. 66–8.

43 Darwin's *Beagle* journal, quoted by Paul Theroux in Bruce Chatwin & Paul Theroux, *Patagonia Revisited* (London, 1985, 1992), pp. 42–3.

44 Charles Darwin and other quotes from Alan Moorehead, *Darwin and the Beagle* (London, 1969), pp. 90–103.

45 Darwin, quoted in Moorehead, p. 103.

46 Samuel Kirkland Lothrop, *The Indians of Tierra del Fuego* (New York, 1928), p. 25; Revd Ben Garrett, cited in Piotr Klafkowski, 'Who remembers the people of Fireland ... A contribution to the study of linguistic extermination', *Lingua Posnaniensis*, 40 (1998), p. 210.

8. Ill Winds

1   Mary Gilmore to W. A. Woods, 11 June 1903, in W. H. Wilde & T. Inglis Moore, eds., *Letters of Mary Gilmore* (Melbourne, 1980).

2   Mary to Will, 24 November 1901.

3   Gilmore to Woods, as above, *n*. 1.

4   Mary to Will, 24 November 1901.

5   Gilmore to Woods, as above, *n*. 1.

6   Andrew Graham-Yooll, *The Forgotten Colony: A History of the English-speaking Communities in Argentina* (London, 1981), p. 21.

7   Mary to Will, 25 November 1901.

8   Mary to Will, 28 November 1901.

9   Gilmore to Woods, as above, *n*. 1.

10 Mary to Will, 28 November 1901.

11 The Banco Londres y Tarapacá founded in 1899, had become, by the time it was robbed in 1905, allegedly by Butch Cassidy and the Sundance Kid, the Banco Tarapacá y Argentina.

12 Quoted in W. H. Wilde, *Courage a Grace: A Biography of Dame Mary*

Gilmore (Melbourne, 1988), p. 120.

13 Mary to Will, 30 November 1901.

14 Gilmore to Woods, as above, *n*. 1.

15 Mary to Will, 30 November 1901.

16 Gilmore to Woods, as above, *n*. 1.

17 Graham-Yooll, p. 138.

18 Mary to Will, 30 November & 1, 2 & 5 December 1901.

19 Mary Gilmore, 'Mary Gilmore – achievements', written 1946–7, NLA Papers of Dame Mary Gilmore, MS 8766/5/2.

20 Graham-Yooll, p. 159.

21 Gilmore, 'Mary Gilmore – achievements'.

22 Mary to Will, 2 December 1901.

23 Bruce Chatwin, *In Patagonia* (London, 1977), p. 88.

24 Mary to Will, 3 & 8 December 1901.

25 Mary to Will, 2 & 11 December 1901.

26 Mary to Will 12, 14 & 16 December 1901.

27 Mary to Will, 18 December 1901.

28 Mary to Will, 21 December 1901.

29 As above.

30 Mary to Will, 22 December 1901.

31 Mary to Will, 23 December 1901.

32 Mary to Will, 26 December 1901.

33 Mary to Will, 1 January 1902.

34 As above.

35 Mary gives this information in 'Henry Lawson: Personal History – Henry Lawson and I', Diary vol. 41, October–November 1922, ML Papers of Dame Mary Gilmore A3292.

36 Mary to Will, 13 January 1902.

37 Mary Gilmore, poem 'Patagonia in the South', written 12 January 1902, NLA Papers of Dame Mary Gilmore, MS 727/2 Folder '1900'.

38 Mary to Will, 16 January 1902.

39 Gilmore, 'Mary Gilmore – achievements', as above, *n*. 19.

9. **Homecoming**

1 Mary Gilmore, 'Montevideo', 'Prose 1902–04', ML Papers of Dame Mary Gilmore, ML MSS 123 box 8.

2 Mary Gilmore, 'America: The Sea Lions', NLA Papers of Dame Mary Gilmore, MS 8766/5/1.

3   Mary Gilmore to W. A. Woods, 11 June 1903, in W. H. Wilde & T. Inglis Moore, eds., *Letters of Mary Gilmore* (Melbourne, 1980).

4   Mary Gilmore, 'Henry Lawson: Personal History – Henry Lawson and I', Diary vol. 41, October–November 1922, ML Papers of Dame Mary Gilmore A3292.

5   Gilmore to Woods, as above, *n.* 3.

6   Richard Curle, introduction to W. H. Hudson, *Adventures Among Birds* (London, 1951), p. vi.

7   Entries on William Ernest Henley in *Encyclopaedia Britannica* and *Penguin Companion to English Literature* (Harmondsworth, 1971).

8   Mary Gilmore to Judith Wright, 23 February 1952, Wilde & Moore, pp. 273–4.

9   Gilmore, 'Henry Lawson: Personal History – Henry Lawson and I', as above, *n.* 4.

10 Quoted in Hubert Herring, *A History of Latin America: From the Beginnings to the Present* (London, 1954), p. 630.

11 Mary Gilmore, draft of letter to *Sydney Morning Herald*, 14 May 1942, ML Papers of Dame Mary Gilmore, ML MSS 123.

12 Archaeologist A. J. Vogan, quoted in Dymphna Cusack, T. Inglis Moore & Barrie Ovenden, eds., *Mary Gilmore: A Tribute* (Sydney 1965), p. 10.

13 Mary Gilmore, poem 'Never Admit the Pain', from *The Wild Swan*, reprinted in *Selected Verse* (Sydney, 1948).

14 Mary Gilmore, poem 'When I Am Gone', *Tribune*, 6 December 1962.

15 Mary Gilmore, quoted in Cusack *et al.*, p. 25.

16 Mary Gilmore, poem 'Yea I Have Lived', from *Marri'd and Other Verses* (Melbourne, Sydney, 1910).

Afterwards

1   Ronaldo Munck, with Ricardo Falcon & Bernardo Galitelli, *Argentina: From Anarchism to Peronism* (London, 1987), pp. 84–7.

2   As above, p. 88.

3   As above, p. 89.

4   Antonio Soto, addressing the strikers in Patagonia in 1921, quoted in Munck *et al.*, p. x.

5   Bruce Chatwin, *Anatomy of Restlessness: Uncollected Writings* (London, 1996), p. 122.

6   As above, p. 124.

7   For the suppression of Patagonian rebellion, see Osvaldo Bayer, *Los Vengadores de la Patagonia trágica*, vols. 1–3, (Buenos Aires, 1972–4); vol. 4 (Fed. Republic Germany, 1978); Bruce Chatwin, *In Patagonia* (London, 1977), pp. 96–101, *Anatomy of Restlessness*, pp. 115–28; Munck *et al.*, pp. 88–9; Andrew Graham-Yooll, *The Forgotten Colony: A History of the English-speaking Communities in Argentina* (London, 1981), p. 236; Jorge Abelardo Ramos, *Revolución y contrarevolución en la Argentina* (Buenos Aires, 1976); José María Borrero, *La Patagonia Tragica* (Ushuaia & Buenos Aires, 1989); María Brunswig de Bamberg, *Allá en la Patagonia* (Buenos Aires, 1995), pp. 30–32.

8   Munck *et al.*, pp. 88–9.

9   Graham-Yooll, p. 236.

10   *Buenos Aires Herald*, 23 October 2002.

11   Dan Krishock, 'Business Outlook: Short memories', *Buenos Aires Herald*, 23 October 2002.

12   Gwynne Dyer, 'Media Phenomenon', *Buenos Aires Herald*, 21 October 2002.

BIBLIOGRAPHY

Primary sources

ML = Mitchell Library of State Library of New South Wales
NLA = National Library of Australia
USL = University of Sydney Library

Darwin, Charles, *Journal of the Voyage of the 'Beagle'* (London, 1845; facsimile edition, Geneva, 1968)

Gilmore, Mary, 'Verse Notebook', ML Papers of Dame Mary Gilmore, ML MSS 123 box 3

Gilmore, Mary, 'Letters from Mary to Will Gilmore in Patagonia 23–9–1899 to 26–12–1901' (typescripts loaned by Dr George Mackaness), ML microfilm copy FM4/2280

Gilmore, Mary, 'Prose 1902–04', ML Papers of Dame Mary Gilmore, ML MSS 123 box 8: ('Paraguay and Elsewhere in South America'; 'Recollections of Colonia Cosme'; 'El Ejercito Salvacion: Buenos Aires'; 'The Gaucho'; 'General Roca'; 'In Buenos Aires'; 'The Welsh Colony at Chubut, Patagonia'; untitled essay about Philomena de González; 'America'; 'Patagonia Night'; 'We Called Him José'; 'Montevideo')

Gilmore, Mary, poem 'To Gallegos and the Gallegans', ML Papers of Dame Mary Gilmore, ML MSS 123 box 4

Gilmore, Mary, 'Henry Lawson: Personal History – Henry Lawson and I', written Goulburn October–November 1922, Diary vol. 41, ML Papers of Dame Mary Gilmore, A3292

Gilmore, Mary, Diary vol. 3, 7 March 1942, ML Papers of Dame Mary Gilmore, A3254

Gilmore, Mary, Prose: ('America. The Sea Lions'; 'Cortes'; 'Magellan';

'South American', NLA Papers of Dame Mary Gilmore, MS 8766/5/1

Gilmore, Mary, Prose: ('Mary Gilmore – achievements', written 1946–7), NLA Papers of Dame Mary Gilmore, MS 8766/5/2

Gilmore, Mary, 'Notes for Patagonia'; draft short story 'Patagonia in the South', NLA Papers of Dame Mary Gilmore, MS 8766/14/3/Folder '1900'

Gilmore, Mary, poem 'Patagonia in the South', NLA Papers of Dame Mary Gilmore, MS 727/2/

Gilmore, Mary, 'Life in Cosme, Pt 1', *The New Idea,* June 1904

Gilmore, Mary, *Marri'd and Other Verses* (Melbourne, Sydney, 1910)

Gilmore, Mary, *Old Days: Old Ways: A Book of Recollections* (Sydney, 1934)

Gilmore, Mary, *More Recollections* (Sydney, 1935)

Gilmore, Mary, *Selected Verse* (Sydney, London, 1948)

Gilmore, Mary, *The Passionate Heart and Other Poems by Mary Gilmore* (Sydney, 1948, 1969, 1979)

Hatcher, J. B., *Bonehunters in Patagonia: Narrative of the Princeton University Expeditions to Patagonia – March 1896 to September 1899* (Woodbridge, Conn., 1901)

Jones, Jack *et al., Henry Lawson – By His Mates* (Sydney, 1931)

Killik Aike wages book 1896–1902, courtesy of John Blake

Lane, John, Papers, Cosme Colony Collection, Rare Books Library, USL

Lane, William, as 'John Miller', *The Workingman's Paradise: An Australian Labour Novel* (Sydney, 1892 facsimile edition, Sydney, 1980)

Lawson, Henry, 'Freedom on the Wallaby', Queensland *Worker,* 16 May 1891

Lawson, Henry, 'The Rejection', *Bulletin,* 21 October 1893

Lawson, Henry, correspondence, Papers of Henry Lawson, ML AL 29/23

Pigafetta, Antonio, *The First Voyage round the World, by Magellan, translated from the accounts of Pigafetta, and other contemporary writers,* Lord Stanley of Alderley, ed. (London, 1874)

Prichard, Hesketh, 'Search for the Giant Sloth', New York *Sunday Herald,* reprinted *Buenos Aires Herald,* 20 September 1900

Spence, W. G. Papers, ML A1562/2

Stevenson, D. R., Notebook, Cosme Colony Collection, Rare Books Library, USL

Wilde, W. H. & T. Inglis Moore, eds., *Letters of Mary Gilmore* (Melbourne, 1980)

New Australia (The Journal of the New Australia Co-operative Settlement Association)
Cosme Monthly
Bulletin (Sydney)
Worker (Queensland)
Worker (NSW)
Tribune (Sydney)
Sydney Morning Herald
Buenos Aires Herald
Standard (Buenos Aires)
La Prensa (Buenos Aires)
La Nación (Buenos Aires)
El Antarctico (Río Gallegos)

Secondary sources

Archetti, Eduardo P., *Masculinities: Football, Polo and the Tango in Argentina* (Oxford, 1999)

Ball, Deirdre, ed., *Insight Guide – Argentina* (Hong Kong, 1988)

Bao, Sandra, *Argentina, Uruguay and Paraguay* (Hawthorn, 2002)

Bayer, Osvaldo, *Los Vengadores de la Patagonia Trágica*, vols. 1–3 (Buenos Aires, 1972–74); vol. 4 (Federal Republic of Germany, 1978)

Bayer, Osvaldo, *La Patagonia Rebelde* (Mexico, 1980)

Borges, Jorge Luis, 'The Captive', *Dreamtigers*, translated by Mildred Boyer & Harold Morland (New York, 1964, 1970)

Borrero, José María, *La Patagonia Tragica: Asesinatos, piratería y Esclavitud* (Ushuaia & Buenos Aires, 1989, 1997)

Bridges, E. Lucas, *Uttermost Part of the Earth* (London, 1948)

Bruce, James, *Those Perplexing Argentines* (London, 1954)

Brunswig de Bamberg, María, *Allá en la Patagonia: La vida de una mujer en una tierra inhóspita*, Javier Vergara, ed. (Buenos Aires, 1995, 1999)

Chatwin, Bruce, *In Patagonia* (London, 1977)

Chatwin, Bruce & Paul Theroux, *Patagonia Revisited* (London, 1985, 1992)

Chatwin, Bruce, *Bruce Chatwin: Photographs and Notebooks*, David King & Francis Wyndham, eds. (London, 1993)

Chatwin, Bruce, *Anatomy of Restlessness: Uncollected Writings*, Jan Borm & Matthew Graves, eds. (London, 1996)

Collier, Simon *et al.*, *Tango! The Dance, the Song, the Story* (New York, 1995)

Collier, Simon, *The Life, Music & Times of Carlos Gardel* (Pittsburgh, 1986)

Cusack, Dymphna, T. Inglis Moore & Barrie Ovenden, eds., *Mary Gilmore: A Tribute* (Sydney, 1965)

Dijkink, Gertjan, 'Peripheral Dignity and Pain: Argentina', in *National Identity and Geopolitical Visions* (London, 1996)

Duncan, Tim & John Fogarty, *Australia and Argentina: On Parallel Paths* (Carlton, Vic., 1984)

Ferns, H. S., *Britain and Argentina in the Nineteenth Century* (New York, 1977)

France, Miranda, 'Cry for Me, Argentina', *Spectator,* reprinted in *Sydney Morning Herald Good Weekend,* 3 August 1996

Gibson, Herbert, *The History and Present State of the Sheepbreeding Industry in the Argentine Republic* (Buenos Aires, 1893)

Graham-Yooll, Andrew, *The Forgotten Colony: A History of the English-speaking Communities in Argentina* (London, 1981)

Guy, Donna J., *Sex and Danger in Buenos Aires: Prostitution, Family and Nation in Argentina* (Lincoln & London, 1991)

Haymaker, Richard E., *From Pampas to Hedgerows and Downs: A Study of W. H. Hudson* (New York, 1954)

Herring, Hubert, *A History of Latin America: From the Beginnings to the Present* (London, 1954)

Hosne, Roberto, *Patagonia: History, Myths and Legends,* translated by Carol Duggan (Buenos Aires, 2001)

Hudson, W. H., *Idle Days in Patagonia* (London, 1893; Berkeley, CA, 1979)

Hudson, W. H., *Far Away and Long Ago: A Childhood in Argentina* (London, 1918, 1985)

Hudson, W. H., 'A Second Story of Two Brothers', *A Traveller in Little Things* (London, 1923)

Hudson, W. H., *Adventures Among Birds* (London, 1951)

Isherwood, Christopher, *The Condor and the Cows* (London, 1949)

Keynes, Richard, *Fossils, Finches and Fuegians: Charles Darwin's Adventures and Discoveries on the Beagle, 1832–1836* (London, 2002)

Klafkowski, Piotr, 'Who remembers the people of Fireland … A contribution to the study of linguistic extermination', *Lingua Posnaniensis,* 40 (1998)

Koebel, W.H. *Argentina Past & Present* (London, 1914)

Larden, Walter, *Estancia Life: Agricultural, Economic and Cultural Aspects of Argentine Farming* (Detroit, 1974)

Lothrop, Samuel Kirkland, *The Indians of Tierra del Fuego* (New York, 1928)

Macqueen, Angus, director/producer of documentary *Cry for Argentina,* October Films & BBC, 2002

McCarthy, Pete, *McCarthy's Bar* (London, 2002)

McEwan, Colin, Luis A.Borrero & Alfredo Prieto eds., *Patagonia: Natural History, Prehistory and Ethnography at the Uttermost End of the Earth* (Princeton, NJ, 1997)

Mielche, Hakon, *Journey to the World's End* (Edinburgh & London, 1943)

Moorehead, Alan, *Darwin and the* Beagle (London, 1969)

Morris, Jan, *Farewell the Trumpets: An Imperial Retreat* (London, 1978)

Munck, Ronaldo, with Ricardo Falcon & Bernardo Galitelli, *Argentina: From Anarchism to Peronism – Workers, Unions and Politics 1855–1985* (London, 1987)

Musters, George Chaworth, *At Home with the Patagonians: A Year's Wanderings* (London, 1871)

Owen, Geraint, *Crisis in Chubut: A Chapter in the History of the Welsh Colony* (Swansea, 1977)

Palmer, Vance, *The Legend of the Nineties* (Melbourne, 1954)

Pendle, George, *A History of Latin America* (Harmondsworth, 1963)

Perry, Roger, *Patagonia: Windswept Land of the South* (New York, 1974)

Puig, Manuel, *Heartbreak Tango: A Serial,* translated by Jill Levine (London, 1987)

Queiroz, Juan Pablo & Tomás de Elia eds., text by César Aira, *Argentina: The Great Estancias* (New York, 1995)

Quesada, Fernando, *Argentine Anarchism and 'La Protesta',* translated by Scott Johnson (New York, 1978)

Ramos, Jorge Abelardo, *Revolución y contrarevolución en la Argentina* (Buenos Aires, 1976)

Rock, David, *Argentina 1515–1982: From Spanish Colonization to the Falklands War* (London, 1986)

Savigliano, M., *Tango and the Political Economy of Passion* (Boulder, 1995)

Scobie, James R., *Argentina: A City and a Nation* (New York, 1971)

Scobie, James R., *Buenos Aires: Plaza to Suburb, 1870–1910* (New York, 1974)

Shakespeare, Nicholas, *Bruce Chatwin* (London, 1999)

Shumway, Nicolas, *The Invention of Argentina* (Berkeley, 1991)

Simpson, George Gaylord, *Attending Marvels: A Patagonian Journal* (New York, 1934)

Skottsberg, Carl, *The Wilds of Patagonia: A Narrative of the Swedish Expedition to Patagonia, Tierra del Fuego and the Falkland Islands in 1907–1909* (London, 1911)

Solberg, Carl, *Immigration and Nationalism: Argentina and Chile 1890–1914* (Austin, 1970)

Souter, Gavin, *A Peculiar People: The Australians in Paraguay* (Sydney, 1968, 1981; St Lucia, 1991)

Strange, Ian J., *The Falkland Islands* (Newton Abbot & London, 1972)

Theroux, Paul, *The Old Patagonian Express: By Train through the Americas* (London, 1979)

Topcic, Osvaldo, 'Butch Cassidy and the Sundance Kid and the Río Gallegos Bank Robbery', *Old West* (Fall 1993)

Trehearne, Mary, *Falkland Heritage: A Record of Pioneer Settlement* (Ilfracombe, 1978)

Tschiffely, A. F., *This Way Southward: An Account of a Journey through Patagonia to Tierra del Fuego* (London, 1945)

Walter, Richard J., *Politics and Urban Growth in Buenos Aires, 1919–1942* (Cambridge & New York, 1993)

Wheaton, Kathleen, ed., *Buenos Aires* (Buenos Aires, 1988)

Whitaker, Arthur P., *Argentina* (New Jersey, 1964)

Whitehead, Anne, *Paradise Mislaid: In Search of the Australian Tribe of Paraguay* (St Lucia, Qld, 1997)

Wilde, W. H., *Courage a Grace: A Biography of Dame Mary Gilmore* (Melbourne, 1988)

Wilkinson, Susan, ed., unpublished ms., 'Memoirs of Robert Nathaniel Greene', copy held by John and Minnie Boote.

Williams, Glyn, *The Desert and the Dream: A Study of Welsh Colonization in Chubut 1865–1915* (Cardiff, 1975)

Wilson, Jason, *Buenos Aires: A Cultural and Literary Companion* (Oxford, 1999)

Guardian
Buenos Aires Herald
La Opinión Austral

ACKNOWLEDGEMENTS

I am grateful to the following organisations and their staff for making manuscript and pictorial material available to me and assisting me with my research: the Public Trustee of New South Wales, executor of the Dame Mary Gilmore Estate; State Library of New South Wales and its Mitchell Library, particularly Paul Brunton, Jennifer Broomhead and Jerelynn Brown; National Library of Australia and Graeme Powell, Wendy Morrow and James Nornarhas; the Rare Book and Special Collections Library of the University of Sydney Library and Neil Boness and Sara Hilder; also John Fairfax Limited. Mary Gilmore's poetry is reproduced with kind permission of the publishers from *Selected Poems* (ETT Imprint, Sydney, 2003). I am grateful to Tom Thompson and ETT Imprint also for material from Mary's *Old Days, Old Ways*.

I wish to thank Aerolineas Argentinas for its generous assistance with travel and the Argentine Consul General to Australia, Enrique Rubio, and Deputy Consul General, Ana Celia Pisano, for facilitating research in Buenos Aires.

In Argentina I was greatly aided by the staff of the Biblioteca Nacional and the Archivo General de la Nación in Buenos Aires, also the Gaimán Regional Museum, the Bariloche Regional Library and Museo de la Patagonia, the Museo de los Pioneros and the British Club in Río Gallegos. Many Argentine friends were more than generous with their hospitality and assistance, although not all will necessarily agree with some opinions I express: John and Elisa Magrane ('Minnie') Boote of Estancia Los Yngleses, Lulu Boote, Herbert Gibson, John and Monica Blake of Estancia Killik Aike, Professor Oswaldo Topcic and Pablo Beecher. Luis María González was generous beyond measure as travelling companion, translator and guide to his country.

I give special thanks to all those other individuals who helped me in manifold ways in the preparation of this book, including Gil Appleton, Janet Bell, Axel Bendixsen, Gil Brealey, Tony Bremner, Murray Brown, Peter Brown, Bob Connolly, Mary-Jane Field, Robyn Fookes, Steve Gregory, Alan Hall, Michael and Alicia Karelicki, Dr Judith Keene, Anna Lanyon, Jennifer Lionetti, Peter McGregor, Tom Molomby, Debbie Mortimer, Silvia Ordoñez, Vincent Plush, Greg Price, Rodolfo and Nancy Rivarola, Dr Tim Rowse, Rod Sangwell, Di Simmonds, Gavin Souter, Dr Jennifer Strauss, Christina Thompson, Suzi Whitehead, Florence Wood de White and Eleanor Witcombe.

I am especially grateful to Tom Keneally for reading the manuscript and his comments on it; to Brian Turner, whose stories about his youthful wool-classing days in Patagonia started me on this journey; to John Kerr, always my first, most caring and critical reader and ruthless blue-penciller; to Dr David and Pam Martin who offered a haven when it was needed; to John and Adrienne Whitehead, constantly available with loving support, and to my indefatigable agents, Rose Creswell and Annette Hughes and the staff of Cameron Creswell Management.

Finally I want to thank the wonderful people at Profile Books (UK) – Kate Griffin, Sally Holloway, Penny Daniel and Peter Carson – and also Patrick Gallagher, Andrew Hawkins and the staff of Allen and Unwin in Australia.

Illustrations acknowledgements

Author: pages 54, 66, 75, 95, 185, 193, 218, 240, 278; Archivo General de la Nación, Buenos Aires: pages 42, 46, 49, 275; Cosme Colony Collection of Rare Books Library of University of Sydney Library: pages 30, 268; Felton family photographs, courtesy of John Blake: title pages, pages 183, 189, 201, 255; Gaimán Regional Museum: page 130; *Illustrated London News*, July 1889: page 155; John Byron's *A Voyage Round the World* (London, 1767): page 143; John Fairfax Limited, Sydney: page 271; Mitchell Library of State Library of New South Wales: pages 16, 26; Museo de la Patagonia, Bariloche: pages 126, 223; Pinkerton Detective Agency photograph: page 157; Roil Fotografía, Río Gallegos: page 233; Thomas Gibson painting, courtesy of John Boote: page 96.

INDEX

Index

Index